THE GENTEEL
TRADITION
AND THE
SACRED RAGE

CULTURAL STUDIES

OF THE

UNITED STATES

ALAN TRACHTENBERG

EDITOR

ROBERT DAWIDOFF

THE GENTEEL TRADITION AND THE SACRED RAGE

HIGH CULTURE VS. DEMOCRACY IN ADAMS, JAMES, & SANTAYANA

THE UNIVERSITY OF NORTH CAROLINA PRESS

CHAPEL HILL & LONDON

The paper in this book meets

the guidelines for permanence

and durability of the Committee

on Production Guidelines for

Book Longevity of the Council

on Library Resources.

Manufactured in the United States of America

96 95 94 93 92   5 4 3 2 1

Library of Congress Cataloging-in-Publication Data

Dawidoff, Robert.

The genteel tradition and the sacred rage : high culture vs.

democracy in Adams, James, and Santayana / Robert Dawidoff.

p.   cm.—(Cultural studies of the United States)

Includes bibliographical references and index.

ISBN 0-8078-2017-2 (cloth : alk. paper)

1. American prose literature—History and criticism.

2. National characteristics, American, in literature.

3. Santayana, George, 1863–1952—Knowledge—America.

4. Tocqueville, Alexis de, 1805–1859—Influence.

5. Literature and society—United States.   6. James, Henry,

1843–1916. Ambassadors.   7. Adams, Henry, 1838–1918.

Democracy.   8. United States—Civilization.   9. Democracy

in literature.   I. Title.   II. Series.

PS362.D38   1992

818'.40809'358—dc20   91-30746

CIP

For my friend Richard Rouilard

CONTENTS

FOREWORD

Something of a taboo seems to have fallen over the word *democracy*. It is rarely encountered anymore in humanistic studies, snubbed in favor of gender, class, race, region. The particularist emphasis of these terms may represent a deliberate refusal of the universalist implications of grand concepts like democracy. Of course, reasons abound for suspicion of the word, its unsavory nationalist resonances, countless betrayals undertaken in its name. But its dropping out of serious use among cultural historians and critics may signify something more fundamental and significant, an unease and embarrassment with a term so charged with challenges to the very enterprise of *studying* the culture in which we participate. The posture of the cultural critic implies detachment, a certain degree of apartness. Doesn't the idea of a democratic order, of social and political equality, put the serious critic at risk of estrangement, of seeming superior, ungrateful, ungenerous? To think of yourself as cultured, as detached enough to make judgments, isn't this already to think of oneself as unequal, superior, set apart from the mass? Criticism demands distance, it asserts difference, it enacts discrimination. Democracy seems to impose compliance, acceptance of common norms and collective opinion, all that Tocqueville meant by the "tyranny of the majority." Disenchantment with the system of popular government in America, a defining aspect of cultural criticism at least since Emerson, has only driven the word *democracy* further into the background. Seeming irreconcilable, the antinomies of culture and democracy have receded from the foreground of attention they once commanded, say, in the works of Whitman and of the generation of Van Wyck Brooks, Constance Rourke, and John Dewey.

Robert Dawidoff's book restores the question of culture and democracy to the prominence it once had. It revives the relevance of the word *democracy* to cultural studies, indeed to cultural change and reconstruction. The book does so by exploring sources of the trouble the word continues to make for students of American culture, for the field of American Studies itself.

While the heart of the book lies in three remarkable chapters on Henry Adams, Henry James, and George Santayana, Dawidoff places the careers and works of these central figures within a more inclusive structure defined by a polarity of opposing stances, the Tocquevillian and the Jeffersonian.

In Tocqueville's simultaneous celebration of political democracy and disdain for its cultural effects, Dawidoff locates his core theme. Through the lens of Tocqueville's *Democracy in America* American intellectuals have seen democracy, political and social equality, as a particular dilemma. If to claim identity as an American assumes acceptance of equality as the founding principle of nationality, is it possible to be "smart" and remain American at the same time? Jefferson and his side of the argument answer yes and place the reconciliation of culture and democracy high on the American agenda. The Tocquevillian program, inherited by Adams, James, and Santayana, was to figure out a way of living within political democracy but outside its culture, detached from its popular life, the everyday sphere in which cultivation and taste invite stigma rather than honor. Participation versus detachment, leadership founded on commitment to equality even in the presence of unequal privilege versus cultural oligarchism: these are the issues engaged by the Jefferson-Tocqueville polarity.

The figures Dawidoff places at the center of the book bequeathed a distinctive heritage of antidemocratic bias in successive generations of American scholars, even many overtly committed to democratic goals. Linked by friendship, by common ties to Harvard and to New England (the foreign-born Santayana an exception), each saw American democracy as a burden, a challenge to distinguish oneself, rather than an opportunity for positive cultural change. Each registers in his writings and career the pain of difference, of experiencing himself as disdained, disregarded, held in a certain contempt, or, even worse, indifference, by the popular realm he identified with democratic culture. In their own eyes they suffered the fate of intelligence when masses are empowered with self-importance, or, most vividly in the case of Santayana, of sexual difference forced to closet itself from moralistic surveillance. Estranged by their sense of an imposed marginality, they fashioned in their works a seductive paradigm of an American elitist predicament.

Dawidoff rejects the paradigm, sees it as a mode of self-protection from the jarring realities and democratic pleasures of popular life and its culture. But he writes of these figures with remarkable empathy and original insight. The readings of Adams's novel *Democracy*, Santayana's well-trodden essay

"The Genteel Tradition in American Philosophy," and, notably, James's *The Ambassadors*, reap major new insights: for example, his interpretation of Lambert Strether as a turn-of-the-century intellectual in an exquisite agonized moment of partial liberation from servitude to gentility, capitalism, and sexual parochialism. Dawidoff teaches us how to read such texts as at once personal and cultural documents, expressions of particular histories yet speaking to a common history of embattled Americanness.

The Tocquevillian formula, he reveals, earns its enduring strength because it speaks to the needs of disenchanted intellectuals, including many of the dissident Americans who founded the field of American Studies. Dawidoff's readings offer monitory tales. His book speaks finally about the relation of Americanists to their own subject, which is themselves, their own implication in the conscious and unconscious democracy of popular life. Dawidoff affectingly portrays the temptation to court alienation for the sake of confirming our own difference, our own superiority to the culture in which we breathe. This is to separate ourselves "from ourselves." The final word of his Adams chapter can stand for the lesson of the entire book: "Beware."

The Jefferson-Tocqueville opposition remains an unresolved issue. Do recent cultural studies, the remapping of the field of study into newly named realms of gender, race, class, offer hope of a resolution? For Dawidoff what matters are not the labels one employs but the quality of desire and willingness to search for a democratic stance toward the subject of popular life. The book not only argues the point but demonstrates it, not least by recreating a history of lives and ideas and texts from which contemporary debates spring and have much to learn. Here is an example of how a reconciliation of modes might be achieved, the high and the popular, the historical and the critical, the cultivated, the smart, and the democratic. *The Genteel Tradition and the Sacred Rage* returns the question of democracy to center stage, not as political theory alone but as cultural and personal experience.

—Alan Trachtenberg

ACKNOWLEDGMENTS

The John Simon Guggenheim Foundation awarded me a fellowship to write this book, and a Claremont Graduate School research fellowship enabled me to accept it. Leonard Levy urged me to do my own work and gave a bracing example of a scholar who does his. Robert Mezey read poetry with me, including the poems cited here. Daniel Aaron's unsentimental early reading of the whole manuscript was enormously helpful. Douglas Greenberg, Richard Howard, Elizabeth Keyser, Dan McCall, Elizabeth Minnich, Eve Kosofsky Sedgwick, Nathan Tarcov, and Helena Wall read all or parts of the manuscript and talked it over with me to my great benefit. Barry Weller read the manuscript with an editor's eye and a friend's care. Blame Gunther Freehill if you don't like this book—without his help with my computer, the manuscript would surely have been lost.

Students in seminars at the Claremont Graduate School over several years helped me talk and think about the subjects of this book. Charles Mitchell gave me valuable assistance and many good suggestions in preparing the manuscript. John Walsh prepared the index. Lelah Mullican and Martha Vance cheerfully kept things going at the office.

Alan Trachtenberg gave me splendid and shrewd advice about finishing the book. His and J. C. Levenson's readings guided my revisions. Kate Torrey of the University of North Carolina Press has been a good editor and a good-natured one. Linda Pickett's copyediting was a model of helpful attention.

I owe William Spengemann thanks for years of encouragement and conversation; his counsel, generosity, patience, and interest have been a treasure.

Michael Roth has given me invaluable fellow feeling, criticism, and confidence. I am grateful for his company and his remarkable example.

Rena Fraden is this book's ideal reader, and I had her intelligent advice, informed interest, and constant lively encouragement while I was writing it.

Even rough times are good times with friends like Margaret Ecker, Richard Rouilard, and Chuck Young.

I am fortunate to have had Ann Coffey's guidance and support in this as in all my adventures.

I wish my aunt Helen Tenney Davidoff had lived to read this book, although she probably wouldn't have liked it; my uncle Milton Davidoff had better read it at least twice.

Robert Dawidoff
Los Angeles, April 1991

INTRODUCTION

It was quite an adventure in 1831. Two young, ambitious French aristocrats took ship for the New World to see what this American democratic regime was like. Theirs was the paradigmatic neoconservative voyage, a trip to an inevitable future to see how best to cope with the changes it was bound to bring to a French regime they were interested in reforming, but whose essential civilization they hoped to save.

The future is a good place to think about the present and is as likely as the past to offer the contrast and clarity perspective wants. Young people go elsewhere to find out what they really think about home, and young writers create from their wanderings the alternative places that express their views of home. You may not be able to go home again, but most literary careers near home as they go on.

Young Alexis de Tocqueville was no exception. He went with his friend Gustave de Beaumont to the United States on an adventure, a serious-minded grand tour of the future. The declared object of their inquiry was prison reform, but Tocqueville thought the future was certain to be egalitarian, and he visited the only place he knew where a political regime had been instituted along democratic lines. *Democracy in America* is Tocqueville's early masterpiece about what Europeans could reasonably expect democracy to be like. Tocqueville left America and the subject of America behind him when he finished the book, devoting his energy and his intelligence to what had always been his interest—France and French politics and civilization. He did not become an Americanist or even an *Americaniste*.

From Tocqueville's and Beaumont's accounts of their travels, it is evident that these two young French aristocrats plunged into the tumult of Jacksonian America with the eager cooperation of Americans. New York fell at their feet even before their arrival; the prison doors swung open, town after rising town jostled to greet and sweet-talk and do research for these two ancien régime charmers. Even Boston, frostily holding out for a day or two, came around. Only the frontier kept a grave aloofness, and the travelers soon learned that frontier Americans were being as expressive as they could be.[1]

Why did Americans welcome these visitors so warmly? It seems that the Yankees were eager to cultivate that good opinion to which Thomas Jefferson had alluded in the Declaration of Independence; even revolutionary new nations crave acceptance. The New World had always played out its drama, in part, for a European audience. Moreover, Americans thought they had a real good thing in this democratic republic of theirs, and they befriended the Frenchmen with the kind of bragging that reveals both pride and insecurity. Their need to share seems inseparable from their need to boast. Tocqueville resisted most of his urges to mock this braggadocio. Perhaps he understood the insecurity.

The archetypal encounter of Tocqueville and the Americans was his commerce of sympathy with the American critics of democracy. He found his best informants, his readiest collaborators, and his destined audience in people who, like him, had reservations about democracy and enjoyed the chance to express those reservations to sympathetic, aristocratic, non-English Europeans.

Such Americans were ambitious to gain what Tocqueville was concerned to preserve. Their counsel and agreement encouraged Tocqueville to think well of the American regime and its political prospects. They did not cause him to revise his doubts about the things in democratic civilization that he disliked, because they disliked so many of them, too. He could project onto them his own sense of potential victimization by an egalitarian majority. His observer's detachment was something the Americans rose to ape. They took his tone about their own people, assuming that they shared what they granted as his capacity to look at the development of the regime from a detached point of view. They got what readers of *Democracy in America* can get, a sense of detachment from democracy as a way of controlling one's experience in it. That detachment was suspect in them and in him.[2]

An irony of Tocqueville and Beaumont's visit to America is that what mattered not very much to them turned out to matter so much to their American hosts. *Democracy in America*, read in France and much read in England, is a staple of American self-understanding, a classic reading of American political and cultural life. The French visitors passed out of the American sphere but left behind them Tocqueville's written artifact, the two volumes of views of America. Like that other text found in those years, the *Book of Mormon*, it was seized upon by Americans.

And, like that other passing angel's gift, *Democracy in America* has formed a basis for a cult of sensible American living. Its essential understanding is that you must view democratic life from a detached horizon—not from within its daily rounds—adopting the visitor's perspective on your own life. The cult of Tocqueville uses his conclusions about democracy to judge the proper distance from it that a civilized life in America requires.

Democracy historically interferes with the feeling that smart Americans have that they are better than the rest of us. America inflicts a particular hurt on those with a stake in the nondemocratic institutionalization of the expressive. That feeling, and its interpretive consequences, which I call "Tocquevillian," are the subject of this book. The Tocquevillian responds to the irritating challenge of democratic culture to the traditionally expressed self-consequence of intelligence. Its premise is an experience of intellectual and creative discontent and the possibility of detached observation of the source of that discontent.

Tocqueville wished to demystify democracy, to remove it from the index of European political thinking, and to give back to it enough complicated meaning so that people of education and expectations could see themselves as doing something other than blindly opposing it. It is not the only irony of Tocqueville's American career that, although he was not especially interested in American civilization, his views of it in *Democracy in America* have proved lastingly influential within it.

The American interpretive experience has become more common, if not necessarily more interesting and heroic. Being an Americanist, professionally or not—that is, someone who spends time estimating American civilization on the scales of primitive to civilized, decline and fall, good or bad, one to ten, then and now—has become a form of national self-consciousness in this media age. The study of its exemplary past is therefore all the more interesting.

The appeal of Tocqueville, and especially of the Tocquevillian claim of detachment, constitutes one strategy smart Americans have used to cope with American democratic culture—usually to place themselves outside of its context. An alternative tradition, beholden to Jefferson, attempts to place smart Americans within a culture they find in many ways uncomfortable. This book only glimpses that alternative possibility.

After an initial chapter on Tocqueville's visit to America and his version of it as *Democracy in America*, the present study treats Henry Adams, Henry James, and George Santayana. They shared the milieu and ambience of

Boston and Harvard and were American cosmopolitan aristocrats. Santa-yana's instance was an American expatriation, while James's was European, and all three held a central place in the world of American expatriates. Their writings manifested an important unease with American democratic cul-ture, and a disenchantment with the native solutions to its moral control linked them. All three remain influential American writers on American subjects. Together, they broke the ground for much of American interpreta-tion from the point of view of the intellectually and artistically advantaged. How America felt to them has much to do with how the American educated classes say it seems to us.

This book explores these writers' views and also, in understanding them, tries to show how their authors' profound implication in the dilemmas of American democratic culture, especially as Tocqueville outlined them in *Democracy in America*, shaped their claims to have detached themselves from that culture. This must affect any taking up of their views by Americanists.

Chapter 1 discusses Tocqueville's American visit in the hope of framing a tradition of response that Adams, James, and Santayana exemplify. It is a tradition widely shared but, perhaps, mistakenly adopted by liberally edu-cated Americans. The point of retreading this familiar ground is to suggest how subjective Tocqueville's detachment was when it came to his cultural observations. His own expectations and traditionalist views created a per-spective—and it is that perspective his American readers borrow.

Henry Adams's career is the subject of chapter 2. His whole career can be viewed in terms of his attempt to attach the Tocquevillian perspective, and the whole of his writings share in the attempt. Chapter 3, on Henry James, looks at what James thought was his best book. *The Ambassadors* is profoundly about how America makes Americanists of its creative intel-ligentsia. Lambert Strether's escape from Woollett is also an interpretive leave-taking, first, from the moral strictures of the Puritan New England provincial past (what James called the "sacred rage") and, then, from the moral and aesthetic compromise that imperial, cosmopolitan America worked out for the reception of the world's artistic goods (what Santayana called "the genteel tradition").

In Strether, James identified the moral dilemma of the modern American "thinking" person. In order to do so, wonderfully enough, *The Ambas-sadors* had to explore the terrain made familiar elsewhere in the formulae of American generic fiction; it worked through that terrain to become an instance of art that one finds through—not despite—grappling with an American democratic reality that implicates one.

Chapter 4 treats George Santayana's Americanist writings. Along with John Dewey, Santayana decisively influenced modern Americanist writing. His experience and his interpretive writing, therefore, rather than the body of his philosophical work, form the core of my interest. The Conclusion looks at some of the questions raised by Tocquevillian interpretation.

The book's title reflects, albeit in euphonious rather than chronological order, the conflict that seems to me to lie at the heart of the interpretive tangle Americanists must face. Americanists are self-conscious Americans who have to interpret democratic culture to live within it. That turns out to include more of us than just the academic contingent to whom we generally assign the name. Americans have interpretive opinions rather than simple allegiances binding them to the United States. This sophistication in allegiance is what the Constitution requires in return for its abstemious regimen of required patriotic beliefs. Americanist*ism* in recent history has been, in effect, a response to Americanism.

In *The Ambassadors*, Lambert Strether and his new friend Maria Gostrey talk over his old friend Waymarsh's toxic reaction to Europe. They joke about the fits of American provincial reaction to which he is subject and call them eruptions of the "sacred rage." Although Waymarsh tends to have spending rather than preaching fits, Strether and Gostrey recognize that spending is a form that moralism assumes. In their joke, the great moral zealousness that founded the good old "city upon the hill" of New England Puritanism and stoked the fires of American republicanism—the backbone of the American democratic experiment, its conscience, and its native protection from the corruptions to which democracies are liable—has dwindled into a boorish uneasiness with Old World luxury. The sacred rage had once marked, equally in Benjamin Franklin's ease and John Adams's unease, the conscious separateness that Americans cultivated in their constant pains to remind Europeans that America represented an improvement on European civilization.

The sacred rage was especially active in preventing Americans from feeling comfortable with refinements and luxurious corruptions such as sophistication, belles lettres, or anything other than *dulce* and *utile* (and better *utile* than *dulce*). Ironically to call this driving moral energy, which the abolitionists also enacted, a "sacred rage," implying something primitive, awkward, and funny, is to say that the once terrible, founding moral seriousness of New England has turned out to be laughable. *The Ambassadors* shows that Strether's own liberation from what he dares call the "sacred rage" is but a prelude to his confrontation with what, in America, had replaced it.

The genteel tradition replaced the sacred rage in America. Essentially, it was an attempt to retain the moral assurance that New England Calvinism and republican independence had given, without the denial of pleasure or empire they respectively required. It was the attempt to have the cake of virtue and eat it, too. In literature and philosophy, it amounted to a way of controlled, moralistic reading. The sacred rage knew that you should only read books that taught certain things; the genteel tradition thought you could make books teach you anything you wanted. It was like liberalism, but it was not relativist or pragmatic. It presupposed all the structures that were convenient but none of the staunchness, not to mention self-denial, that played so crucial a part in the earlier republican and Calvinist dispensations. It was the moralizing compromise that enabled American cosmopolitan, capitalist, and imperial expansion but was ambitious to continue to exercise social control; it hoped particularly to withhold from the democracy the freedom of the few who understood themselves to be distinguished no longer by stringent virtue, but by the less stringent signs of superiority—money, education, exclusivity, and cultivation. It was a fateful development and continues to characterize American culture, poisoning the relation of the educated individual to democracy by offering a false distinction on the basis of taste.

In *Democracy in America*, Tocqueville worried that the cultural side of democracy would undermine the standing and the possibility of traditional wisdom in the expressive sphere. He believed that traditional wisdom was necessary to gentle life. Henry Adams came to view the unsuitedness of the special likes of him for democratic leadership as indicative of the rejection by democracy of all that once had properly constituted the great public man. In his own work, he reclaimed what he had expected to be the rich preparation for leadership for the private space of cultivation, with the accompanying anathema of the very possibilities of public life.

Henry James's choices and much of his writing reflected the dilemma of a traditionalist sensibility confronted with American capitalist, democratic culture. In *The Ambassadors*, Strether and Miss Gostrey, in joking about the sacred rage, note the passing of the religious fervor that had once made New England morally independent and formidable. What had once fired a zealous religion now but warmed a confused materialism. But the subsequent moralism of genteel culture and provincial ambition made Strether long for the true old sacred rage, despite all its awkwardnesses. *The Ambassadors* concludes with Strether's seeing through the American present order, which left him free and bound to return to democratic America.

George Santayana suggested that the dichotomy in American culture was hard and fast. Democracy might foster energetic, barbarian, physical, expansive culture that traditional culture, meaning to reform and control, would inevitably fail to grasp. The "genteel tradition" was Santayana's phrase for the particular dilemma of conscious, traditional cultivation as it interacted with American material energy. The hope of improvement and the possibility of an American home for Western civilization invariably, in this view, was compromised by America's native high-minded, moralist Protestantism. Santayana's conception of the genteel tradition pointedly captured the dismaying orthodoxy that resulted from the attempt to harness American democratic (often material, athletic, entrepreneurial, but always at some level from-the-bottom) popular energy to a European-originating high culture.

The American compromise was not unusual among middle-class cultures, but the clear field and institutional vigor of its enactment and the morally obsessive tone that New England gave to formal culture were noteworthy. The genteel tradition was distinguished by its belief that good men were made from good books—although this transformation tended to become the responsibility of good women. The moral agency of the middle classes was assumed. These good books had a special role to play in the taming of America. They were meant to guide, uplift, and control the lower classes and to civilize and control the newly rich.

The cultural hegemony of the genteel classes was to be perpetuated by this tradition. Its very blindness toward what Santayana recognized as the interesting material and popular energies of America was matched by its dim feeling for the great works of Western art and thought. It represented a bloodless compromise.

Sometimes, as Strether found out, the genteel tradition fronted grim, relentless moral narrowness and material ambition—the attempt to control the individual. It also verged on the expertise-fueled social control of the

Progressive movement. As Santayana suggested to a long line of Americanist interpreters, the genteel tradition ended up discouraging originality through preclusive acceptance. One of the worst things the genteel tradition could do to a writer was to invite him into the parlor, as Mark Twain found out. The genteel tradition has come to stand for what American culture does to truth and vitality in art.

Lurking in the notion of the genteel, however, is another level of criticism, clear to Santayana but perhaps not so clear to many who have taken up his views. It says that the cultural situation in a democracy is by definition problematic. The genteel makes the mistake of trying to civilize what is best left alone. The genteel tradition itself can be protested, as Vernon Louis Parrington did in *Main Currents in American Thought*, in the name of "the People." The genteel does have an agenda of control, and it depends on an analytical complex that, in turn, assumes certain views of what art and culture are, how they should be discussed, and how American civilization should be viewed. Essentially, this discourse perpetuates American Tocquevillian views about democracy. These, in effect, claim that democracy is inhospitable to the best and highest in expression and thought. To this way of thinking, America might be better as a liberal democratic home for traditional values than for democratic culture.

The genteel assumptions about American culture are that Star Kist wants tuna with good taste and that democracy by its nature corrupts the higher things.[3] American Tocquevillians assert the status of traditional knowledge within the democratic regime by claiming detachment for it. They explain its value in terms of its alternative to the democratic, about which they are analytical, and in terms of the self-description of the traditional, toward which they are reverent. They tend to take the leap to detachment as if it were the renunciation of what is familiar, as if it were a leap of faith.

The attachment of the American Tocquevillian has been to certain values —cultural values that are seen to be not shared by the democracy. It is not so much a case of cultural elitism (although it is probably also that) as it is one of cultural separatism. The feeling of implication in the culture you describe disappeared in favor of feeling embarrassed by its possible claim. The identity of self with the detached perspective, brought to bear in observation, gained the private agenda of the American Tocquevillian an unexamined license. Since the essential claim about civilization is made in the name of human values, claims about culture must be read as claims about people. The claim is that there are different standards for behavior that proceed from different sensibilities and different talents. The Jeffersonian notion that talent creates responsibilities before privileges conflicts with the Tocquevillian notion that talent creates privileges that lead to responsibilities.[4]

THE GENTEEL
TRADITION
AND THE
SACRED RAGE

CHAPTER ONE

TOCQUEVILLE AND THE AMERICAN MIND

TOCQUEVILLE'S AMERICAN PROJECT

One way to start an argument among educated Americans is to suggest that Alexis de Tocqueville was wrong about democracy in America. If there is any orthodoxy in the study of American civilization, it is some sort of Tocquevillian one. The objectivity, the detached observational quality of the young Frenchman's remarkable study of democratic civilization in the United States remains a polestar for American self-study. Its accuracy, its method, and its importance constitute an assumption of the American literate classes. Pounded into our brains in college and reinforced by journalism and academic commentary, Tocqueville's observations have a privileged status. Much of the influence his *Democracy in America* exercises can be attributed to the book's power. It is an authoritative and persuasive rendering of American political culture and of democratic political culture. It was the first and remains the best comprehensive study of what Tocqueville presciently saw as a great modern subject.

The Tocqueville story is attuned to the view of the Robert Burns maxim that distills the Protestant and social scientific tenet that it is best to see yourself as others see you—the "others" being the province of wise men to posit, and the proof of the pudding being the acquired taste of the eating. And, like those traditions, it leaves it to the subject to define the appropriate judging "other"; it is a fantasy of self, not of difference. But it remains an odd fact of American interpretation that a young foreigner's observations on his first visit to a phenomenal new regime have such credibility. The accuracy of his observations, especially as they concern the cultural life of the American democratic regime, has great limits. But the attractiveness of his method and the allure of his claim to detachment persist, and it is worth thinking about why they do. It is one suggestion of this book that the Tocquevillian strain in American interpretation bespeaks a response to democracy on the part of Americans for whom its implications—especially its cultural implications— are unhappy and whose experience of the intellectual life of the American democracy is painful.

Democracy, for Tocqueville, was something that was bound to happen— and America the only place to look to see how it happened. This is why it mattered so much to him to distinguish those aspects of American life that were exceptional, that could not be counted upon or ought not to be worried about in Europe, from those that were democratic in the general sense. *Democracy in America* renders America as a *kind* of democracy. With its remnant hints of something actually seen, it also suggests a people born of historical circumstance and shaped by luck and inheritance, bodying themselves in the democratic form.

Tocqueville disciplined his information about America to his serious purposes. Here and there, however, his own youthful experience of America's exciting youth burst out—in all the moments in the two big volumes where the rough-and-ready American detail resists Tocqueville's categorizing generalizations, refusing to assemble like iron filings under magnetic sway—in a tribute to the movement westward. In his attempts to generalize about the gravity of frontiersmen, for instance, it is possible to see the Americans Tocqueville encountered crowding his archetypes with their interesting particularities. He happened to encounter more frontier gravity than hilarity. And it seems clear that, like any journalist, he could not resist working up what he saw into an American and democratic archetype; hence his observations on the gravity of the frontiersmen. *Democracy in America* is studded with undigested nuggets that tell about the ways in which Tocqueville was in a particular place and time, as well as in a class of regime.[1]

In his predictions of the course of democratic civilization, Tocqueville's abstractions from the particular case leave the impression of a formidable observer's detachment. He filtered his observations through his aristocratic biases, which remained relatively undiluted and virtually unchallenged in the sphere of culture—however tempered in matters political. He questioned the ancien régime but appeared not to have questioned the value of its civilization. In his presentation of democracy, Tocqueville meant to render and distinguish the things about America that were special to it— the frontier, the English Puritan heritage, the low and busy political life, its civilization, and its peoples—but presumably were accidental to democracy. The things that made American democracy work, in Tocqueville's account, were the things most interpreters have found to be the makings of the "American mind" and civilization. They also tended to be the things he was least able to recognize as elements of civilization, as he knew it.

The notion of the American mind has had a curious American history. It is presently an unfashionable notion among historians, although its attributes as an interpretive mode, called by other names, do persist. America recently has had a *mentalité*, but no mind. But modern American historians learned from ancient American founders, like John Adams and Thomas Jefferson, to consider the collective category of American thinking. Tocqueville has been particularly influential among those who have written about this subject. Henry Adams and Henry Steele Commager, David Potter and Daniel Boorstin, and the classic phase of American Studies form some of the links in the great chain of Tocquevillian being. Inexplicit Tocquevillians, like George Santayana, Richard Hofstadter, and Lionel Trilling, are friendly to his understandings. Even decidedly non-Tocquevillian historians of American culture, like Vernon Louis Parrington, Perry Miller, and Merle Curti, depended on the general notion of an American mind that Tocqueville did so much to define.[2]

Tocqueville's primary interest remained politics and the ordering of civil society into a regime. Issues of *moeurs* seemed to him inevitably conjoined to the nature of the regime. Although he grounded his observations of American political life in a study of documents and laws and institutions, as well as in observations and conversations, the phenomena that informed his discussions of expressive life were considerably less certain and more subject to the influence of taste and the opinions of the interlocutors. Did he inspect an American college? Did he read an American book? Tocqueville did not know much about American art, but he knew what he liked.[3]

American culture was harder to find than American politics in the Jacksonian period. Tocqueville was poorly placed to find out about it on his own or to appreciate what he might encounter of it. His encounter with American culture really amounted to interactions with Americans who were subject to the worried claim of traditional civilization on the democratic future and subject to their own provincial, Anglo-American cultural anxieties to boot. He had neither motive nor skill to question their outlook. They agreed with him that what was good about American civilization was European and that what threatened it was democratic. Tocqueville described lasting political structures from what he saw of American politics, crediting their capacity to grow. He boiled down the lasting dynamics of democratic civilization to the particular, unsatisfactory moment of cultural history he observed superficially and without much interest. American civil society did not do away with Tocqueville's doubts about democracy, but it eased his mind. Culturally, the case was virtually opposite.

In matters of civilization, *Democracy in America* loosed those doubts about democracy and equality that remained under control in Tocqueville's discussion of politics. His fears about what equality would do to political life notwithstanding, he advanced the cause of democracy by translating his experience of visiting a democracy into his generalizations about democracy itself. As his journals reveal, Tocqueville met a host of people with whom he might share a civil society. Patriotic Americans though they were, many expressed reservations about American politics that resembled his own.

Tocqueville was as ill-prepared to welcome cultural change as he was well-disposed to welcome liberalizing political reform. Indeed, the prospect alarmed him.[4] Civilization, as he knew it, might not end with the advent of democracy. Nevertheless, the pell-mell of American culture did not reassure him; it tired and bored, confused and depressed him.

It was only in the American woods that Tocqueville found the contrasting quiet that soothed his soul. In Michigan, Tocqueville had reached at last, he thought, the imaginative destination of his journey. "Now as we advanced further the last signs of man disappeared. Soon there was nothing even to indicate the presence of savages, and we had before us the spectacle which we had been so long pursuing, the depths of a virgin forest." There, he experienced that a kind of sublime majestic order reigns above your head. But near the ground there is a general picture of confusion and chaos. Trunks that can no longer support the weight of their branches, are split half-way up and left with pointed and torn tops. Others, long shaken by the wind, have been thrown all complete on the ground; torn out of the soil, their roots form so many natural ramparts behind which several men could easily take cover. Immense trees, held up by the surrounding branches, stay suspended in the air, and fall to dust without touching the ground. . . . In the solitudes of America nature in all her strength is the only instrument of ruin and also the only creative force. As in forests subject to man's control, death strikes continually here; but no one is concerned to clear the debris away. Every day adds to the number; they fall and pile up one on top of the other; time cannot reduce them quickly enough to dust and make fresh places ready. There many generations of the dead lie side by side. Some that have come to the last stage of dissolution, show as no more than a train of red dust along the grass. Others already half consumed by time, still yet preserve their shape.[5]

In a remarkable passage, Tocqueville summarizes how the scene affects the traveler. "This repose of all nature is no less impressive in the solitudes of the New World than on the immensity of the sea. At midday when the sun darts its beams on the forest, one often hears in its depths something like a long sigh, a plaintive cry lingering in the distance. It is the last stir of the dying wind. Then everything around you falls back into a silence so deep, a stillness so complete that the soul is invaded by a kind of religious terror."

Looking around, the traveler sees the signs of nature in perpetual war and at perpetual peace and hears no sound, not even the one Daniel Boone kept his ears sharp for—the axe striking. "Here not only is man lacking, but no sound can be heard from the animals either. The smallest of them have left these parts to come close to human habitations, and the largest have gone to get even further away. Those that remain stay hidden from the sun's rays. So all is still in the woods, all is silent under their leaves. One would say that for a moment the Creator had turned his face away and the forces of nature are paralyzed."[6] Like so many intelligent travelers, Tocqueville confronted nature with ideas he had learned from books.

Democracy in America emphasized that Americans cherished no aesthetic feelings toward their forests, seeing them only as a field for expansion. Tocqueville contrasted the man-made with the deep, powerful workings of nature. Nobody reading the above excerpts would think of him as a detached observer. He saw what he wanted to see, viewing nature as Jean-Jacques Rousseau or William Wordsworth might—with the highest human feeling and intelligence but with an ear that banished the sound of animals and a second sight that could discern the chaotic order of nature and the Creator's moods (even in the gloom of a Michigan forest not very far from settlements of all kinds). The sublime ordered his feelings.

This experience of the primeval, the natural, and the sublime—for which his aristocratic, traditional, aesthetic education had conditioned him—was the emotional high point of his journey. In this passage, he shows an ambition not unlike that of American painters, poets, and writers of the day, and of the richer cultural age to come, to find the proper terms in which to understand the panorama of the American setting. But Tocqueville appears to have blamed Americans for not seeing what he saw, and for not being able to appreciate it. The democratic soul and the American soul seemed to him as distant as the Native American from his own experience. Tocqueville banished the Native American from this forest primeval, where the forces of nature are in control and the animal and the human are absent. He found an eerie place out in the woods, and it surely is significant that the Creator's face is turned away when this, at best, troubled *dévot* had his communion with his deepest feelings.

In the Michigan woods (one wonders how near the Big Two-Hearted River), Tocqueville found what he says he had looked for elsewhere in vain on his American journey. He had expected a living panorama. "It was there, in a word, that I counted on finding the history of the whole of humanity framed within a few degrees of longitude." He wrote:

> Nothing is true in this picture. Of all the countries in the world America is the least adapted to provide the sight that I went to seek. In America, even more than in Europe, there is one society only. It may be rich or poor, humble or brilliant, trading or agricultural, but it is made up everywhere of the same elements; it has been levelled out by an egalitarian civilisation. The man you left behind in the streets of New York, you will find him again in the midst of almost impenetrable solitude: same dress, same spirit, same language, same habits and the same pleasures. Nothing rustic, nothing naive, nothing that smells of the wilds, nothing even that resembles our villages.[7]

Other testimony of the time remarked a big difference in human society and conditions throughout America. The sameness Tocqueville saw must be observed from a distance, indeed.

The things that seemed to many observers of the frontier so at variance from the conditions "back east" hardly struck Tocqueville, who was looking for the great chain of human social being. It is almost funny how little difference the Frenchman noticed between the city merchants and the rude frontiersmen. America had disappointed his hope of finding the history of human civil society. One may wonder how he could have recognized such a tableau, except in French shapes and forms. He was a poor cultural-anthropological analogist. It bears on Tocqueville's importance to Americans that through him we can, presumably, see ourselves as others saw us. But it is worth keeping in mind how much of his view consisted of his *not* seeing what Americans were used to seeing. What was there for Tocqueville was the absence of what he had expected to see.

What he experienced as the sameness and the "present tense" of American life depressed him. There was no differentiation, no adventure, nothing to stir this young, romantic, conservative Frenchman's imagination or to stimulate his emotions. And, then, he found himself in the forest at last. In the absence of these unfeeling, doubly familiar Americans, and sunk in that ennui with the regular round of human existence that so often feeds the sublime experience of nature, Tocqueville encountered the American, the western, woods—the archetypal home of the primeval for Europeans, too. The vision he had there punished the Americans. His excitement sprang from satiation with observation. He had a profound internal experience and returned to his job, refreshed by the forests.

What he found there was what he had missed in the human sights he had been viewing. He found the generations, the traditions, the tangled evidence of war and peace, the passage of time, the averted face of God— all the things which, many years later, Henry James (in a famous passage on Nathaniel Hawthorne) noted the frustrating absence of from the imaginative viewpoint in American democracy.[8] Tocqueville projected it onto nature and populated the forest with the drama he missed among Americans. A wonderful moment, it inspires tremendous fellow feeling for the too often, too wonderfully, distanced observer.[9]

This should also be kept in mind as an instance of how Tocqueville's private agenda of feeling and attachment created his detachment. If he saw a disappointing democratic sameness in Americans, if American aesthetics disappointed, disappointment was partially his object. The experience of the sublime in nature characteristically generates a moral hierarchy by which to judge people who do not see the natural world in the same way. Tocqueville used his strictures on democratic civilization to establish standards that protected his own aesthetics from American infection and democratic competition. Delight and fellow feeling did not tinge Tocqueville's appreciation of American civilization. The version of civilization, public and private, that America had to offer him was seldom beguiling or ennobling, only intermittently recognizable, and never tempting. He yielded little of his heart of hearts to the expressive life of the United States.

In the name of the traditions that had formed him, Tocqueville suggested that in the opposition between aristocratic and democratic civilizations is revealed the true price democracy makes the superior individual pay. His chapters catalogue the risks to which democracy must expose cherished notions of literature, philosophy, morals, language, intellect, the self, human nature, and the possibilities of civilized life. They prepare the reader to see the democratic as an adversary to traditional civilization. The detached, observant Tocqueville attributed the debasing effect of democracy to the twin forces of individualism (materialist individualism) and equality. They reduce human life to the individual's unaided experience and subject that already devalued coin of experience to the inflationary pressure of democratic egalitarianism. And the superior human being imagines how insupportable it would be to have to live under such conditions.

Most of Tocqueville's informants were Whigs. With them, Tocqueville saw a bustling society so full of project that it could be forgiven its failure to develop a more refined and theoretical intellectual life. He also remarked that Americans were, after all, provincials, even before they were democrats, and the provinces countrywide. Luckily for the Americans, they had Europe to depend on in their past and present and, should they act prudently, in their future. One senses here, as elsewhere, the abiding cultural conservatism that buttressed Tocqueville's political moderation. But how did Tocqueville disentangle the American and the democratic? The democratic was general, the American particular. His abstract description of the democratic described varieties of American things or tendencies, however loath he was to identify them as such. American particulars informed his fantasy of the educated individual trapped in the democratic future. He described democratic despotism as a kind of counter-utopia. "When I conceive a democratic society of this kind, I fancy myself in one of those low, close, and gloomy abodes where the light which breaks in from without soon faints and fades away. A sudden heaviness overpowers me, and I grope through the surrounding darkness to find an opening that will restore me to the air and the light of day."

In his account of *Tocqueville and Beaumont in America*, George Pierson tells a story that sheds light on the sources of this dark passage. It is the story of their stay in the country cabin in Tennessee where Beaumont found lodging for Tocqueville, who had taken sick in a terrible winter storm. Pierson points out that this cabin reappears in a somewhat altered form in Tocqueville's book, as a typical frontier dwelling. We have no account from Tocqueville of this interlude, but Beaumont's survives.

> Thirteenth of December; what a day! what a night! The bed where Tocqueville is lying is in a chamber whose walls are made of oak logs not even squared, placed one on top of the other. It is so cold it would crack a stone. I light a monster fire; the flame crackles on the hearth fed by the wind which rushes in on us from all sides. The moon sends its rays through the interstices between the chunks of wood. Tocqueville gets warm only by stifling himself under his blanket and the pile of coverings I load on him. No succor to be gotten from our hosts. Depth of our isolation and abandonment.[10]

Perhaps Tocqueville dreamed his dream of the cave of democratic barbarism from under those covers in that rude cabin, shaken with chills in the "depth of our isolation and abandonment." Tocqueville's American nightmare energized his reservations about democracy and is the clue to his discussions of democratic civilization. The detached observation masks the resisting individual.

Tocqueville's account of democratic philosophizing shadows his account of American philosophy. The chapters feature a curious interplay between American and democratic subjects, the "philosophical method of the Americans" yielding to the "principal source of belief among democratic nations." The chapters that treat democratic tendencies summarize and generalize and advance the specific observational claims of the American chapters. Tocqueville named the Americans "Cartesians," reflected upon them as progeny of seventeenth- and eighteenth-century philosophical discourse, and reflected upon their English religious foundations. He credited them with an intellectual history rather than a philosophical habit: "That is to say, without ever having taken the trouble to define the rules, they have a philosophical method common to the whole people." Tocqueville talked to William Ellery Channing, but not about philosophy, and he missed Ralph Waldo Emerson. He believed the American habits of thought might yield a kind of philosophy in democratic times, but he was far from crediting Americans with the conscious practice of the philosophy their habitual thoughts implied.

Tocqueville states succinctly at the start of his discussion what the following chapters amplify: "In most of the operations of the mind each American appeals only to the individual effort of his own understanding." Here, their unconscious Cartesianism and their fundamental democracy unite. The effect of democratic and American life on the habit of philosophy was, in Tocqueville's view, to sever the mind from the authority of tradition and throw it back on a falsely individual notion of authority, mandated by democracy but not understood as the limited and partial view it really was.

Philosophy should herald the freedom of the human mind, but the American mistakes individualism for individuality, separateness for originality, ignorance for conclusions, self-interest for wisdom, canniness for philosophy, smugness for perfectibility. Americans confuse the techniques of pursuing their self-interest (even rightly understood) within the commercial and political metabolism of their society with the reflection and serious questioning appropriate to philosophy. In this, they form a subset of the modern. In this, they also exist within the horizons of their society and not outside them, where philosophy properly dwells.

One difficulty with Tocqueville's discussion is that he judges philosophical habits among the Americans by a standard that presumably makes philosophy impossible in a democratic state: one of the conditions he sees in democracy is that it is impossible for individuals to rise above their horizons enough to see beyond them. Put another way, he contrasts democratic individualism with the example of aristocratic individuality as expounded in the section in *Democracy in America* on "honor." [11]

Americans think effectively only within the lowering horizons of their own society. They can calculate and generalize but find it hard, perhaps impossible, to philosophize. The notion of philosophy as the exercise of human individuality at its highest beggars Tocqueville's American and his democracy. Was Tocqueville's problem over philosophy with America or democracy? Tocqueville's *democracy* sounds mighty like the *modern*. Much of what democracy seems to do is to make the ancient inoperable. Tocqueville sensed that exactly what made democratic life work subverted much of what, in his opinion, made life worth living.

AMERICAN EXCEPTIONS

The philosophical traditions Tocqueville cited as having formed the American habit of thinking—the enlightened and the Protestant—were reformed, if not rejected, by the very philosopher who comes to mind when Tocqueville is discussing American philosophy: Ralph Waldo Emerson. The resemblance between what Emerson might be said to have done and what Tocqueville said an American democratic philosophy must end up doing is uncanny. Individual authority, general ideas, pantheism, and an implicit Cartesianism all go a long way toward identifying Emerson.

Emerson addressed his high-flown eloquence (his language substantiates Tocqueville's guess at how Americans would write such things) to Americans in terms very similar to Tocqueville's words to the French about the Americans. They both worried about the lack of individuality in American individualism, the materialism of democracy, and the dangerous tyranny of the egalitarian majority. Emerson's "The American Scholar" exemplifies and echoes the very things that Tocqueville noticed. Emerson's status and politics would have made him one of Tocqueville's congenial Americans. What stands in the way of this ex post facto association is that Tocqueville inescapably would have thought that what Emerson did was *not* philosophy.[12]

Emerson tried to find a way for the isolated, weak individual to develop a strong and original individuality. He would teach the individual to thrive, in the course of life within a democracy, by making decisions from the inside out—to oppose democracy, if necessary, but from the inside out. One reason for Emerson's tremendous influence on the American middle classes was the profound help he gave to the kinds of individuals that Tocqueville appeared to value, in the very conditions of democratic materialism that Tocqueville described. Tocqueville acutely suggested that the frequent resort to private judgment in a democracy would support stability but also narrow the limits of individual freedom of thought. Emerson thought this, too. Tocqueville thought that democratic individualism was not really positioned to improve this problem. Emerson proposed his variety of transcendentalism to solve it.

Tocqueville guessed pretty well what transcendentalism eventually would involve, and his comments on pantheism show what he thought of its essentially false understanding of individuality:

> If there is a philosophical system which teaches that all things material and immaterial, visible and invisible, which the world contains are to be considered only as the several parts of an immense Being, who alone remains eternal amidst the continual change and ceaseless transformation of all that constitutes him, we may readily infer that such a system, although it destroy the individuality of man, or rather because it destroys that individuality, will have secret charms for men living in democracies. . . . Among the different systems by whose aid philosophy endeavors to explain the universe I believe pantheism to be one of those most fitted to seduce the human mind in democratic times. Against it all who abide in their attachment to the true greatness of man should combine and struggle. (*Democracy in America*, vol. 2, book 1, chap. 7)

Like Emerson, Tocqueville invoked "the true greatness of man" as a standard by which thought might be measured. Since he already knew what it amounted to, he left it undefined. Emerson made its definition the object of his philosophizing.

The influence of German philosophy was critical to Emerson's thinking. Tocqueville resolutely opposed that tendency in nineteenth-century philosophy. He connected it to the human failure to choose among alternatives. "When the conditions of society are becoming more equal and each individual man becomes more like all the rest, more weak and insignificant, a habit grows up of ceasing to notice the citizens and considering only the people, of overlooking individuals to think only of their kind. At such times the human mind seeks to embrace a multitude of different objects at once, and it constantly strives to connect a variety of consequences with a single cause" (*Democracy in America*, vol. 2, book 1, chap. 7). Weak and bewildered by choices, the American individual was an object of interest to Tocqueville as an instance of the democratic tendency toward the debilitating mental habits of the modern temper.

For Emerson, this weak and isolated individual presented a potentiality. To whom else, and in empathic recognition of whom else, could Emerson's "The American Scholar" have been addressed? Emerson's was surely the sort of rhetorical philosophizing that Tocqueville predicted American philosophy must be. In its encouragement of democratic individuals to cultivate and seize and insist on their individuality in lieu of their individualism, it may have been the very example of culture Tocqueville believed in. Emerson's call to "Man Thinking" to awaken to the possibilities inherent in democratic America resembled the simultaneous courting of mutually exclusive alternatives, the refusal to choose masquerading as choice, that Tocqueville had imagined when he dismissed the kinds of philosophies democracy in America would yield.

It is easy to imagine Tocqueville regarding Emersonian injunctions like the following with a categorizing, even a scornful, smile.

> The world,—this shadow of the soul, or *other me*, lies wide around. Its attractions are the keys which unlock my thoughts and make me acquainted with myself. I run eagerly into this resounding tumult. I grasp the hands of those next to me, and take my place in the ring to suffer and to work, taught by an instinct, that so shall the dumb abyss be vocal with speech. I pierce its order; I dissipate its fear; I dispose of it within the circuit of my expanding life. So much only of life as I know by experience, so much of the wilderness have I vanquished and planted, or so far have I extended my being, my dominion. I do not see how any man can afford, for the sake of his nerves and his nap, to spare any action in which he can partake. It is pearls and rubies to his discourse. Drudgery, calamity, exasperation, want, are instructors in eloquence and wisdom. The true scholar grudges every opportunity of action past [*sic*] by, as a loss of power.[13]

Now, imagine Emerson addressing Tocqueville, who saw so many of the same things in America, but who typified the response of the Old to the New and opposed observation to participation.

Emerson would surely have thought "Nature" had things to say to Tocqueville in the Michigan woods. He might also have welcomed Tocqueville's characterization of the sort of thought democracies would encourage. It is a change of tone or a shift in attitude that makes Emersonisms symptomatic rather than specific. Emerson made a philosophy out of the conditions Tocqueville remarked in America, and his thinking resembled the very philosophy (with its individualist concern, its generality, its pantheism, its style of argument) that Tocqueville thought must characterize such a creed. He called the scholar a hero of culture, not its detached observer.

Emersonian philosophizing even appears to have contributed to the general moral improvement that Tocqueville conceded would be one happy tendency of the democratic age. But there is no getting around the fact that Emerson thought his way would help individualists achieve individuality and that he expected the American scholar effectively to counter the tyranny of the majority. He imagined an American culture that would make of common clay a magnificent and a new art and wisdom. This was what Tocqueville thought could not happen.

For Tocqueville, Emersonian notions would not advance the greatness of humankind. Tocqueville's detachment from the American situation enabled him to suggest that what would seem like a real philosophy to the Americans might be merely a philosophical ideology, bounded by the horizons of the American democracy and sharing its Anglo-American origins and the generalized requirements of a democratic philosophy. This point of view was undeniably telling, if not final. Democracy is presumably beggared by this judgment. Emerson, in fact, was not. There is no reason to believe that "The American Scholar" or "Nature" did not in fact comprehend what Tocqueville was getting at. On the contrary, "The American Scholar" starts where Tocqueville left off, saying that it is precisely from the humble everyday tools of the democratic age that one must make a philosophy, that this indeed is what philosophy is—enlightenment not by ancient lights but by one's own. Detachment within American culture means detachment as a selection, not as a line drawing. Living in a culture need not prevent one from rising above it when the moral occasion dictates. To begin by rising above it, however, is a way of avoiding it. The specific American case could provide responses to Tocqueville's views that the generalized democratic case by definition could not. Democracy may not have understood the alternatives to it by which Tocqueville judged it, but some Americans clearly did.

In discussing the literary characteristics of democratic times, Tocqueville contrasted two styles of literary work: aristocratic and democratic. Literary progress is from democratic to aristocratic—from the exuberant, untutored energy of popular expression to the mannered, overrefined preoccupation with style. Literary greatness reflects the stages of cultural competition between the aristocratic and democratic—the exclusive and the popular, the highbrow and the lowbrow—elements within cultures.

Tocqueville's discussion of the aristocratic literary performance bears consequentially on the American instance.

The slightest work will be carefully wrought in its least details; art and labor will be conspicuous in everything; each kind of writing will have rules of its own, from which it will not be allowed to swerve and which distinguish it from all others. Style will be thought of almost as much importance as thought, and the form will be no less considered than the matter; the diction will be polished, measured, and uniform. The tone of the mind will be always dignified, seldom very animated, and writers will care more to perfect what they produce than to multiply their productions. It will sometimes happen that the members of the literary class, always living among themselves and writing for themselves alone, will entirely lose sight of the rest of the world, which will infect them with a false and labored style; they will lay down minute literary rules for their exclusive use, which will insensibly lead them to deviate from common sense and finally to transgress the bounds of nature. (*Democracy in America*, vol. 2, book 1, chap. 13)

Tocqueville little thought that America would produce such writers soon. Yet his version of the aristocratic propensity in writing previews the caricatures of the writings of James that commenced during his lifetime and have continued since. It makes up a part of what Santayana named "the genteel tradition." What Tocqueville described as something outside democracy was indeed a feature of American literary life by the end of the nineteenth century.

James's own book about American democratic culture, his 1879 study of Hawthorne, echoed many of Tocqueville's observations and has been used to confirm them. Whereas Tocqueville said that "the inhabitants of the United States have, then, at present properly speaking, no literature," however, James emphasized the poor *makings* for literature, "properly speaking," in his time in the United States. James's solution to his cultural situation was expatriation. Surely, this confirms the Tocquevillian prediction of the democratic principle driving the aristocratic out.

It did not interest Tocqueville that American democracy might supply its own actors of the aristocratic principle in literature, as in other things. Tocqueville's description of great ages of literature could describe several periods in American literature and culture; the "American Renaissance" of the 1850s was just the first. James's work and life, like Emerson's, suggests that Tocqueville's version of democracy delimited America. Tocqueville's keen insights into the ground of cultural enterprise suffered because he abstracted what he saw in America into a model of the democratic mind, when his observations were more properly clues than conclusions. The elements that constitute American culture are present in Tocqueville's writings, astoundingly, but missing is what it was really like—the drama, the story, the conflict, the feelings, the culture. It was detachment before the fact.

Think of Tocqueville's encounter with America not only as a solemn, social scientific observation but also as a Jamesian comedy of transatlantic manners, misunderstandings, and cultural collisions. Tocqueville ultimately reasoned from a fear that America could not produce, had no place for, and could never understand someone like himself. His journals suggest that he felt the Americans he met seldom understood him. He, of course, felt that he understood them perfectly. In *The Europeans*, James explored this sort of feeling. He was as little at home in the American future as Tocqueville was in the French. His was an artist's alienation, so he left home; Tocqueville's was clearly a cultural alienation, so he hurried home.

THE AMERICAN TOCQUEVILLIAN

The American Tocquevillian is divided in allegiance to the American regime, believing both that its people are the enemies of intellectual freedom and that America is yet the world's defender of freedom. The Tocquevillian is willing to fight for liberal democracy because of the freedom and protection it gives but does not recognize as easily the bounty of cultural democracy because that is the principle that interferes with the individual need for distinction. ("Of *course*, you are as good as I am, but the books I read are better than the ones you read.") Reading Tocqueville provided Americanists with a perspective from which they could see American culture; they could free themselves of certain plaguing issues and could emphasize those qualities that were thought best suited to a modern American geopolitical role at the center of the free world. The notion of liberal democracy as a best possible, rather than a transcendently ordained, regime looked in the post–World-War-II period especially attractive. The nonideological claim of Americans vis-à-vis, first, the Nazis and, then, the Communists—the notion of a form of government that required enlightened self-interested adherence rather than true belief—held an attraction for educated Americans. There was something grown-up in Tocqueville's Old World view of America.

There was a growth in the educated, socially conservative, and yet in many ways politically as well as culturally internationalist segment of the population that, Whiglike perhaps, identified with a transatlantic world. The tiny American intelligentsia of Tocqueville's time, which always had been an alternative to the "native" American impulse, now had become powerful. Some of the most important scholarly work of the postwar period depends on the kind of clear-eyed view of the democratic that a reading of Tocqueville can encourage.[14]

The elaboration and growth of the institutional educational life of the United States after World War II required a movement away from the culturally provincial. World responsibility required a sense of America's place in the history of the West, and the particular politics of the Cold War required a separation from the simplest kind of litmus test for understanding democracy. The influence of Tocqueville essentially shadowed the move of the American polity from the democracy of America to the democracy of Tocqueville's inevitable Western future.

When America at last became the leader of the West, it became the thing Tocqueville was writing about: a world in which democracy could have custody of the West. The Tocquevillian always looked at America in terms of how the democratic affected what was prized in previous orders. Making the world safe for democracy and democracy safe for world leadership compromises an American politics that can be liberal or conservative but is open to the antidemocratic cultural understanding. Belief in the improvement of American democracy through grafting, or through somehow making it a resting place for the world's modern and traditionalist cultures, helped create that remarkable intellectual sophistication that is an element in the cultural formidability of the United States as a world power.

Making a homegrown, "native" culture sophisticated enough to respect an imported one had been, in a sense, the American interpretive project from the start, or so the American Tocquevillian historians and interpreters said. American cultural history is the story of successful appropriations trying, in turn, to resist appropriation. Descriptions of American culture as a melting pot, as an ethnic pluralism in terms of dualities in tension, claim as the characteristic American cultural process the very one that in its highest phase would produce discrepancies for the American Tocquevillian view. This view held that democracy was put in the world to make thought and art of the most advanced sort for the discriminating to enjoy, free of cultural rootedness or mores or control or social obligation. The obligation was to the regime that made learning free, not to the principle of freedom on democratic terms, as it might inflect the learning.[15]

Tocqueville's prominence in American interpretation since World War II has amounted almost to an orthodoxy.[16] Even those who dispute him and the consensus views that derive from his observations have not restored the Parringtonian liberal interpretation to its previous place. Our view of the liberal past has been chastened, and we interpret within a Tocquevillian paradigm—one might even say horizon. It has been a subtle and consequential ascendancy, but the most important thing that his influence has signified is that the democratic is in principle unfriendly to individual expression and that individual civil freedom, although the regime may have figured out how to protect it within majoritarian democracy, has not been achieved on the cultural level. The American interpretation that the Tocquevillian replaced looked to the popular for the free; the Tocquevillian sees the popular as the natural enemy of the intellectually free—by which it means the intellectually individual, by which it means the intellectually and artistically good (better, best, beautiful, subtle, traditional, interesting, true).

One senses in many influential Americanist interpretations a habit of attitude toward the popular. Hofstadter's historical writings make a consistent case that popular understandings of the American regime are usually wrong, subversive of pluralism, superstitious, liable to demagogic manipulation, uncomprehending of freedom, and better left in the sheath of the larger workings of American conventional politics. The notion that "the people" are there to be liberated into utopian self-realization is countered in Hofstadter by a picture of the popular as myth-ridden, paranoid, anti-intellectual, and not the proper natural defender of its own or anyone else's freedom.[17]

An astringent realism about the limits of heroes, idealistic pictures, and the hopes of Left or Right for transforming the limits of human character led many Americanists to prize the restrained, even cynical, wisdom and the lowered expectations of James Madison. Embracing Madison need not be a politically conservative position, but it was culturally conservative. It staked out a conservative liberal position in a time of liberal hegemony. It was acutely a conclusion drawn from liberal experience, as Parrington's was a conclusion drawn from liberal expectation. The ideological excesses of Left and Right prompted such views; McCarthyism and Stalinism were seen as simultaneously threatening, and the analysis was supposed to express an awareness of the simultaneity of their threat.[18]

It is not surprising that the American Tocquevillian also midwived the birth of Madison as favored founder. Madison emerged as someone with a commitment to ordered liberty. He resisted the chaotic transformations of Jeffersonian hopes, and his realistic view of human nature was located in Hume and not in the utopian French Enlightenment. He looked to self-interest, not the people, as the salvation for democratic republican institutions. It was a chastened faith, and its antidemocratic cultural implications made so much political sense that no one seemed to take very clear note of where they led. Madison was a good choice for those who were skeptical of what had passed for ideology, especially the Jeffersonian/Hamiltonian, Manichaean view of American history. It particularly undermined the ideologizing of democracy that had been considered Jeffersonian. Madison was seen as all the founder that liberal democracy needed, and the neo-Madisonians jettisoned the Jeffersonian expression of democratic faith, the sense of "the people" as a conscience and ideal for the gifted individual.

Merrill Peterson's *The Jefferson Image in the American Mind* suggested that the fact that Jefferson was put to use, however many ways he was used, was a constant of American history and signified an awareness of the democratic and the libertarian. Abraham Lincoln and Robert Frost had said as much.[19] It was a characteristic of the 1960s that Jefferson was not put to use but out to pasture. Jefferson the slaveholder, the imperfect civil libertarian, "the aristocrat as democrat" (in Hofstadter's earlier phrase), as human being, revealed the strains and exhaustions of the liberal democratic hope. Such a figure could not sponsor a search for a guiding transcendent purpose. Madison soothed what Jefferson disappointed—the wounded hopes of high ideals. Jefferson came to stand for liberal hypocrisy, Madison for a tough-minded realism that freed the intellectual from the utopian. And it particularly freed the dry-eyed calculation of the intellectual's enlightened self-interest from the prompting of the inner voice of democratic Jeffersonian idealism. Madison and Tocqueville were an ideological partnership that replaced the historical association of Madison with Jefferson.

The replacement of Jefferson with Madison was never complete. President John F. Kennedy welcomed a glittering, prize-winning American elite to the White House by saying that never had so much talent been gathered there since Thomas Jefferson dined alone—this garnered Jeffer-

son for the meritocracy. That meritocracy was at once true and a different coming true of the Jeffersonian dream. The "best and the brightest"
could claim the Jeffersonian mantle, but theirs was a Madisonian understanding and sometimes, it seemed, even Tocquevillian. The people must
be served, but they were to be told, by those best suited to serve them,
how they were to be served best. The class of modern natural aristocrats,
liberated for public service in a burst of energetic idealism, for various
reasons were not imbued with a sense of democratic conscience. Democratic institutions themselves—a sluggish Congress, an entrenched segre-
gationist establishment, complacent constituencies throughout the land—
seemed at odds with democratic sincerity and justice. This second sight into
democratic institutions, which saw through them to their essential character, helped speed the rush to serve and modernize and reform. American
progress in the late 1960s depended on an inspiring level of American self-
understanding and self-scrutiny. Comparing reality to promise and seeing
through promises to reality constituted the dual method of the time. It
was an interpretive process that emphasized high ideals and tough-minded
action.

Intellectual, enlightened self-interest was not, at first, subject to the same
scrutiny as material self-interest. When that happened in the 1960s, all
Tocquevillian hell broke loose. The great Hofstadterian agenda of academic
freedom did not question the possession of the academy by orthodoxies
that were culturally antidemocratic in tone and were constituted without
reference to democracy. It was assumed that professional scholarship was
neutral with respect to interest, and that its essential white male character was a reflection, at the very worst, of a history of prejudice that was
being counteracted with all deliberate speed. That protected, professionalized academic knowledge might itself be particularist in character was
hard enough to take in; that its premise of detachment might prove antidemocratic was a charge too reminiscent of the well-known anti-intellectual
tendency of the American people to be taken seriously.

The antipopular tone of Hofstadter's work made much sense. The people
were anti-intellectual and democracy was not much help in improving that
situation. What, from this liberal point of view, democracy could do was
to increase the advantage of education and enlightenment within society
and somehow undercut the democratic delusions about history and about
life. Hofstadter's liberalism took the Tocquevillian insight to different conclusions than the American Tocquevillian. Nevertheless, Hofstadter never

allowed that the knowledge he defended was antipopular in a way that needed to be explored.[20]

This, of course, is what Parrington, for all of his own mistakes, had recognized and conceptualized in his *Main Currents in American Thought* as the Jeffersonian/Hamiltonian, democratic/antidemocratic dichotomy in American thought. Curti followed Parrington in emphasizing the democratic, Deweyite teleology in *The Growth of American Thought*. One reason Commager's *The American Mind* remains so gripping is his attempt to reconcile his own Parringtonian and Tocquevillian views within one synthetic cultural understanding. Arthur Schlesinger, Jr., paradigmatically takes the democratic into account in his interpretations of American intellectual life. Their trends of thought, like Parrington's, which both denied the inherent anti-intellectualism of the popular and made it the cause of scholarship to close the gap in American intellectual life between liberal and democratic principles, departed from Tocqueville. Parrington and Curti did not rate the Frenchman highly. What the Tocquevillian must see as an inherent opposition between the individual and the democratic, they saw rather as the potential mix—not oil and water, but flour and yeast.[21]

The Tocquevillian replaced the liberal in the postwar period on this very question. Even the Left was Tocquevillian on the central issues. The educated young expected an American majority to be wrong and created a politics and a counterculture that was democratic in theory but not in terms of American democracy, which was assumed to be itself undemocratic and faulty. The sixties loosed the Left from its studious pursuit of an actual democratic working-class majority, electoral or cultural. The still noteworthy elimination of Parrington as an element in the interpretive scene bears attention. Who reads Parrington any more? His most influential critics were Trilling and Hofstadter, whose by no means identical projects shared the elaboration of the protected place within America for disinterested or detached scholarship that the university and its nondemocratic allegiances afforded.[22] The academy was hospitable to a realistic look at popular energies, an examination that tended to undermine anyone's extravagant faith in democracy.

America's interpretation of its civilization in the last fifty years has been much beholden to American Tocquevillian views. It has eased the way for America's hosting of the culture of modernism and for the sophisticated intellectual and scholarly structure that has defined the cultural home of the free world. Without rehearsing the history of America's emergence as host country of Western ideas and intentions, it is worth noting that a view of American civilization that was compatible with America's increased role as metropolitan in the modern world was necessary.[23] What Max Lerner intoned about America, *as a civilization*, has been the modern subtext, just as Tocqueville said it would be. The powerful irony of American democratic civilization's inheriting the burden of protecting and advancing what remains of those things Tocqueville valued in culture is matched by the assimilation by American intellectuals of a Tocquevillian self-conceit to go along with their stewardship.

In a sense, American intellectual life has spawned a culture of guardians who function as a teaching priesthood and curating bureaucracy for lodging the booty of the ages in America. The public-arts culture of the United States has made a success of high culture that would have astonished Henry James. What was once available only to the rich is there for general consumption.

This expansion of a complacent consumer culture has, of course, much of the taint of the genteel tradition. The moralism of high art, the moralism of cultural engagement, and the moralism of liberal education have fused into a culturewide nostrum that is best distilled in the appeals to the individual heard when the Public Broadcasting Service raises money. Americans have elaborated the drawing of distinctions about human beings that presumably goes along with high culture. American popular culture diffuses the suggestion that better books, higher-class television, and foreign films and foods make better people, and that better people are more easily recognized by shared tastes. Even popular culture can become a better taste, if spoken about in the right way. Santayana would have felt vindicated. Consumer moralism represents the apex of the genteel tradition, the diffusion of self-consciousness and Western civilization in the place of morals among the high-minded American middle classes, and the substitution of the palate for the sensibility, of taste for art, of received opinion for philosophy.

The human inevitability of such transformations of cultures into orthodoxies is not at issue. But the cultural implications for a democracy of confusing what distinguishes one from the other, in terms of sensibility, with what makes one morally a better person, is at issue. If the role of letters and philosophy in a democracy is to distinguish one person from another, one might well ask to what end. The view of art and letters as the testing place for status within a democracy is established and ritualized—and that is the Tocquevillian view. The worth of the civilization is determined by the fate within it of traditional views of civilization, as interpreted by their traditionalist guardians. American Tocquevillian interpretation sometimes amounts almost to a ritual of purification with respect to the democratic and the popular.

The Tocquevillian makes assumptions about the possession of individual wisdom and the democratic potential to come up with something better. The first assumption is the humanist axiom that good books make good men. It was the axiom of the genteel tradition and was encumbered by, among other things, central assumptions about the relation of money to culture, sexuality, and gender; the relation of manners to morals as expressed in cultural attainment; and the thicket of assumptions and irresolutions through which Lambert Strether must find his way in *The Ambassadors*. The second assumption is that, left to itself, the democracy will quickly produce a diminished, majoritarian cultural alternative to the past. This more powerful assumption remains at the core of that critique of American intellectual life that would subject even the genteel tradition to criticism because it represents the inevitable cultural corruption brought on by a democratic society.

TOCQUEVILLIAN COMPENSATION AND BEYOND

One limitation of Tocquevillian detachment is discovered in his strictures on democratic language. It is easy to agree with his worried comments about the disappearance of precise meaning, as the habit of treating language as a democratic convenience, not a fixed galaxy of definitions, overwhelms. There may well be something poignant in the disappearance in the modern age of the patois, along with the cultural and class distinctions it represented. One may even be tempted, in Tocqueville's wake, to make language, traditionally defined and used according to traditional authority, a measure of civilization. Tocqueville chose meaning over form. "I had rather that the language should be made hideous with words imported from the Chinese, the Tatars, or the Hurons than that the meaning of a word in our own language should become indeterminate" (*Democracy in America*, vol. 2, book 1, chap. 16).

Even as the Edwin Newman/William Safire schoolmarm in everyone nods agreement, the beauties in American speech come to mind—its livewire democratic expressiveness, and the concessions it is formed to make to all the newcomers who would speak it, rise through it, express and imagine in it. How hard it is to call that American speech a patois also comes to mind. Tocqueville was willing to suffer the barbarities of common speech only if they were necessary to preserve a traditional core of ancient meaning in a context of social control. He did not shy away from freezing the growth of language to preserve certain meanings, to privilege certain views and social structures. He grasped what the linguistic symbols stood for in real life. Democratic language offered a double affront, and, if he must choose, he preferred the affront to his sensibilities to the subversion of his authorities. No one need blame him.

American culture has witnessed an extraordinary change in the sound and use of languages. Like it or not, the story of this civilization is told in a language that has fulfilled Tocqueville's worst fears. The detachment that reads or hears this language from the Tocquevillian certainty about language must always deplore the direction of the culture. James shared Tocqueville's ear in many ways. He detested the generality of speech. He made his novels out of the shaded meanings of words. But, in a revealing moment, he showed another side. In youth, James had been severe about Walt Whitman. In later life, he read some Whitman poetry to Edith Wharton, his voice filling "the hushed room like an organ adagio" as he recited from "Song of Myself." "At the end, the Master flung his hands upward, a characteristic gesture, and with the eyes twinkling said: 'Oh, yes, a great genius, undoubtedly a very great genius! Only one cannot help deploring his too-extensive acquaintance with the foreign languages.' "[24]

James had the order right. Whitman's too eager delight in adding words from the Chinese, the Tartar, and the Huron, like Emerson's frustrating generalities, might embarrass finer-grained readers. But, to James, it was a delicate joke's worth, a small price to pay for the beauty and originating power of the work. Democracy, in Whitman's instance of that very amendment in language Tocqueville understandably deplored, was too much the moving spirit of America for James to refuse it in this form, however much he might prefer life elsewhere. His distance was a defense, but he did not want it to confuse his judgment about good and great American things. James loved Whitman, and he made Isabel Archer an Emersonian. He sent his most admirable character, Lambert Strether, home to America, clear-eyed, at the end of *The Ambassadors*.

For Tocqueville, the detachment with which he viewed America and democracy kept him always aloof from its human beauties. For James, that detachment had always the comic shrug of one who knew how funny it was to feel that way, hailing from such a country. His American characters, after all, are memorably American. That ironic shrug and twinkling eye, the expatriation, and even the lifetime of dissenting feeling that contributed to it are only one tithe the amount that Tocqueville's aristocracy had to pay to the democracy in the American regime. Like Jefferson or Oliver Wendell Holmes, Jr., James understood this, albeit in different ways. It was not a price Tocqueville was called upon to pay, nor was he willing to imagine the advantages of paying. But it proves a consequential and perilous price for Americans to refuse. It admits one to a rich and beautiful world that Tocqueville neither discerned nor would have liked had he discerned it, but which may soothe even the highest-toned American soul, given half a chance.

Tocqueville's discussions of poetry "among democratic nations" bring some of these questions to a head. Poetry, he believed, concerns the "Ideal." "The Poet is he who, by suppressing a part of what exists, by adding some imaginary touches to the picture, and by combining certain real circumstances that do not in fact happen together, completes and extends the work of nature. Thus the object of poetry is not to represent what is true, but to adorn it and to present to the mind some loftier image" (*Democracy in America*, vol. 2, book 1, chap. 17). He reasoned about the forms poetry would take in democratic ages. The principle of equality seemed likely to do more direct dirty work on poetry than on almost any other form of expression that Tocqueville discussed. He loved poetry as he understood it and loathed what he feared would replace it. The principle of equality must rob poetry of its past and its present and make impossible those ideals the rendering of which is poetry's true function. His imagination of what democratic poetry would be like was shrewd and powerful. The democratic poet would have to pander to the democratic audience's incapacity to stay interested in anything but itself. Reflecting on the limits that ordinary objects and the regular round of life have as subjects for the ideal, he wrote, "These things are not poetical in themselves. . . . This forces the poet constantly to search below the external surface which is palpable to the senses, in order to read the inner soul. . . . I need not traverse earth and sky to discover a wondrous object woven of contrasts, of infinite greatness and littleness, of intense gloom and amazing brightness, capable at once of exciting pity, admiration, terror, contempt. *I have only to look at myself* [emphasis added]" (*Democracy in America*, vol. 2, book 1, chap. 17).

Tocqueville here predicted Whitman. His mind grudging his heart's creation its aesthetic approval all the way, Tocqueville said in his own voice what Whitman said over and over again in his: "I have only to look at myself." This nearness was not an identity. Tocqueville and Whitman, like Tocqueville and Emerson, would not have agreed about the nature of the self any more than they agreed on the subjects of poetry. Tocqueville called the future democracy the "modern democracy," thereby elevating his perceptive abstractions to something static—this is a moment in which the gathered standards of the past can predict and understand and have their say to the future. He predicted what he would not acknowledge.

Tocqueville's work was profoundly anti-modern. It offered the lights of the past as a guide to living in an unwelcome future. For all its welcoming of political democracy, it insisted in cultural matters on the propagation and superiority of cultural views that refused democratic mores. This was never clearer than in the case of poetry, where Tocqueville's luminous mind suggested the American democratic bard and, in the very moment of prediction, refused him a welcome. Emerson, who less cogently predicted Whitman, extended the welcome Whitman required.

Tocqueville's insights into poetry are barren. They discourage the very openness his political views encourage. His wonderful view of the American westward movement as poetry depended on his mean-spirited and suspect claim that Americans could not appreciate the beauties of the forest. His own view of those woods was partial and cluttered. Tocqueville's detached observation erected a wonderful system to contain the realities of American democracy. The American Tocquevillian builds on that system an understanding of democracy that is meant to cure enthusiasm for it. Conceived before the fact of the things it teaches one to despise, *Democracy in America* deals in the perpetuation of its own values rather than in the sympathetic understanding of democracy. In cultural matters, especially, Tocqueville exalts distance from surrounding phenomena, the fear of annexation excusing one from participation. The point is to consider phenomena as symptomatic of a previously arrived at account of democratic culture. The love of and pleasure in things, their flavor, gets lost in the placing of them. It is supposed to. The taste for democratic civilization is regarded as evidence that one is lost to it. The traditional is assumed, the democratic examined.

If one identifies as Tocquevillian a class of intelligent observers who live under the democratic regime yet see it with reserve—a class of Whigs with civilized second sight about values—America has had its Tocquevillians. There is that tradition of political and cultural conservatism that has fielded groups of Americans who view with determined skepticism the claims of the modern and the democratic and the egalitarian in cultural, as in political, life. The tradition of interpretation that Tocqueville can be said to have founded has flourished in American letters. American scholarship has followed Tocqueville's suggestions and venerated his methods and understanding. Such monuments of American interpretation as the classic American Studies movement are difficult to imagine without *Democracy in America*.

The American Tocquevillian haunts American intellectual and cultural life. A collection of attitudes and a pose, it extends from Adams through Santayana to American Studies and into present-day neoconservatism/conservatism. Above all, it is a way of distancing the democratic community in the interests of traditional understandings of civilization. It has had a powerful impact on the American interpretation of democratic civilization. It is not always self-consciously Tocquevillian. Matthew Arnold guided Trilling's critique of American culture. The cultural critique of democracy and the claim of detachment in observing American democratic civilization equip the American Tocquevillian project of distancing the self from the engulfing and lowering democratic community. When Americans draw the line on cultural matters, when they seek out Tocqueville's detached perspective—in domestic or real expatriation, in conscious poses of disdain or conservatism or eccentricity, and in regional refusal of the streamlined modern (sometimes wrapped in the difficult modern itself)—one encounters that challenge to the horizons of democracy that distinguishes the Tocquevillian.

The sources of American detachment about America are bound to differ from Tocqueville's own. Too, the resulting views will not always echo his. But American history abounds in homegrown traditionalist critiques of American culture that echo Tocqueville's specific reserves about America and the generalized critique of democratic culture he fashioned from them. The genteel tradition, that sturdy mainstream of American high culture, was distinguished by a worry similar to Tocqueville's about the effect individualist materialism and democracy would have on the progress of morals as reflected in letters. The Tocquevillian does not shrug a *de gustibus* shrug of dislike but drives home with judgment the teleology of aesthetic and cultural choice.

Culture, for the American Tocquevillian, is where the healthy and dis-eased regimes breed and where the superior individual can take a stand. Tocqueville never endorsed the independence of art from culture or from what it expressed. He hoped for, rather than predicted, the maturation of the best Americans into a class who understood their self-interest rightly. In matters of manners and civilization, he did suggest that he knew such people would exist, but he could not imagine their developing in the American or in a democratic setting. At best, he saw them as developing in controlling relation to, not in creative identification with, democracy. Every age has featured line-drawing, status-seeking, or status-preserving would-be American aristocrats articulating Tocquevillian and other con-servative principles of association and differentiation, claiming distance and detachment from the democracy. The American arts began with aristocratic tendencies bothered as much as buoyed by the possibilities of democracy.

The inner American Tocquevillian voice demands that one see through American things to their debased democratic skeleton. The American Tocquevillian reduces the stakes of the specific phenomena of American intellectual history in relation to the ultimate stakes of the democratic mod-ern departure from the aristocratic traditional. Detachment triangulates the view of home through a Tocqueville-like conscience, a kind of ancien régime Jiminy Cricket.

The received reading of Tocqueville perpetuates the initial encounter. We end up in a one-way conversation with this French aristocratic visitor about our own country, justifying it to him, joining him in detached to-and-fro about it and the people who live here. It is a static image of a brief and judgmental encounter that we address. He never changes his mind. He had no care for the world we live in, never imagined belonging to it. His detachment came naturally to him. He had attachments to other values and things.

The American Tocquevillian suffers an interested conversion to a suspect detachment. It was Tocqueville, after all, who warned of too-general ideas:

> General ideas are no proof of the strength, but rather of the insuffi-ciency of the human intellect; for there are in nature no beings exactly alike, no things precisely identical, no rules indiscriminately and alike applicable to several objects at once. The chief merit of general ideas is that they enable the human mind to pass a rapid judgment on a great many objects at once; but, on the other hand, the notions they convey

are never other than incomplete, and they always cause the mind to lose as much in accuracy as it gains in comprehensiveness. (*Democracy in America*, vol. 2, book 1, chap. 3)

It does not surprise that Tocqueville should have fallen prey to this tendency. His abstraction of democracy was bound to get him into trouble. Tocqueville's remarkable view of America purposefully discourages the sympathetic engagement with democracy as a community of value and expression—as a human community of which one forms a part—on its own, democratic terms. The American Tocquevillian takes up that detachment in imitation of his distance, as if Tocqueville had been as detached from his own community. He was not. His detachment was not open but closed, a blind for his vigorous other attachments.

What is heartwarming about contemporary Tocquevillianism is the charming spectacle of a class of Americans draped in gear drawn from the ancients and the moderns—the third, second, first, and next worlds—all expressing that need for something else, which the Constitution merely said could not be legislated and which Tocquevillians thought would not develop but that in fact exists. American civilization is—in addition to being imperial, colonial, colonialist, provincial, materialist, sterile, and unoriginal—grandly, gloriously multitudinous. And the key to its glory is to exchange the Tocquevillian perspective of seeing it at a middle distance for the Whitmanian perspective of seeing it swirling about you (and you swirling with it about others).

In "Song of Myself," Whitman wrote that poem, that quintessentially democratic poem, that Tocqueville could never have loved. It opposes the democratic to the detached experience of America. The conclusion of its fifteenth section recounts the things Whitman has seen and heard in America and makes a good starting place for the further examination of the American Tocquevillian in some of its American guises. Prophylactic or inspirational, Whitman is worth keeping in mind.

Off on the lakes the pike-fisher watches and waits by the hole in the
    frozen surface,
The stumps stand thick round the clearing, the squatter strikes deep
    with his axe,
Flatboatmen make fast towards dusk near the cotton-wood or
    pecan-trees,

Coon-seekers go through the regions of the Red river or through
    those drain'd by the Tennessee, or through those of the Arkansas,
Torches shine in the dark that hangs on the Chattahooche or the
    Altamahaw,
Patriarchs sit at supper with sons and grandsons and great-grandsons
    around them,
In walls of adobie, in canvas tents, rest hunters and trappers after their
    day's sport,
The city sleeps and the country sleeps,
The living sleep for their time, the dead sleep for their time,
The old husband sleeps by his wife and the young husband sleeps by
    his wife;
And these tend inward to me, and I tend outward to them,
And such as it is to be of these more or less I am,
And of these one and all I weave the song of myself.

CHAPTER TWO

HENRY ADAMS: THE FIRST AMERICAN TOCQUEVILLIAN

PROLOGUE

A television commercial promoting a brand of aspirin stages a question-and-answer session. A plausible-looking young man, dressed in a laboratory coat, is standing before an audience of average Americans, pointing to statements of alleged fact about the pain-relief properties of aspirin. His logic goes like this: (*A*) doctors say aspirin is the best over-the-counter home remedy for pain; and (*B*) the best-selling (thus best) aspirin is the brand advertised in this commercial.

A and *B* are different kinds of statements, stemming from different authorities and using different kinds of proof. *A* reflects the agreement of our medicine men: doctors *do* recommend aspirin for many kinds of everyday pain. It does dull pain and bring relief. *B* merely reflects the success of the company that manufactures this brand of aspirin in making aspirin that meets the Food and Drug Administration's standards (it can be sold as aspirin) and the marketing standards of American enterprise (it has been manufactured and distributed successfully enough to be in stores everywhere).

The code for *A*, *doctors recommend*, is a reasonable facsimile of the truth behind the statement. Doctors are accepted as scientific oracles of modern medicine and are thought by most people to know more about sickness than any other group of authorities, although it should be said that many people simultaneously or alternatively believe in folk medicine, prayer or other divine healing, meditation, chiropractic, home remedies and herbal medicine, endurance, denial, psychology, and so forth. The phrase *doctors recommend* distills a cultural consensus about sickness and health. People who have to be told that doctors recommend aspirin, for whom A is a learning statement, ought to be impressed by the scientific ring of it all. People who are used to the wonders of modern medicine ought to be reassured.

B is different. It assumes the legitimating aura of A, connecting the truth that *doctors recommend* aspirin to the notion that one kind of aspirin is better than another. From a scientific point of view, once the legal/chemical standards have been met aspirin is pretty much aspirin. You have to make people buy your brand for some other reason—convenience, price, packaging, ease of ingestion, dosage, and so on. The commercial wants to associate the medical/scientific uses of aspirin with this particular brand and give the impression that *doctors recommend* this brand. Making people believe in a product works part of the cure. People have a stake in what they buy. *Purchase*, as current slang reflects, suggests belief and, presumably, understanding.

The commercial stages a drama of scrutiny and implied skepticism, providing a questioner from the on-screen audience. We see the scientific product spokesman in action. He resembles Rex Morgan, M.D. He looks better groomed and superior to the audience. He speaks in that newscaster's voice that, in effect, turns everybody else into dialect speakers. He seems like someone from the State College giving a lecture to farmers or maybe a public health official explaining sanitation to the poor. He does not look like a traveling salesman.

A woman in a housedress asks the question. She looks like someone Ernest Angley might have tried healing the previous Sunday night. A mournful, serious-looking woman, her weight and drab appearance suggest poor education, hard work, and a luckless and earnest need to know. She looks like she suffers from headaches. She looks like someone whose life gives her pain, who needs more than aspirin to cure what ails her— who needs a new life, some comfort, some contact with a therapist or a lawyer . . . *something*! And she asks, in an underliterate, grammarless whine, what "the most of the people use." The spokesman smoothly replies that his product is the choice of "the most of the people"; that is, it is "the best-selling aspirin."

This commercial dramatizes the intellectual workings of democracy. The woman wants proof that the majority has endorsed this remedy. Science plus the majority equals democratic cure. That more people use something is both the object of the pitch and its most telling claim. Of course, widely shared remedies are not the peculiar feature of democratic regimes. Cures have always attracted people because they have worked, and some cures have always been devised for "the most of the people." The style and logic, however, are democratic. She speaks the democratic speech and is democratically reassured.

When you think about this slatternly woman croaking for her democratic reassurance fix, you may find yourself identifying with the "doctor" and not with her. He is the missionary of capital and science and progress and cure and is not the one in pain; he is ahead of the game and in step with the democratic majority. The commercial plays on our fear that we may resemble her and be stuck in the back streets of ignorance and poverty and pain, denied the promise of American life. That fear may be part of what motivates us to buy the right aspirin.

You may watch this little drama with horror. Or, having been told about it, you may be prouder than you already are that you seldom watch television. Or, if you do watch, you may congratulate yourself that you skip the commercials. If you are willing to go this far, you may also be willing to admit that disgust for mass culture in our democracy that anyone sensible must feel when confronted with anything so cruel, so crass, so dishonest, and so low. Perhaps you entertain a more picturesque and uplifting drama of cure—say, the Virgin Mary and her medieval shrines and cathedrals. You may feel how out-of-place someone with your sensibilities is in the modern world, with its vulgarity and its capitalism and its democracy that cannot bear to empower the talented or distinguish the beautiful. This is the moment in your life for which Henry Adams has been waiting. You are about to enter the twilight zone of the disenchanted and will soon learn the secret of the degradation of the democratic dogma. You are ready to go *beyond the democratic door*. . .

HENRY ADAMS, TOCQUEVILLIAN

Henry Adams ranks with Ralph Waldo Emerson as our most remarkable all-around man of letters. He wrote history, aesthetics, journalism, economics, fiction, criticism, poetry, translations, autobiography, memoir, biography, filiopiety, adventure, natural history, science, pseudoscience, and futurism. Although he was better at some of these genres than others, most of what he wrote remains readable for its own sake. He was as good at some kinds of writing, like history, autobiography, letters, and highbrow guidebooks, as any American has ever been.

Adams's career was remarkable in other respects. He never had a popular success. Even Henry James had the popular success of *Daisy Miller*. Other American literary careers made concessions to public taste or popular myth. The steady widening of Adams's readership has been posthumous and, essentially, on his own terms. The more educated Americans become, the more they read Henry Adams; the more educated they become, the more they see things as he told them they would. The more readers Henry Adams has, the more things become like they seemed to him. Henry Adams was not even one of the discouraged, neglected, tragic, unappreciated geniuses that American literary history dotes upon. He appreciated himself and thrived at the center of a small world of devoted and admiring friends—a small world that just happened to run much of the big world. Adams understood his own unpopularity. He claimed to believe that the end of the world would come before Americans would learn to appreciate him.

Even more than Henry James, Henry Adams narrowed the possibility of readership to the Napoleonic demand that his personal point of view be shared. He ended up naming his protagonist "Henry Adams," but it was a belated naming. "Henry Adams" had been there all along—he is the one over whose shoulder the reader sees. Adams was at pains to distinguish himself from his times and his countrymen. He was ambitious to continue what he regarded as his family tradition of leadership, redacted as literary inaccessibility and individuality. He assumed that Adamses should have been prized by their countrymen for the qualities they displayed in power. He came to believe that he had inherited the qualities that brought them down in public life. He interested himself in how identical were these two sets of qualities. If they were different, he was a second-rate Adams; if the same, he was a true Adams, betrayed by times so brutal that they denied him even the moment of height from which to fall.

From boyhood, Henry Adams believed that being an Adams and receiving the status due to an Adams was part-and-parcel of the life he was to live. In time, birthmark and birthright turned out to be very different, indeed. Axiomatic in his writing is the continuing surprise he felt that it did not suffice to be Henry Adams. Emerson or no Emerson, it seemed to Henry Adams that the great world did not even come close to appreciating him. The surpassing irony of Henry Adams, the one irony that the old codger—whose mastication juice was irony—missed about himself, was that he embodied the Emersonian "American Scholar," or would have, had he but believed. For the world has come round to his writings, year by year, reader by reader. Adams's failure to believe, as Emerson said the American individual must, is not a fault but locates the faultline in his thought. Subtract the belief from the Emersonian and you get an American Tocquevillian.

Adams, like Tocqueville, recalls Jefferson and Emerson. Though Adams deconstructed Jefferson and dismissed Emerson, banishing them from his world as authorities, he was a writer who could be better understood with reference to these two more capaciously expressive souls. They, between them, achieved the power he scorned but missed, the happy relation to democracy that eluded him. Despite their dilution beyond recognition, their distillation into culturewide picker-uppers, Jefferson and Emerson retain their freshness and power. They seem always available on any reader's terms. Henry Adams requires an important allegiance, beyond the literary and stylistic, to the very attitude one must take toward American and democratic and modern life.

The theory of democratic interpretation starts with people making up authoritative explanations for the popularity of a piece of art. When Harry Cohn, who ran Columbia Pictures, said that he could always tell how well a movie would do by whether it caused a tremor in his behind, Herman J. Mankiewicz cracked, "Imagine! The whole world wired to Harry Cohn's ass!"[1] This story is usually told for what it says about moguls and writers, but it captures the problem with democratic interpretation. Democracy requires that art be referred to "the people." Those who know the public taste in a democracy presumably understand democratic culture. Cultural history records the disputes about who "the people" are. Harry Cohn's boast and Mankiewicz's remark occur as events in the dialogue of democratic interpretation. Tocqueville might not have put it quite the same way, but he understood the problem, which is—from the traditional point of view—the detour art takes through democracy, or—from the popular point of view—the wrong turn art takes away from democracy toward the highbrow.

"Smart" Americans like to think they are better than everybody else, as most smart (or pretty, or rich, or strong, or stupid—or human) people do. Democracy properly makes it hard to sustain that superiority. It is, perhaps, harder to accept the special limitations democracy puts on intelligent and expressive people because individual wisdom is always harder to privilege than money or beauty or strength. Democratic culture is about democratic wisdom and what it does to the individual, which to some extent means giving the individual the model of the masses as a comparison and tying democratic reception to individual creativity. This may mean common sense, but it is just as likely to mean conventional superstition or incurious dullness. Henry Adams worked out an attitude toward democracy that made being smarter than everybody else—or thinking you were—legitimate and important. It is more than the preceding Adamses ever did and is more than Jefferson or Lincoln did; they accepted responsibility to or kinship with a democratic people. The arrogance and aggressiveness with which Henry Adams pitted himself against the conditions of the regime and the age keep him interesting. He refused to be bound by the democracy even when he was ambitious to serve it.

Walt Disney's conceptual framework—Fantasyland, Frontierland, Adventureland, and Tomorrowland—usefully crystallizes the American literary project better than any other literary figure's. His categories stem from the practical idealist Disney's grasp of his audience: practical because he had to attract and hold the audience; idealist because he also wanted to entertain it and create for it. Fantasyland includes romance—the romance of Nathaniel Hawthorne and supermarket magazines, of Gothic, racial masquerades, most stories of indoor childhoods, and, indeed, almost anything in America that happens indoors. It makes its business from an alternative to the present in the past; to the hovel in the castle; to the miserable, tragic, and poetically sad in the happy; to the real in the fancied. Fantasyland is a qualitative as well as a substantive theme and tends to be present in most other theme parks. Sleeping Beauty's castle, after all, is as much the symbol of the enterprise as the mouse.

Frontierland recreates the American past. Its primary relationships happen between men and, especially, between boys. Women join Indians, trees, animals, and weather as factors that assert varying degrees of welcome and unwelcome control over the men and the boys and provide the authenticating tests of manhood and boyhood. It includes Americana. Most American history used to be written in Frontierland. Southern history is always a combination of Fantasyland and Frontierland. Social and cultural history seem to combine Frontierland with Tomorrowland.

Walt Whitman mixed American genres without irony, but he merely suggested a concentrated sensibility of enthusiastic welcome; Disney actualized it. Whitman was pre-generic. Disney imposed a categorical order, made a shrine and animated abstracted, anthropomorphic animals and humans out of what Whitman thought needed to be seen as unabstracted, everywhere. Disneyland is not about seeing yourself or things truly but about ideal reflections in that "mirror, mirror, on the wall" or in cute icons. The Disney enterprise animates a protected version of the world and everything in it. It pictures the world made safe for democracy. Creative but interpretively controlling, the Disney version, like classic American fiction, is embarrassed and formal about moods, like sex and anger and violence and art, that are beyond the scope of Jiminy Cricket, Thumper, or those mice.

If Frontierland explores the jolly heart of lightness, Adventureland suggests the heart of darkness (man against nature and animals), its legions not cowboys so much as hunters. The difference is largely in tone; these are the hardest lands to tell apart. In Frontierland, the myth takes care of African Americans, turning them into "darkies," and Native Americans, turning them into "Indians" on a quaint, doomed warpath. Whites in Adventureland are civilized, and others are not. Adventureland is also Darwin country, the most philosophically nineteenth-century of the lands. Fantasyland is medieval and European and Catholic; Frontierland is American, nationalist, and Methodist (or Baptist or Presbyterian); Adventureland is Social Darwinist, capitalist, missionary, Calvinist, determinist, Hemingwayish, and, although names are not named, more about business and the confrontations of the marketplace. Frontierland preserves the illusion of fair play, but Adventureland is about playing pro ball, or professional anything.

Tomorrowland tells the story of the future, especially about how science, the kind from physics on up, tames and makes the universe work. Its Einsteins are Edisons. It also suggests corporate capitalism, the way in which nature is tamed not so much in Baconian as in General Electric fashion. Its classic experiences are the streamlined comforts of the future and the astonishing fabrications of the pleasures of the science-based future—the rides. The human type for Tomorrowland has to be young enough to stand the rides. If you can understand the physics and enjoy the rides, you will prove fit for the future. This calls for a youth that does not need its parents because it is superior to them in being more scientific. The young mind that cannot imagine its own aging and lives in the present moment, understood as the moment with a future, grasps Tomorrowland. It is the most exciting place for its partisans and the most unnerving for its misfits. It favors science fiction, engineering, the predictive, marketing, advertising, the plastic, and demographic realities.

Henry Adams wrote in all the American genres. His Fantasyland centers around *Mont Saint Michel and Chartres*. In his writing, Tomorrowland is the future's flip side of Fantasyland—the streamlined, geometric, unavoidable future. Adams's histories tend to take place more in Frontierland than in Fantasyland, although his Frontierland and Adventureland share as close a relation as Fantasyland and Tomorrowland. His visits to Tahiti, and his geological and scientific writings, are foursquare Adventureland. Fantasyland and Frontierland blend in his filiopietistic biographical writings. *Democracy* is more like Frontierland and especially like Main Street. *Esther* starts in Fantasyland and tours the park. *The Education of Henry Adams* recounts a life lived in all the lands.

Henry Adams borrowed a Tocquevillian attitude that became his improvement upon the old English (or Puritan, or Southern) oppositional stances. It claimed a detachment from what it observed and never acknowledged kinship with what it described. His writing was distinguished and cosmopolitan, deliberately meant to stand apart from the rest of America. His individual explorations map the lands in ways Disney was too anxious for popularity to attempt. But Adams's work constitutes a theme park of unpopularity, an anti-democratic exploration of American themes.

On 1 May 1863, writing to his brother Charles, a captain in the Union cavalry, Henry Adams reflected upon how what they each had seen of life, of war, and of Europe must affect their subsequent careers.

Can a man at your time of life be a Cavalry Captain and remain a briefless solicitor? Can a man of my general appearance pass five years in Europe and remain a candidate for the bar? In short, have we both wholly lost our reckonings and are we driven at random by fate, or have we still a course that we are steering though it is not quite the same as our old one? By the Apostle Paul I know not. Only one fact I feel sure of. We are both no longer able to protect ourselves with the convenient fiction of the law. Let us quit that now useless shelter, and steer if possible for whatever it may have been that once lay beyond it. Neither you nor I can ever do anything at the bar.[2]

The convenient conceit of fraternal comparison did not discard so easily as the law, of course. Henry continued with this interesting view of himself: "My hand could at best use a rapier. It is not made for a sabre. I should be like a bewildered rabbit in action, being only trained to counsel. My place is where I am, and I never was so necessary to it as now. All thoughts of escape, even for a day, have vanished. We are covered with work, and our battles are fierce and obstinate."[3]

Looking back from The Education, Adams's bitter sense of the futility of his trying to make people believe how important his and his father's work had been fused with his general sense of recommending himself to the public opinion of the democracy into his tricky irony about his years as his father's confidential secretary. Unfortunately, the account of those years in The Education was memorably good. Adams's self-proclaimed obscurity set off a hilarious, sharp, and exciting portrait of English intellectual, social, political, and moral life. The triumph of recollection was unfortunate because it obscured his earlier situation as it turned the tables on his English tormentors. At the time of the embassy, in his middle twenties, Adams was beginning to know himself through an enthusiastic, engaged sense of his own important work, a knowledge The Education slights.

Henry's own history hitherto had been that of an undifferentiated Adams. It is not very likely that anyone else thought very specifically, as he said he did, that a Henry Adams—not to mention this Henry Adams— must be president of the United States. But he felt destined with a pointedly American family destiny for a vocation, properly public. A particular path of unlimited possibility may come to the same thing as constriction. Adams wrote his autobiography as the story of a man who had to be president to succeed and who led a remarkable life in the shadow of not "making good." His experience taught him to think better than did every aspect of that foreordination, except how not to judge himself, his life, and the world by its incompletion. Readers of The Education will remember Henry Adams as the guy whose life was determined by the fact of his inherited expectation of being president.

In their very different ways, John Adams and Thomas Jefferson worried about the fate of a country that lacked a system for binding its aristocrats to its best interests and about what interests of the nation its superior individuals would identify with. Jefferson emphasized the hope of the natural aristocrat, Adams the fact of the empowered and the rich. Together, they addressed the relation between the talented individual and the people, which they thought would be the test case of democratic allegiance. Jefferson could not imagine a nation's getting along without winning its intellectually gifted to the good of the less gifted. John Adams could not conceive a nation's preventing the rich from corrupting politics and popular demagogues from inciting the poor against the rich.

One strand of hope remained the attachment that the talented, the privileged, and the ambitious would come to feel toward a regime that had a democratic principle deep in its heart. John Adams and Thomas Jefferson, and even Ralph Waldo Emerson, specialized in how to connect men like themselves to the people, in how to make fellow Americans of those from whom they inescapably, naturally, and properly stood out. They imagined a culture of responsibility in which an American superego talked to the conscious self about being an American. They commenced the garrulous tradition in American letters of Americans talking themselves into—and out of—being Americans, as a way of talking about the meaning of being an American.

The Adams family tradition bore out some of the Jeffersonian hope, cut with the Adams practical high-mindedness and infusions of wealth through marriage. An Adams was reared with that consciousness of public duty that Jefferson hoped to cultivate in the naturally talented, and education was preparation for assuming that duty. But the Adamses bent the twigs themselves, not counting on the public to tend its own interest. Unlike the Jeffersonian avatars, therefore, an Adams did not feel beholden to the people but to the best interests of the public, which involved being true to one's self and stubbornly, almost perversely, keeping one's own best counsel. John Adams trusted his wife, John Quincy Adams his conscience, Charles Francis Adams his father. Henry was not altogether certain, but he knew his vocation involved the assumption of whose counsel he might keep about his all-important relation to the life of that inherited province of Adams responsibility, the United States of America.

Underscoring John Adams's redoubtably cheerful possession of what sometimes seems a melancholy wisdom was the stern New England legacy of toughened response to human actuality. Jefferson's plastic imagination was irresistibly beguiling, even to John Adams, who read the Virginian's brimming letters as one might hear sweet music. But John Adams did not expect life to sway to the harmonious melody of reason. Reason was not life but another of the human tools in hewing from life something better, rather than something worse. Only participation in the business of life redeemed the endless struggle and rescued the individual's life from the bitter, debilitating perception of how endless a struggle the human condition is. This perception stood at the core of the New England strength and informed the public-spiritedness that must be content to be its own reward.

Henry Adams inherited an awareness of this as his legacy. As legatees are, he was prone to the ambivalent belief that he had earned what he had inherited and that he must have deserved it. As he left his education to begin his career, it lay in the balance whether his life was to prove susceptible to the difficult, happy, active peace of this lesson. Henry Adams appears to have understood the message from the inside out. His job was to figure out what he would best do for America; America's part was to let him. How America would use, recognize, accept, reward, welcome, and secure the talent of this supremely and confidently, intellectually and artistically, gifted son was the acid test of regime. He had no thought then that his career would turn out to be his education. Like Charles Foster Kane, Henry Adams was going to need more than one lesson, and he was going to get more than one.

Henry Adams was serving as secretary to his father, Charles Francis Adams, the American ambassador to England during the Civil War, when he encountered *Democracy in America*. As sometimes happens with fateful intellectual encounters, there was small event.[4] His 1863 letter to his brother suggests that Henry Adams was thinking he might well serve by counseling his country. He admired the military virtues and may have felt that envy and guilt about not fighting in the Civil War that historians have attributed to the noncombatants of his class. But the letter also shows his esteem for the nonmilitary virtues that made him useful to his father's embassy, hence useful to his country. He knew how important it was that the Union win the geopolitical as well as the military conflict.

Something struck the private secretary, something he left out of the *The*

Education, that made him envision a role for himself. Although his passing reference to St. Paul should not be too greatly stressed, he does seem clearly to have seen the light of his own calling for the first time.

> Our own position here does not change. We lead a quiet and not un-pleasant life, and I pass my intervals from official work, in studying De Tocqueville and John Stuart Mill, the two high priests of our faith. So I jump from International Law to our foreign history, and am led by that to study the philosophic standing of our republic, which brings me to reflection over the advance of the democratic principle in Euro-pean civilization, and so I go on till some new question of law starts me again on the circle. But I have learned to think De Tocqueville my model, and I study his life and works as the Gospel of my private reli-gion. The great principle of democracy is still capable of rewarding a conscientious servant. And I doubt me much whether the advance of years will increase my toleration of its faults. Hence, my boy, I think I see in the distance a vague and unsteady light in the direction towards which I needs must gravitate, so soon as the present disturbing influ-ences are removed.[5]

In 1863, Henry Adams read Tocqueville and found his model.

Ernest Samuels, in his great biography of Adams, gives an admirably clear account of Henry Adams's readiness to take to Tocqueville. The French-man had interviewed John Quincy Adams, then a former president sitting in the House of Representatives, during the trip to America that produced *Democracy in America*. The informants he trusted had been the Adamsy sort of Whigs. A separateness from the popular element, combined with a value for the constitutional regime and a feeling of responsibility for the public good, infused these politics and made the observation deck of Tocquevillian detachment an easy perch. Charles Francis Adams claimed a long-standing familiarity with Tocqueville's writings. Henry Adams must have read with relief and enthusiasm someone whose writings about the United States were not only informed by the views he had always respected but also treated the lonely wisdom of his grandfather with the honor not accorded it in his own time and country.

Brooks Adams was right to identify Henry with John Quincy Adams in his remarkable essay, "The Heritage of Henry Adams," which introduces the posthumous collection of Henry's essays, *The Degradation of the Demo-*

cratic Dogma.[6] John Quincy Adams's career was the caution. His intellectual and political prescience and integrity had fallen afoul of the democracy. To an Adams, the democracy was the tiger the constitutional scheme must ride. His grandson identified with the very qualities John Quincy Adams had in drastic abundance that did not well suit him for democratic politics. No career illustrates better than John Quincy Adams's how well served America can be in the world by qualities it inevitably disappoints at home. Nothing in Henry Adams is so sweetly or simply shared as those early passages in *The Education* about his grandfather. Such associative credentials went a long way in Tocqueville's favor with young Henry Adams.

In addition, as Samuels makes clear, private secretary Henry Adams was coming of political age in a segment of Anglo-American interest positively soaked in Tocqueville. He came to the book "as a result of the widespread interest inspired by the Civil War, which friends and enemies of America regarded as a crucial test of that system of government. The entire pro-Northern coterie drew strength from de Tocqueville's appraisal of America's power of survival." The Henry Reeve translation was being reissued in America and England. Reeve was an Adams sponsor and a central figure in their English circles. Adams had already learned to appreciate Tocqueville's ideas from other sources, especially from François Guizot. Tocqueville reached an Adams already receptive to the drift of his views and their philosophical presumptions.

Samuels emphasizes that *Democracy in America* crystallized for Adams things about America he already believed:

> Read at a time when he was becoming keenly alive to its implications, *Democracy in America* helped to catch and fix the random criticisms of America that had been cropping out in his letters—public and private—into a kind of catalogue of political imperfections. Where formerly he had written complacently of the American political system as of something perfected, yet destined by a law of necessary progress to indefinite material expansion, he now saw through de Tocqueville's eyes that "The organization and the establishment of democracy in Christendom is the great political problem of our times. The Americans, unquestionably, have not resolved this problem, but they furnish useful data to those who undertake to resolve it. . . . If those nations whose social condition is democratic could remain free only while they inhabit uncultivated regions, we must despair of the future destiny of

the human race." The cogent analysis of the flaws in the American system fell in with the old warnings of his grandfather and father and revived their cankering doubts in him. . . . Still, de Tocqueville's text held open a perilous route of escape. If a great democratic revolution was still going on, it was susceptible of intelligent control. As in de Tocqueville's opinion, the true source of democracy in America lived in the New England character, Adams concluded that the rescue could be effected by the "New England element."[7]

Samuels reads Adams's letter to his brother as the setting out of this course of stewardship.

Tocqueville lulled the reluctance or squeamishness one might feel about the democratic aspects of American public service with the alluring promise of stewardship, or protecting the people from themselves, as aristocrats like to put it. Tocqueville liked about democracy its constitutions, its capacity to free the citizen in the common person, and the stability of free government. He did not like democratic habits of thought and modes of human excellence. To the degree that democracy creates its own views, Tocqueville counseled against being blinded by them. The proper steward of democracy views democracy as a necessary condition, as capable of good as any regime, but always best seen from the standpoint of what it has supplanted and in the light of what it fails to nourish. Tocqueville's perspective on democracy was achieved by his cultural residence in the European past, which was not always antidemocratic but was certainly nondemocratic. This was his counsel.

Henry Adams surely read Tocqueville, in part, to affirm himself in his inherited and temperamental distaste for braving the democratic weather. The service Adams meant to render democracy was a service of the enlightened understanding. But the democracy was not supposed to take or leave his advice at will. He did not opt for a detached role if that meant detachment from the fate of his reflections in the world. He meant to be listened to, but without having to gain the ear of his audience from the electoral to-and-fro. Adams accepted Tocqueville as a role model in a way that would place him near the throne but outside the sway of democracy. This is an inherently problematic choice. The Jeffersonian grants the democratic, but the Tocquevillian would avoid it.

Despite the liberal tendency of his age, Tocqueville's aristocratic connections placed him within an active political center. Henry Adams understood connections and might have wished his own society to be more connected. Some of Tocqueville's appeal to Adams was surely the glamour of the liberal aristocrat whose social and political lives mingled. Henry Adams would have liked to be a titled republican, a steward rather than a champion of the people. Tocqueville's greatest attraction proved his suggestion that one of the chief services to a democracy might be the detached observer who construes the rightly understood self-interest of the whole. In *Democracy in America* shorthand, it would be the wisdom of volume 2 activated in the realm of volume 1.

Adams recognized in Tocqueville a model for an American writer—the possibility of an authoritative interpretive function. The privilege Jefferson claimed for the natural philosopher, the tradition of the New England preacher and moralist that produced Emerson (and that Emerson reformed), and the high-toned examples of New England literati who were also politically engagé combined in Adams's fantasy of the role that reading Tocqueville sparked in his mind. The New England notion of high culture as a contribution to the body politic, and the several traditions of informed comment on American life and the specific Adams history of being right rather than a being a second-term President, also influenced him. The notion that democracy needed observing—as well as governing, championing, celebrating, bemoaning, or exemplifying—and was worth understanding rather than preaching to, would serve his purposes admirably.

Before the democratic age, the twin authorities of religion and the Enlightenment shared the deferentially defined public attention. In their wake, American writers found themselves with plenty on their minds about their country but at somewhat loose ends about how to express it. Washington Irving, James Fenimore Cooper, and their colleague novelists had to fold social comment awkwardly into genres of sentimental and Gothic fiction. They found themselves angrier and angrier at the difference between how they found things at home and how they were taken to its hearth. Harriet Beecher Stowe's definitively successful political use of the novel eventually also suggested its limits. The American novelist of social views who writes in popular genres may influence the American heart but not so reliably direct the American head. Upton Sinclair's lament that in *The Jungle* he aimed for America's heart and hit the American stomach tells the tale. The romantic historians intended an impact. America absorbed rather than heeded these writers. American Studies, the scholarly genre that in the mid-twentieth century evolved to understand them, addressed what Americans could manage to live with, not what truly changed their minds.

The tragedy of the Puritans, as literary historian Perry Miller explained it, and the endlessly compelling odd luck of the founding have inspired attention to powerful wisdom that somehow got through to Americans in a way that made them think difficult thoughts. Emerson created the terrain for the American scholar as a cultural spokesman, but even—or especially—Emerson accepted the conditions of speaking to the great middle-class democracy, the aphoristic homey fate of radical wisdom. The true Emersonian leap of faith is that philosophy can be trusted to the conventional uses to which a people will put it. Thus was his Puritan resignation lightened but not substantially altered by the slipping of Puritan culture's grip on its realm. The Emersonian extended an aerated Puritanism to the American middle class. It featured a high-minded demanding aspect and an applicable breadth. In extending the Puritan type, Emerson pioneered the American type. His own success at the two jobs that an American philosophy must perform was unusual. His movement even managed a successful high culture that, from the heights of its eminence, directed a popularly accepted one. This, of course, is not at all what Tocqueville had in mind. Tocqueville did not aim to enlarge the democratic soul with philosophy but to stiffen its backbone with traditional wisdom. And Adams's choice of Tocqueville over Emerson—and Jefferson—signifies.

There has flourished a continuing culture of privileged Americans learning to talk about their country, taking themselves, their attainments, and their ambitions into account. Ambitious politicians must learn to express their singularity, so that it will join their exceptional talents to the common cause and not alienate the voter. In a like way must highly developed individuals develop some culture of American understanding that explains their individuality and defends it from their fellow Americans. Tocqueville classically set out the different and contending principles of individualism and equality. He understood that each had a necessary development, holding the potential for social and political disruption. His analysis has an abiding appeal to those who believe their individuality threatened by democracy and who do not accept the democratic remedies, which argue that individual claims against the majority have their root in equality.

The habit of speaking of America as a *them* place and not a *we* place is a cultivated American habit. America becomes a place from which one hails, perhaps, but to which one does not exactly belong. It afflicts one with a kind of embarrassment—the way parents afflict a teenager—that prompts condescension even after you leave home. The Tocquevillian language develops to justify the separation that money and success and luck can bring, making firm and defensible the accidental distinctions of life that have no constitutional hold in America or in its myth. The genteel patois serves the need to turn good fortune into good breeding and luck into virtue, to give to individuality a permanence that cannot be ideologically institutionalized in America. The snobbery and desperation and legitimate pride of such efforts abound. Universities, symphonies, museums, and the monuments of our high culture testify to it. They all share an insistence, an aggressive fostering of their function, that lies like a requirement and a burden upon "all ye who enter here." Think about how much easier it is to go to the movies than to go to a museum. One takes you deeper into American culture, the other away from it.

American popular culture is run on mass, democratic, capitalist lines, but its formal culture is run on privileged, elitist, private lines. The first is about the present moment's entertainment and expression and is receptive to the public taste. The second is about the past and the future and tries to make the past count in the present, to insure the future of the distinctions of the past, and also, by the way, to provide a class distinction within present-day democratic society. The movies or popular music are best about what it feels like to be us, now, here. High culture and education are about what it would feel like to enjoy a different us, a different now, an opposing here. No wonder the highbrow mixes with such friction in Americans, strikes such irritating and superior and discordant notes, verges on the pompous, fails of the easy and natural, and requires education.

High culture and genteel culture seek status as an agency of social control. They claim to help brake the popular passions and cultivate the individual virtues and qualities that democracy lacks and needs. Their claim suggests the Jeffersonian natural aristocracy but serves the interest of the more-than-materially privileged who want a special place within American democracy, a place that does not appear to be bought. This claim reveals the Tocquevillian appeal. The real place from which detachment observes America is not outer space or the ideal hold of an uncompromising human brain, but Europe—good old ancien régime, Western, Christian, monarchical, hierarchical Europe.

The Tocquevillian perspective cultivates and brings to bear the European perspective. The Adams ancestry was proudly and quintessentially

American. Since he was stuck with that and was prevented by it from true expatriation, Henry Adams made a point of it. The chosen people of America were his tribe and his line their priests, as he says in *The Education* with an irony that sets off his distinctive, unapproachable specialness with a claim to its exclusivity greater than the modern world can offer. Nobody reading Adams buys the irony. It is borrowed in the spirit he offered it, to costume the fantasy of American aristocracy. Democracy falsifies even its true aristocrats. America fails its natural aristocrats.

Tocqueville's book helped to make the United States respectable. It also taught Americans one way to see themselves reflected in a notion like democracy, and not just in the convex mirrors of their own self-regard or the concave mirrors of their lack of it. The problem is that *Democracy in America* encouraged Americans to look into a mirror and see someone else. The key even to trickle-down American Tocquevillianism is that one must be able to look clearly at democracy by removing oneself from it. Lincoln and Whitman saw themselves in the democratic mirror; Henry Adams never did. To take up the Tocquevillian line, you have to come to feel yourself apart. Adams's own sense of self and family, indeed, everything about him, readied him to accept what would keep him American but separate him from the democracy. He was to be anointed sage, to be recognized, to elect and not to be elected.

Democracy in America put forward a thrilling historical principle that exercised a profound and happy influence on Adams's historical writings. Adams's desire to detach himself from the means and ends of American democracy survived his abating attachment to the historical and political dictates of Tocquevillian insight. Even after his world lay in ashes and the future seemed beyond contemplation, even after human action seemed a myth and a very personal medievalism was his only proper subject, Adams retained the need that found its deepest echo in Tocqueville: to tell the truth about democracy as if that truth did not apply to him, except as its superior victim, someone to whom America had happened. Tocqueville's historical principle of democratic inevitability survived to explain why Henry Adams happened to be caught in the middle of democracy trying to explain it.

The perception of the inevitable future relieves the prophet of responsibility and connection, and the Tocquevillian model is prophetic. Henry Adams cultivated the Tocquevillian prophet's role; he started with suggestion, tried historical explanation, moved to scourging transhistorical generalization, and finally accepted the detaching curse of resignation. Surely, Henry Adams viewed the prospects of his prophetic career as almost certainly likely to be without honor, although it took him twenty years or so to realize that this was so. The strange music in his prose of his signature future past tense (what it must have seemed that it would be going to be like), suggests his double frame of mind—an expectation of honor and a foregone conclusion of disappointment. The odd construction activates much that is haunting and beautiful and felt in his writing.

Henry Adams was willing to accept the destruction of everything—to philosophize, predict, and fantasize the obliteration of the world—rather than to sacrifice his apartness from democracy. To follow his career is to trace his acceptance of the Tocquevillian model. Henry Adams was extreme and idiosyncratic, but it is just those qualities that the individual cultivates when cut off in individuality from fellow human beings. Henry Adams attached himself to medieval things (Fantasyland) and dismissed the rest of us to the dynamo-powered spaceship of an earth hurtling toward destruction (bleakest Tomorrowland). It sounds attractively simple to conceptualize a relation to democracy that frees one of its stylistic burdens and personal degradations and of the frustrations and humiliations of the superior self within it. This temptation launched Henry Adams's magnificent and compelling spiraling off into his memorable, eccentric orbit.

HENRY ADAMS'S VOCATIONAL EXPERIENCE

The following passages are from chapter 17 of *The Education*.

> The difference is slight, to the influence of an author, whether he is read by five hundred readers, or by five hundred thousand; if he can select the five hundred, he reaches the five hundred thousand.

> He knew, without absolutely saying it, that Grant had cut short the life which Adams had laid out for himself in the future. After such a miscarriage, no thought of effectual reform could revive for at least one generation, and he had no fancy for ineffectual politics. What course could he sail next? He had tried so many, and society had barred them all!

As for Adams, all his hopes of success in life turned on his finding an administration to support. He knew well enough the rules of self-interest. He was for sale. He wanted to be bought. His price was excessively cheap, for he did not even ask an office, and had his eye, not on the government, but on New York. All he wanted was something to support; something that would let itself be supported. Luck went dead against him. For once, he was fifty years in advance of his time.

The Tocquevillian program suggested to Henry Adams a busy program of work encompassing reform, the stewardship of the people's best interests through serious political journalism, the exposure of the corruptions in need of reform, political reform activity, and the writing of history. With characteristic discipline and energy, Adams took it on. Throughout his life, he wrote as if his livelihood depended on it. Henry Adams's dilemma was that he returned home to steward a democratic people and, in their stead, he found the American democratic people. The suave savagery and telling ironies of *The Education*'s chapter on this horrible unmasking detail Adam's progress from a hopeful to an angry Tocquevillian. For it is ever in the confrontation between generalized democracy and the particular American brand that the American learns the American Tocquevillian lesson.[8]

The chapter in *The Education* called "President Grant (1869)" remains an astonishing and transparent account of an insufferable disappointment. For all its stylistic trappings, Adams veiled less in it than in his accounts of his other bitter disappointments. Hindsight had sharpened his sense of letdown and whetted his anger. Seminal in many ways, it is a source of that genre of political writing that, in our own day, Norman Mailer and Gore Vidal have used to such advantage. The chapter introduced a self to whom America had happened. As an indictment of the corruption and hopeless, unsalvageable, deliberate idiocy of our political life, it resembles Alexander Pope's satires. Henry Adams named names. In his delightful way, Adams wrote things about President Grant that one cannot quite believe that he was saying but that are still liberating to read—liberating in the way "The Emperor's New Clothes" is. Adams retaliated with his superior intelligence, the very thing Ulysses S. Grant and the American people presumably scorned. *The Education* always has it Adams's own way: that is what autobiography is for. He allowed that, this once, things did not turn out so badly for him after all. Had Adams been as much of a failure as he says he was, his book would have been unreadable. He kept the truly sad and unhappy things in his life out of *The Education*. It abounds in humor, interest, and vitality and is attractive because one feels that one would have loved to live the very life Adams keeps repeating was hardly worth living.

Adams's letters of the time reveal him to have been naive, supercilious, superior, ambitious, and enthusiastic. He really thought he could take America away from the guys who ran it and institute reform. In this, he was fueled by his family's manifest destiny, the ideas that Tocqueville had given him, and his youthful confidence that he could win the righteous battle with his pen, a band of friends, and his principles. Henry Adams clearly traced to this early period of the Grant administration the moment of his deepest disillusionment with America. The emotions of this period reappear in his historical works. Surely, his moments of fellow feeling with (and mockery of) John Randolph struck these sparks. He wrote about it in *Democracy* and returned to the scene of the betrayal in *The Education*. Adams crowded a great number of things into a deceptively lofty account.

In chapter 17 of *The Education*, "Henry Adams" comes to Washington as part of his Tocquevillian writing project.

> In England, Lord Robert Cecil had invented for the *London Quarterly* an annual review of politics which he called the *Session*. Adams stole the idea and the name . . . and began what he meant for a permanent series of annual political reviews which he hoped to make, in time, a political authority. With his sources of information, and his social intimacies at Washington, he could not help saying something that would command attention. He had the field to himself, and he meant to give himself a free hand, as he went on. Whether the newspapers liked it or not, they would have to reckon with him; for such a power, once established, was more effective than all the speeches in Congress or reports to the President that could be crammed into the government presses.

The self-mockery here shades only slightly the regulation Tocquevillian doctrine of Henry Adams's expectations, which he recounted accurately. He did expect his coverage of the Washington scene to make him powerful. He had in mind as well the foreign audience, which belief that there is an effective alternative to American democratic opinion in the reflection of American conduct in the large perspective, philosophic and detached, was a characteristic American Tocquevillian twist.

In a letter to his brother Charles from Washington in January 1869,

Adams referred to his work, which clearly meant the work of cleaning out the reunited house:

> There is no news here. Everyone is in the dark. I am very hard at work and care very little for the new administration as I find I can get on without it. What do you say to this? Our labored work does not gain us all it ought. I want to be advertised and the easiest way is to do something obnoxious and do it well. I can work up an article on "rings" which, if *published in England*, would I think create excitement and react through political feeling on America in such a way as to cover me with odium. Wells says, don't disgrace us abroad. I say: Rot! The truth is open to expression anywhere. No home publication will act on America like foreign opinion. I am not afraid of unpopularity and I will do it.[9]

This attractive, youthful hope is touching in its fantasy that a reformer/ writer like Henry Adams could really get anywhere in cleaning up the mess of American public life in the Gilded Age. It also indicates that Adams really was detached from American life, not merely philosophically but actually. As he admits elsewhere, it was human beings who always tripped him up. There are no human beings in Tocqueville, only democratic human types. Tocqueville's model is an intellectual model of philosophic manipulation, not practical political dealing, which is a necessary skill in any regime's real world, after all.

Adams failed to gain enough odium to do himself or his cause much good. But he laced his sense of himself, in the thick of the reform alternative, with a deliberate invitation to unpopularity that has a warning sound to it. Was he more committed to reform or to unpopularity? Five days later, he wrote to Charles that he was not satisfied with his work or himself: "We are small enough creatures absolutely, but relatively to the mass of fools who make mankind, we are at the top of the ladder. . . . As for me, I have bluffed people so damnably on the idea of my wanting office, that they are now humbled at my feet and if someone would only offer me something handsome so that I could refuse, I should be secure from such suspicions for ever."[10] Perhaps he was waiting for the offer he could not refuse, the one so tempting he would have to take. His fevered involvement in the public realm, mixed with a justified but unintegrated sense of his own superiority, was pretty heady stuff. But, although the Tocquevillian model proposes the engagement of the aristocrat in public business, it is not clear that it proposes that the democracy belonged where Henry Adams clearly thought it did: "humbled at my feet."

What he proposed in *The Session* resembled being the first-string drama critic on the *New York Times*. It claimed to be about observation but was about power, not the power to do but the power to criticize and thereby to reform what others were doing. In this instance, "reform" meant to throw the rascals out and thus create a better climate for the future. His nerve survived his disappointments, and even the Adams irony cannot cut it down to size. He must have imagined himself on some balcony or other eminence as the parade of America showed itself for his inspection and approval. Unlike Henry James, Adams disdained to invent new worlds and characters. He wrote about this world with every intention of control. Even his fiction took place in the world he was living in. And, all those years later, Adams the autobiographer was unforgiving and youthful in his fury. President Grant turned out to be dangerously susceptible to the temptations of the corruptions that surrounded him. Henry Adams's seems to have been the only offer Grant refused.

Adams believed, in 1869, that the problem with democracy was that its materialism and interest-oriented politics made money the private language of the public business. Inevitably, the public good became a contest of rapacious private interests to gain control of enough votes to legislate their interest, as if that constituted the public interest. The people could not be counted on to recognize their proper leaders any more than their best interests. This extended the family understanding, rooted in John Adams's understanding of the problem that wealth presents to free government, full of John Quincy Adams's views about the harmony of a public good that can be achieved by transcending the din of private interest, and continuing the explicit reform politics of Charles Francis Adams, who may have been the highest-minded politician in American history.

Henry was the first Adams to begin by despising popularity. The others wanted it but refused to choose it when it seemed to them a choice over something even more important. Sometimes their unpopular choices made them popular—after all, they got somewhere in politics. They made choices that were unpopular, but they only seemed in hindsight to have been themselves unpopular. Only in the filiopietistic disappointment of Henry Adams did the Adams point become deliberate, principled unpopularity. I think his grandfather or great-grandfather would have counseled him to let his unpopularity find him, not to insist on his lonely stance before it should turn out to be the necessary fact. But it unlocks Henry Adams's experience of America that his individuality was more important to him than anything else. He fulfilled John Adams's prophecy about his descendants, but in a way that would have worried as well as gratified the sire of the line. Henry Adams never cleared up whose battles he was fighting and never could quite admit what his own battles were.

Adams's portrait of President Grant's failures was shrewd. His understanding of the man's character and his portrait of the politics of the Gilded Age were sound, if harsh. He had confidence in his own audience, the remnant of the old-fashioned, American conservative elite: "Adams was not the only relic of the eighteenth century, and he could still depend on a certain number of listeners,—mostly respectable, and some rich" (*The Education*, chap. 17). The American people had elected Grant president because, Adams thought, they saw in Grant another George Washington. Washington, although "in education and experience a mere cave-dweller," at least had known how to run a government. Grant not only failed to do this but also showed himself to be a primitive, commonplace, uncaring, stupid man. To some extent, this was revealed by his policies and by the craven way he submitted to "boss" rule in his cabinet selections and positions.

The proof of the pudding was Grant's lack of interest in Henry Adams. He was like Garibaldi: "Of the two, Garibaldi seemed to him a trifle the more intellectual, but, in both, the intellect counted for nothing;—only the energy counted. The type was pre-intellectual, archaic, and would have seemed so even to the cave dwellers. Adam, according to legend, was such a man" (*The Education*, chap. 17). Adam betrayed paradise because a snake offered his wife a bauble. Grant irritated Adams—he reversed evolution. The following is from chapter 17 of *The Education*.

> He had no right to exist. He should have been extinct for ages. The idea that, as society grew older, it grew one-sided, upset evolution, and made of education a fraud. That, two thousand years after Alexander the Great and Julius Caesar, a man like Grant should be called—and should actually and truly be—the highest product of the most advanced evolution, made evolution ludicrous. One must be as common-place as Grant's own common-places to maintain such an absurdity. The progress of evolution from President Washington to President Grant, was alone evidence enough to upset Darwin.

We know, of course, who Adams thought stood at the top of the ladder of evolution.

Adams's comparison of himself (as the proper type of advanced man) to Grant (as the primitive specimen chosen by democracy to lead) orchestrated a remarkable assertion. The counterpoint is the highly individual and the commonplace, the smart and the dumb, the eccentric and the conventional, the successful and the failed. Adams was saying that he was a higher human type than Grant, that as the individual has evolved the mass of men have regressed. Adams may have appeared to be saying how ridiculous it was for young "Henry Adams" to have made this comparison, but he was in fact making it again. There is something breathtaking about the way Adams could say in retrospect that the American nation did not measure up. It's worth a pause for reflection, after the pause for delight.

In February 1869, Adams wrote to John Gorham Palfrey about the cabinet and the prospects of reform. A good administration may improve things, he said,

> so far as to make the system endurable, and so blind our people to the necessity of true reform. The idea that democracy in itself, by the mere fact of giving power to the masses, will elevate and purify human nature, seems to me to have now turned out one of those flattering fictions which have in all ages deluded philanthropists. The great problem of every system of Government has been to place administration and legislation in the hands of the best men. We have tried our formula and find that it has failed in consequence of its clashing with our other fundamental principle that one man is as good as another. How to escape the logical consequences of this failure, common to all systems yet invented, I confess I do not see.[11]

This is sound, if sad, traditional wisdom, coming from a man in his late twenties, who might well have thought that the Civil War redeemed the moral elevation democracy provides to its people. But look how it worked. It posited the failure of democracy to choose the best men to run it and blamed equality. Adams, however, refused to offer himself to the public to be chosen. He would not stand for inspection and election. His own superiority must be taken, as he took it, for granted. He "did" politics as if the United States of America were a private holding company. He was being thrown off the board by upstart scoundrels who had managed to make it a public company. They had floated stock that was bought up by unqualified speculators, thereby reducing to nothing the power of the family shares.

John Adams had helped to offer America to the public and had helped to structure it so each generation could buy a large share but not a controlling interest. The latter was Jefferson's idea. But it was the principle of human equality that Henry Adams rightly discerned was the opposing principle to his own. No detached observer, Adams fought with the weapons the Tocquevillian arsenal provided him. Energized by a sense of grievance and fired by unfulfilled ambition and, especially, by being asked to compete for what he felt was properly his already, Henry Adams expressed that sense of the superior self opposing America. Henry Adams made a comparison of individual to mass: Henry Adams the individual, America the mass. The character of "Henry Adams" engrosses individuality and denies community by objectifying it.

In the wartime letter to his brother Charles, Adams had contrasted the military and the intellectual in hopeful terms. By the time of *The Education*, Adams regarded his youthful hopefulness with irony, but he did not retract his view that he knew what would have been best. He rather said that the problem was that the world of human beings was at fault. His problem had been that he did not understand how stupid and venial human beings were, from the first Adam on down. He knew this because they did not appreciate him. It is so simple and so big that it is hard to take in. The sharp encounter of Henry Adams and President Grant in *The Education* is an encounter between the natural and ancestral American aristocrat and the will of the people incarnated in the man of action. It is also the tantrum of a frustrated individual will.

It sometimes seems that nothing pleased the inside Henry Adams more than throwing off the yoke of his family's sobersided public duty to enjoy the true privilege of the aristocrat, which was to do as he damn well pleased. This was hard for an Adams to do and hard for an old-style American to do. One way Henry Adams managed it was to create his lasting and enchanting fiction of the serious public servant he really wanted to be but that his country would not let him be. There is a fantastic quality in *The Education*'s "Henry Adams" that capped a lifetime of Adams's literary work. He wrote about the world an Adams knows but experienced it in a clever, annihilating way that no earlier Adams dared admit. His final doom-obsessed works only make obvious—if sometimes tedious in the dire predictions of their peculiar equations—the energies that informed a lifetime of an inside mischief that animated an outside sobriety.

Henry Adams must have been glad to get America off his back so he could get his views of America off his chest. He would not admit it, but he was delighted to have an excuse for getting out of the family business and becoming a rentier rather than an entrepreneur of the Adams's properties—known collectively as the United States of America. He says in chapter 17 of *The Education*:

> The difficulty was not the want of friends, and had the whole government been filled with them, it would have helped little without the President and the Treasury. Grant avowed from the start a policy of drift; and a policy of drift attaches only barnacles. At thirty, one has no interest in becoming a barnacle, but even in that character Henry Adams would have been ill seen. His friends were reformers, critics, doubtful in party allegiance, and he was himself an object of suspicion.

Adams spoke for a small group of independents, as we would call them, who refused to sacrifice their independent, active grasp of public affairs to the conformities of office-seeking, party allegiance, corruption, and laissez-faire at the top. The drift Adams discerned was, of course, the mess someone who wishes control always sees when he cannot bear to participate in a relationship, the metabolism that he suddenly sees as outside himself.

Adams created with the Tocquevillian perspective the very terms of his own alienation. His letters and writings of the time reveal the interest, ambition, and gusto—and even the good humor—with which Adams tried to be effective in public life, but they do not contradict the summing up of *The Education* that it finally came down to a contest of wills in which Henry Adams pitted his individual intelligence against the workings of the American system, which he understood from Tocqueville to require his sort of contribution, but which he found resisted it on the only terms he could imagine it. He was not willing to become a part of it, even to save it. What marked Henry Adams's writings was that he really was as relieved as he was angry not to be running America. His divided ambition stamped his Tocquevillian passport.

Henry Adams wrote distinctive and compelling American history. His individual studies, as well as his extraordinary nine-volume *History of the Administrations of Jefferson and Madison*, baffle summary in the variety of the

American pasts they capture and the suggestive lines they reveal. Teaching medieval history at Harvard after his strategic retreat from Washington, Adams trained himself to history. Although he was later to tell George Santayana, who was beginning his own Harvard teaching career, that "nothing could really be taught," he taught for a while, memorably, influentially, but not happily for long.[12] He returned to Washington, where, with John Hay, he built twin Henry H. Richardson houses that faced the White House. He wrote his *History* and anticipated the American smashup.

His histories challenge the modern reader. Significant, interpretively adhesive incidents crowd them. His Tocquevillian enthusiasm had proceeded in part from a natural predilection for the indication of general law on the face of any particular evidence. He was also a resolute Darwinist. The habit of observation partnered the habit of collecting. He collected American information as one might collect, as Jefferson did, spars, specimens of natural history, which he read as he did fossils. The fossils with which he lined his seminar room were not only Darwinist decor but also a clear signal of method. Adams read a fossil by considering it as a particular instance of the operation of a general law, as evolution's track. The law of evolution preempted the craze for fossils. The Tocquevillian-derived law of democracy preempted Adams's American histories. The explanatory law always fences, although loosely, the Adams intellectual range. And the wider open the spaces, of course, the more barbed the wire.

The habit has the aroma of decayed Puritanism. It bears the psychological, italicizing imprint of that almost imperial self-regard bred in gifted children by ambivalently offered family myth. In time, with Adams, everything came to be doubted except that a collection of particulars made a pattern. The reading of the pattern would discover the law that would explain what was happening and what would happen next. Of course, the right law would also explain what had happened in a way that would change it from seeming that the wrong things had happened. A general law must explain the simple disappointing discrepancy between the life Adams led and liked leading and its failure to bring him power and centrality. Since he could not change things, it was essential that he know everything. Everything must amount to something he knew.

Jefferson's positive basking in enlightened ease about knowledge being power and *dulce et utile* must have taunted Henry Adams. Jefferson's capacity blithely to take the leap of enlightened faith, to believe that knowledge was power and the sweet and useful, was the bane of Henry Adams's historical career. He caught Jefferson in contradictions, faulted him for his failures of knowledge, but had to chronicle his unstoppable rise to power. Nothing even Henry Adams could say could shake the evidence that Jefferson's career and popularity validated his abiding faiths. The Americans resoundingly preferred the Jefferson faith to the Adams knowledge that the human condition must make one suspect the connection between knowledge and power and reject outright that the sweet was the useful. Even when they were willing to use the Adams character and talent, Americans repudiated the men, crediting even their achievements to a Jefferson-derived common philosophy of the natural progress of a democratic people. In the American drama, the Adamses always got the role of Captain Hook to Jefferson's Peter Pan, who was forever untouched by life.

How this must have galled Henry Adams, especially since he himself had no trouble hearing the Jeffersonian siren song. It was Jefferson, rather than John Adams, John Quincy Adams, or Charles Francis Adams, who had the kind of career Henry Adams might have envied and imagined for himself. He kept trying to make the Jeffersonian connection between himself as a man of talent and the good of the democratic regime, and he kept trying to find his disinterested attachment to the people. But he pursued the Jeffersonian ideal with the Adams spirit. The chasm between the sweets of knowledge and the power of the law remained ever wide and altogether problematic for Henry Adams. Like his grandfather, he was a failed Jeffersonian.

What Adams knew about the world and what he believed he should know about the world stalemated, fatally at war. His episodes of intellectual lawmaking invariably exploded in cheerful frustration. They always began with Adams making the world comprehensible, from the point of view of effective action. Tocqueville created for him an arena and a role, and the role gave his life its theme of tutorial relation to his culture. Henry Adams had no stomach for enduring the disappointments of his forebears. He understood what they endured and was not sustained by any faith—in the here-and-now, the hereafter, or even in himself—that would make the ancient or modern creeds of such endurance possible for him. He was a complainer, not a Stoic; a fantasist, not a Cynic; an ironist, not an Epicurean.

Each new possibility of action inched closer to the cloistered, the isolated, the removed, the singular, and the individual, and each phase cast less and less of a shadow in the world. With the shrinking of the shadow, grew the pall Henry Adams cast over a world whose meaning beyond himself he doubted. Finally, he denied that the world could be understood and completed the destruction of meaningful action in the old-fashioned Adams vocational sense. *The Education* moves between Adams's thorough ransacking of the possibility that he could have led the life that was expected of him and his obvious pleasure at the life that he had led. It shifts between a sneer and a private smile. The anger in the book is sometimes directed at the world for being so resistant to his claims and at other times is directed at whatever there was that made him take his own claims in such a world seriously.

In chapter 13 of Henry Adams's anonymous political novel of 1880, *Democracy*, Silas Ratcliffe tries to overbear Mrs. Madeleine Lee's refusal of his marriage proposal:

> He meant to crush opposition by force. More and more vehement as he spoke he actually bent over and tried to seize her hand. She drew it back as though he were a reptile. She was exasperated by his obstinate disregard of her forbearance, this gross attempt to bribe her with office, this flagrant abandonment of even a pretense of public virtue; the mere thought of his touch on her person was more repulsive than a loathsome disease. . . . "Mr. Ratcliffe! I have listened to you with a great deal more patience and respect than you deserve. For one long hour I have degraded myself by discussing with you the question of whether I should marry a man who by his own confession has betrayed the highest trusts that could be placed in him, who has taken money for his votes as a Senator and who is now in public office by means of a successful fraud of his own, when in justice he should be in a State's prison. I will have no more of this. Understand, once for all, that there is an impassable gulf between your life and mine, I do not doubt that you will make yourself President, but whatever or wherever you are, never speak to me or recognize me again!"

Moments afterward, Madeleine Lee puts her feelings this way: " 'I want to go to Egypt,' said Madeleine, still smiling faintly: 'democracy has shaken my nerves to pieces. Oh what rest it would be to live in the Great Pyramid and look out forever at the polar star' " (*Democracy*, chap. 13). This is what Henry Adams did after the *History*.

Democracy tells the story of Henry Adams's Tocquevillian earnestness. The rich and high-minded widow, Madeleine Lee, embarks on a social career in Washington after she is disappointed with the life available to a late-nineteenth-century American woman of cultivation and leisure; Philadelphia, Boston, New York, and even Europe have disappointed her:

> Here, then, was the explanation of her restlessness, discontent, ambition,—call it what you will. It was the feeling of a passenger on an ocean steamer whose mind will not give him rest until he has been in the engine-room and talked with the engineer. She wanted to see with her own eyes the action of primary forces; to touch with her own hand the massive machinery of society; to measure with her own mind the capacity of the motive power. She was bent upon getting to the heart of the great American mystery of democracy and government. . . . What she wished to see, she thought, was the clash of interests, the interests of forty millions of people and a whole continent, centering at Washington; guided, restrained, controlled, or unrestrained and uncontrollable, by men of ordinary mould; the tremendous forces of government, and the machinery of society, at work. What she wanted, was POWER. (*Democracy*, chap. 1)

Mrs. Lee took the Tocquevillian gambit, as had Henry Adams. His casting of her temptation shrewdly gets to the heart of his own or anyone's wishes to have an uncorrupted and disinterested observational relation to the workings of the "good ship Democracy." The knowledge you find when you are on the inside looking in is daunting and tempting. If you make yourself desirable to the democracy, it will corrupt you.

This was keen-sighted fantasy on Adams's part. The Tocquevillian must resist the blandishments of office and yet gain the ear of the nation. No disinterested voice can be heard, let alone listened to, trusted, or believed. John Carrington, the dilapidated, high-minded, disappointed Southern gentleman, a fixture of such novels as *Democracy* and *The Bostonians* and the ghost of the better days of the republic, suggests that there was a dignified history to the present democratic wreck. He also manages to provoke the "Prairie Giant," Senator Ratcliffe, who woos and almost wins Mrs. Lee and embodies the American politics of the time as Adams sees them—swollen, vulgar, corrupt, powerful, shrewd, and probably successful. Public men, Ratcliffe declares, "cannot be dressing themselves today in Washington's old clothes. If Washington were President now, he would have to learn our ways or lose the next election. Only fools and theorists imagine that our society can be handled with gloves or long poles. One must make one's self a part of it. If virtue won't answer our purpose, we must use vice, or our opponents will put us out of office, and this was as true in Washington's day as it is now, and always will be" (*Democracy*, chap. 6).

The novel explores the conflict between Mrs. Lee, who wishes to handle the heart of America with gloves, and Senator Ratcliffe, who offers her the power she wants only if she will take off her gloves and come up close to get it from him. The novel boasts marvelous observation and clever depiction. Ambassadors, reformers, eccentric Washington characters, and charming society ladies talk about American politics, its principles, and its personalities, much as one imagines the Hay-Adams circle did—with great unreserve and sophistication and also with a searching quality. They ask questions such as: What is this all about?; How could that man and that woman really be the president and first lady?; Must not democracy amount to more than this?; What must America be to send such dull, grotesque, corrupt reflections of herself to govern at Washington? Mrs. Lee asks what there is for the likes of her in such a regime and, throughout, Adams whispers, "This is what Tocqueville meant."

The point appears to be that one cannot remain unsullied within or heeded without American democratic life. The book advances a personal morality in which honor and virtue, not to mention every single detail of good taste, are worth more than the degradations of democratic life. You cannot clean hands dirtied with participation in democracy. Even sympathetic observation ends up a snare. Madeleine Lee, of course, unlike Henry Adams, did not set herself up as a tutor to the people; rather, the funny reverse, she is Adams's Tocquevillian beard, disguising just how seriously he had intended his Tocquevillian ambition. He presents his own ambition to advise as her desire to learn. In his novels and in the biography of John Randolph, Henry Adams experimented with what would become his characteristic conceit that lives are best understood in terms of how their reasonable expectations have been disappointed. Adams reverses the American dream.

Mrs. Lee, a young childless widow whose life is already burdened with anomie and sadness, learns a bitter lesson. Had Adams been less concentrated on the politics of how the modern world betrays people, he could have written about her as Henrik Ibsen might have. Madeleine Lee was a talented woman—bored, missing something, missing a vocation to still her desperation. Adams understood this in women and in men, in his wife and in himself. Mrs. Lee's solution is the possibility, hinted at in the letter from her sister to the devoted Carrington that ends the book, that she will come home from the Old World ready to settle down in a well-bred quiet corner of America. This is not a happy ending. Although it adds to the store of the best American society, that society will be all the more cut off from American society and will not admit the likes of Silas Ratcliffe.

Adams staged Carrington's argument with Ratcliffe about Washington as a *ronde* at Mount Vernon. Its Washington theme and variations show Adams at his most artful. His social comedy was always best when it dramatized his own divided sentiments. But, knowing his way around Mount Vernon and Washington and the American past, Henry Adams still made up a Madeleine Lee whose reaction to the knowledge of the present day daunts her into choosing a principled past that is beyond reproach (because beyond recall), and in which ancestry and the ancestral will become the same and keen observation will lead not to power but into supper. Virtue must retreat into private discrimination. The last words of the novel, Madeleine Lee's postscript, sound the motto of an exclusive refuge: "The bitterest part of all this horrid story is that nine out of ten of our countrymen would say I had made a mistake" (*Democracy*, "Conclusion"). All that America could do for Mrs. Lee was nearly ruin her life. Henry Adams believed the same of himself.

The histories still retain and honor the Tocquevillian vocation, the sense of democracy as somehow inevitable and worth observing, but the vocational possibility has diminished. *Democracy* marked Adams's awareness of the conflicted part the American Tocquevillian must play. The democratic embrace is as horrifying as Silas Ratcliffe's to the lovely Mrs. Lee. The relationship between Adams and democracy is like the romance in the novel. But the romance in the novel requires that Ratcliffe allow Mrs. Lee to know him without his responding in any way to her attentions. He must treat her like a lady, but she may use him as she pleases. Adams wrote in the novel what it felt like when America did not treat him like "a lady." The falseness of Mrs. Lee's position expresses the falseness of the Tocquevillian position: she demands prerogative without returning even affection, requires intimacy while keeping her distance, desires power without surrendering control, and retreats from passion in the name of morals and good taste.

Good taste was *non disputandum*, established among the genteel classes in a way that rivaled religion and kept morals company. *Mont-Saint-Michel and Chartres* shows the mark of the broader ideology of high culture that stamped America; but Henry Adams was too individual and too difficult, too serious and too original, too gifted and too mischief-prone, to make common cause with the genteel tradition. High culture and morals blended into the socially and morally unarguable and the indicative. Good taste is a clearer mark of salvation and grace than ever the Puritans could have devised.

Good taste made everything of manners and pronunciation and a kind of insider knowledge—all those things for which American democracy had no ear, no taste, no patience, no time, no money, no liking, no understanding, no gift, and—if we follow Tocqueville—no vocation. Good taste could identify the private society within American society, the place to which one must privately gain an admittance, the place that the people came to believe was the natural aristocracy that Jefferson talked about. Good taste took the sting out of Emerson as well as Jefferson. Believe that this is where Madeleine Lee ended up, in a very interesting, cosmopolitan, private world in which the signals of language, wit, art, and literature were also founded on social distinctions of a highly nonegalitarian discrimination. Here, even riches would not suffice to insulate a social life from ordinary life and democratic feelings. This cosmopolitan refuge was a halfway house for American Tocquevillians. What Mrs. Lee learned about democracy devastated her. It turned her inward to a self no longer interested in democratic connection, a self no world could come round to, a self by definition apart from the world. For his own part, Henry Adams was, perhaps, relieved.

Tocqueville fashioned an immense and beautiful generalization about democracy's place in history that judged from the American case and supported the various generalizations about what democracy was and would become. The particulars of American observation cling to the Tocquevillian generalization like piglets to a nursing sow. This is where Henry Adams began and where the American Tocquevillian always begins. But, as the *History* makes clear, Henry Adams lost the nurturing connection between generalizations and particulars. American Tocquevillians who take an outsider's view of their own country's doings have this central problem of finding the meaning in the horizons they claim to have seen beyond.

Henry Adams began to see, with evolution (as he had with Tocqueville and with reform), the possibilities for meaningful action in the knowledge that evolution brought him, giving him ground back for human choice and freedom. In Adams's writing, it always turns out that human action is futile. The story of each of his intellectual adventures parallels the stories of his two novels. They begin with high hopes and end with resignation to a limited sphere because of the futility of high hopes and because of the pleasures the reduced sphere affords.

Here, Adams shone. He granted the greatness and pursued its existence on the level of his laws and his generalizations and yet found it nowhere in the details. He looked up from his stacked deck with the wide eyes of innocent, surprised hurt and disappointment. It was as if he said, "Honest, no offense intended, but the Emperor just hasn't got any clothes that I can see, no matter how hard I look." Followed by, "I blame myself for looking." If greatness is about self-deception, faith, belief, and those grand leaderly qualities he dissects in *The Education*, his histories, unlike Francis Parkman's, did not celebrate them. They explored achievement in despair of the heroic. They were sophisticated, indeed.

For Adams, human action cannot skate on the thin ice of law. Adams allows any person almost no intentional effect on things, and how relentlessly he strips such effect as humans have of their admirable qualities! This was the theme of his study of Albert Gallatin, who did the work for which Jefferson got the credit. It is not what makes things happen that the people admire and vaunt. The acid biography of John Randolph isolates Randolph's clear seeing in a wild mix of irrelevance. The most irrelevant thing about John Randolph was his capacity to see what was going on in America. The difference between Adams's history and his fiction was that his fictional characters accept observation and understanding as the human actions that really matter. Even Henry Adams could not get his historical characters to admit or his *History* to prove this.

Adams placed his examples from history in a control fluid—the law, the evolutionary, explanatory, metahistorical culture where the germs of particulars grow into law and truth. He characteristically told a version of his immediate story in universal terms: another instance of the recurring human comedy. He also maintained an awareness of the way particular incidents cast a philosophic explanatory shadow. The search through the particulars to find the law is how Henry Adams justified to himself all his delight in stray unearnest particulars, which were the things that amused and interested him. Had Adams wanted a law to keep, he could have found one and kept it. The discard of his laws has satisfied many another. But Adams apparently needed to see himself doing the important thing, finding the law that would explain, that was important enough to constitute a worthy spending of his time, even in the gimlet eye of the Adams expectations for an Adams. He was Adams enough to think he needed to justify his interests in a public-spirited way; and he was enough himself to be restless, irritable, and angry about it. Enough himself to blame it on America, he was Adams enough to blame it on himself.

What did Henry Adams have to substitute for his sires' first-handedness? He had clarity, a secondhand candor and borrowed participant's intimacy of judgment and feeling for the scene that memoirs could not even in hindsight accomplish. He was like a fly on the wall. Then, there was the law, the possibility of seeing more deeply into the situation than can a participant who believes in the importance of his own participation. But the difficulty remained that Adams's freedom from participation so often soured into a contempt for participation. Perhaps the laws codified the meaninglessness of human action, but they sometimes appeared to mock those who believed in the meaning of human action, which is something else again from fate mocking the vanity of human wishes. His laws furnished a detachment that was Olympian only in that they licensed a godlike interference in human events. One cannot help feeling that Henry Adams was always changing his law because it was meant to serve the purposes of a hanging judge.

With characteristic insight and false precision, Jefferson imagined the nature of the relation of intellect to American culture. He imagined an enlightened paradise, but it grew into a positive briar patch of thwartedness and consequent ambivalence, an unresolved situation of blighted nurture and guilty, infuriated aggression. The democratic demand and the mantle of specialness clashed. This is the true American Tocquevillian insight, or the observations of the second volume of *Democracy in America* rendered as a grievance, an angry indictment against a culture that works for the interests of the money- or power-smart, not the truth-smart. This is nothing more than what Socrates found out in Athens: the city does not want advice that is beholden to the philosopher's inner voice.

HENRY ADAMS, AMERICAN TOCQUEVILLIAN

There is a democratic discipline of the soul that is not a democratic horizon but, like any joining, is a conscious and principled leverage on the individual by a perceived higher good of community. This requires the acceptance of democracy as something you must listen to rather than as something that must listen to you. The study of American history convinced Henry

Adams that individuals were powerless to affect the important events, even in the sense that the Tocquevillian role model might have allowed. This was a welcome relief from his increasingly burdensome sense of his own vocation. But, with it, he also threw off the last traces of that sense that the democratic or American community had a claim on his individuality. His by-the-book Tocquevillian days were over. He yet retained the mark of the American Tocquevillian—the need for a detached observation of America because of the need to defend himself from the embrace of democratic identity.

What he needed to find out was what he had thought history would tell him. That is one reason for the twenty-year gap in *The Education*. At a certain point, both the Tocquevillian ambition and the belief that the answer could be found in America ceased to interest Adams, and his law became increasingly the sponsoring interest for other things, such as himself, the objects of his aesthetic curiosity, and his European and Pacific excursions. The discrepancy between the richness of the things he noticed and the automatic, decapitating equations of his law, is striking; the law, chopping the head off the life, has little to do with anything except in moments of ecstatic fantasy—as in "The Virgin and the Dynamo"—when the law and the life come together in a burst of the sublime. The intensity of the observed illuminates the abstractions of the laws with feeling, an emotion that is reserved for the artist Adams was, not for the statesman he was meant to be. Here resides the failure of Adams's Tocquevillianism. He could despise but never steward a people.

Any law that did not do away with Adams's own sense of "failure," which seems to have meant his failure to be the center of the world without having to make any essential compromises in it, was replaced. Each law successively explained a series of facts until, finally, in his last two books, Adams considered the facts of his "life" and his "expression" and concluded laws from them, too. Perhaps the most characteristic intensity of the Adams narrative is the to-and-fro of general principle: will this or that piece of evidence, so interesting in itself, so carefully and variously examined before our eyes by this connoisseur of whatever it is the subject involves, turn out to be a true instance of the trend, the law, the characteristic, or whatever it is that is under discussion? Adams's apprehension of experience, his handling of the documents, weighing of the evidence, hefting of the detritus, and teasing out of the messages of life, inches between the Tocquevillian Scylla and the Adams Charybdis.

He remained a stranger in his own country, even though he lived there and his authority was local and ancient. He felt like a returned traveler, like Rip Van Winkle. "I used to live here, these are my ancestral parts," he seemed to say, "but I feel like a stranger. You have made me feel like a traveler in my own country." *The Education* bears this burden, but it lurks in all his writings after the 1870s. The freshness of his history writing came from his odd combination of knowing everything and nothing at the same time. George Bancroft knew everything and then some. Adams conveyed discovery in the course of his writing. The narrative never dulled discovery. Adams flavored his knowing nothing with his knowing everything, as in this picture of America in 1800 in volume 1 and chapter 1 of the *History*: "A Government capable of sketching a magnificent plan, and willing to give only a half-hearted pledge for its fulfillment; a people eager to advertise a vast undertaking beyond their present powers, which when completed would become an object of jealousy and fear." This was the impression made upon the traveler who visited Washington in 1800 and mused among the unraised columns of the Capitol upon the destiny of the United States. Adams offers a characteristically sound reading of the American historical mood and situation, firmly situated in the traveler's reports he refers to.

Sometimes—in his novels, for instance—Adams tried to season his knowing everything with his knowing nothing. Any time he tried to create a character with common sense, as opposed to experience, he broke down into stock characters. Not having common sense, he could not regard it. He knew better than common sense and usually characterized it as a standard American ingenue. On the other hand, as Madeleine Lee in *Democracy* begins to see how great her ambition was and how bitter its price would be, we almost feel with her. "Almost" is pretty far for Henry Adams, who could never let go of his fictional characters. He never had to let go of his historical ones. Adams learned that fiction must be an ingredient in his essentially historical and autobiographical work, not the other way around. He decided to rest everything on his own case.

Lonely connoisseurship, to which Adams, it seems now, inevitably ascended, always tufted the Tocquevillian catbird seat. To study your horizons as if from the outside requires that you be always judging them and "the most of the people" who comfortably live within them. This inevitably intensifies one's sense of difference from them. *The Education* crystallizes Adams's principled scrutiny of America as if from the outside, from inside himself, and from the centers of power of the age. He has become a literary hero because his unique adventures made every inside an outside. The fact remains that what he found to be ironically meaningless was the same feeling of purpose and activity others might gain within the horizons of American democratic life. This probably includes the lives of those who are alienated, privileged, self-conscious, and literary enough to read Adams. Not least, it includes those who write at length about him.

Henry Adams ended up pretty far from the rest of us. *The Education* abounds, luxuriates, in soured Tocquevillian objectivity about a people whose capacity for civilization and for offending Henry Adams seems to amount to the same thing.

> The American character showed singular limitations which sometimes drove the student of civilised man to despair. Crushed by his own ignorance,—lost on the darkness of his own gropings,—the scholar finds himself jostled of a sudden by a crowd of men who seem to him ignorant that there is a thing called ignorance; who have forgotten how to amuse themselves; who cannot even understand that they are bored. . . . That the American, by temperament, worked to excess, was true; work and whiskey were his stimulants; work was a form of vice; but he never cared much for money or power after he earned them. The amusement of the pursuit was all the amusement he got from it; he had no use for wealth. . . . Bored, patient, helpless; pathetically dependent on his wife and daughters; indulgent to excess; mostly a modest, decent, excellent, valuable citizen; the American was to be met at every railway station in Europe, carefully explaining to every listener that the happiest day of his life would be the day he should land on the pier at New York. He was ashamed to be amused; his mind no longer answered to the stimulus of variety; he could not face a new thought. (*The Education*, chap. 19)

This American scholar should have paid attention to Emerson's. His writing reflects the difference in the views of the American Tocquevillian and the Emersonian: one is outside looking on, in, and through; the other is within, albeit solitary and apart within, the self. The first wants to run things, the second is content to be "right" inside; the first is narcissistic and the second egotistic. They propound two kinds of individualism, one alienated and reactive and the other accepting and participating.

We again meet Adams's American in *The Ambassadors*, this time in the form of Waymarsh. Henry James had a more complete understanding of him because, of course, he was not at pains to distinguish himself from him. Henry Adams always had to make it clear that he himself was not one of the Americans he was describing, as if this needed remarking. The tone of this unpleasant reflection on the national character, settling on the offensive successful classes, neared the kind of understanding of the civilization that caused Santayana to talk about a "genteel tradition" and James to ponder the "sacred rage."

Writing about the Augustus Saint-Gaudens figure he commissioned and placed in Rock Creek Park in memory of his wife, Adams makes his point even clearer: American reaction to the figure confirmed his sense that the American mind "shunned, distrusted, disliked, the dangerous attraction of ideals, and stood alone in history for its ignorance of the past." He further says about the statue, in chapter 21 of *The Education*:

> He supposed its meaning to be the one common-place about it,—the oldest idea known to human thought. He knew that if he asked an Asiatic its meaning, not a man, woman or child from Cairo to Kamschatka would have needed more than a glance to reply. From the Egyptian Sphinx to the Kamakura Daibuts; from Prometheus to Christ; from Michael Angelo [*sic*] to Shelley, art had wrought on this eternal figure almost as though it had nothing else to say. The interest of the figure was not in its meaning, but in the response of the observer. . . . The American layman had lost sight of ideals; the American priest had lost sight of faith. Both were more American than the old, half-witted soldiers who denounced the wasting, on a mere grave, of money which should have been given for drink.

He made himself unspeakably clear. Nothing about America was as compelling as the infallibly disappointing responses of its people to the admirable and beautiful and true. All Adams would see in his countrymen was how unutterably degraded was their response to the best universal and shared human things. Who Adams thought he was had nothing to do with who he thought most of the people were. And the conclusion followed inexorably, in chapter 22 of *The Education*. The growth of America was "the whole mechanical consolidation of force, which ruthlessly stamped out the life of the class into which Adams was born, but created monopolies capable of controlling the new energies that America adored."

As for himself, Adams finally surrendered his old Tocquevillian role. He said he was surrendering the semblance of understanding, but it was responsibility that he threw over at last. In chapter 34 of *The Education*, he said:

> Fortunately, a student of history had no responsibility for the problem; he took it as science gave it, and waited only to be taught. With science or with society, he had no quarrel and claimed no share of authority. He had never been able to acquire knowledge, still less to impart it; and if he had, at times, felt serious differences with the American of the nineteenth century, he felt none with the American of the twentieth. For this new creation, born since 1900, a historian asked no longer to be teacher or even friend; he asked only to be a pupil, and promised to be docile, for once, even though trodden under foot; for he could see that the new American,—the child of incalculable coal-power, chemical power, electric power, and radiating energy, as well as of new forces yet undetermined,—must be a sort of God compared with any former creation of nature. At the rate of progress since 1800, every American who lived into the year 2000 would know how to control unlimited power. He would think in complexities unimaginable to an earlier mind. He would deal with problems altogether beyond the range of earlier society. . . . Perhaps even he might go back, in 1964, to sit with Gibbon on the steps of the Ara Coeli.

This silken curse thrown in the teeth of the future hits its mark. Giving up on us, he suggests that we will come to view the past—as he does, as Edward Gibbon does—as the decline and fall of something preferable, admirable, smaller, better. He pictures a horrific future with delight. He congratulates us on our titanic barbarism. And, as he ends his autobiography, he tells us how he feels. John Hay has died.

> Education had ended for all three [Adams, Hay, and Clarence King], and only beyond some remoter horizon could its values be fixed or renewed. Perhaps some day—say 1938, their centenary,—they might be allowed to return together for a holiday, to see the mistakes of their own lives made clear in the light of the mistakes of their successors; and perhaps then, for the first time since man began his education among the carnivores, they would find a world that sensitive and timid natures could regard without a shudder. (*The Education*, chap. 35)

Well, before you soften your heart at these tender feelings, you might recall that the whole history of civilization is being called witness to the pain that the sensibility of Henry Adams suffered just by being alive in his time, in our civilization, and surrounded by the likes of you and me.

Adams composed a masterpiece that would dissociate us all from our own situations and feelings for the sake of his disappointment. Like most of his late work, *The Education* takes revenge. *Mont-Saint-Michel and Chartres* creates the alternative to the modern allegiance for the individual sensibility—controlled, willed, picked, and chosen—the way a real world cannot be. *Mont-Saint-Michel and Chartres* is every bit as self-centered as *The Education* and bears equal witness to Adams's disappointment with his times. It suggests the alternative to the engagement with the democratic, the modern, the contemporary, and with one's own time, that bespeaks a preference for older values. The older values of *Mont-Saint-Michel and Chartres* look almost punitively related to the belabored absence of certain values in democratic modern America.

Things "worked" for Henry Adams because he lived much the way he wanted to and produced a remarkable and satisfying body of writing. The tone of *The Education* is satisfied and smug, no matter what he seems to be saying. "Education" is what cultures do to train and include. Adams's threnody of the failure of his education attests to his proud isolation at the heart of every American thing—no America must/can garner him. He refused his education, and we, his readers, have cause to be glad. But his refusal is a Tocquevillian strain and deserves wary attention. It is, in Adams, an artist's or a philosopher's refusal. To be "in" on everything and responsible to nothing is a privilege that must not be viewed lightly, even if you are right about everything. Adams stands forth, the very instance of natural talent loosed from the bonds of connection that Jefferson worried about.

It may be harder for a person of talent to accept than to reject democracy. With its egalitarian comparisons with others, democracy often feels like a denial of one's special quality. For the likes of Henry Adams to find content in the moral or political, not to mention the intellectual, community of equality is difficult, if not impossible. In a democracy, one has to look for something different from what Adams insisted on looking for. The medieval offered him a refuge where he could find the sorts of things he was looking for in a community and that vindicated his highly individual sensibility with the illusion of community. Democracy never offered him satisfactory imaginative community, to say nothing of any kind of refuge.

The tip-off may be Henry Adams's shrewd awareness of the divisions within the American culture that the genteel tradition addressed. He side-stepped its terms. It was all grist for his mill, but nothing that he would engage. His mill ground everything to dust. He identified with the mill, as he did with the dynamo, however ironically. Henry Adams refused to see himself as engaged within American culture. Few American writers achieved what Adams did, and even a defensive reader of his books will delight in them. But they remain heartless and merciless in their refusal of community. The true is animated by an exclusive spirit that corrodes inter-estedly, angrily, as it claims to speak ironically, loftily, and disinterestedly. The identification it offers is with the superior. It reverses the story of the democratic dream, tells how a boy grew up and did not become president.

Adams makes the unthinkable easy. His readers identify with a figure of palpable and remarkable individuality whose essential message is that the primary way to understand American civilization is to rise above it. Democracy makes life unbearable to a sensitive nature like Adams's. And it does grate on sensitive natures—any system does. It must be hard to be smarter, better educated, better informed, richer, readier (and readier able) to identify with the public good than most people. The Adams crowd led fabulous lives. But an understanding of one's own ability does not auto-matically excuse one from the moral obligations of community, nor do the pleasures of exclusive association.

Adams chose to write about America, and he borrowed from Tocque-ville the conceit that structured his work with tension and interest. But his initial attempt to look objectively at American civilization with the idea of serving its best interests turned into an obsession to distinguish himself from it. The sweets of his writing were marinated in the juices of his re-sentment and baked in the crust of his disappointment. What Adams plays upon is important—the hurts that democracy inescapably inflicts on the intelligent, cultivated, high culture, the traditionally artistic sensibility, the individual. The genteel tradition codified that hurt into a culture of control. Henry Adams, like other American Tocquevillians, made believe that one could be detached from the culture and observe it, without consequence. To feel that one is beyond "the most of the people" means one has tran-scended democratic community. It is hard to distinguish transcended from refused allegiance. But to take up his detached tone about America as if one were talking (as Tocqueville might) about "them" and not "us" is a consequential, alienating, and intellectually confused position that no mere ironies will soothe.

Smart as Henry Adams was, and as well as he wrote, his writing had an agenda. The flattering identification with him it offers us, *echt* American Tocquevillian, involves an alienation from the democracy he felt had alienated him. That boils down to our courting alienation from ourselves. BEWARE.

CHAPTER THREE

HENRY JAMES
AND THE
SACRED RAGE

THE STORY OF *THE AMBASSADORS*

In *The Ambassadors*, Henry James wrote about what it really felt like to be a certain kind of "superior" American around the turn of the twentieth century. Lambert Strether's reluctant eye-opening in Paris made American waves. James thought that civilized life was morally and socially expressive, and that the kind of person one could be and the kind of life one could live in a society were art's proper concern. *The Ambassadors* tells the story of an American Tocquevillian and how he arrived at a different answer than the Tocquevillian answer to the American question. Strether's Parisian adventure is, among other things, a pointed and poignant dramatic interpretation of American civilization.[1]

Although *The Ambassadors* is not the only novel about American characters analyzing the characteristics of America, it is the best. The story of its protagonist, Lambert Strether, is an adventure story of thinking and considering and reflecting and agonizing and weighing and trying, above all, to figure America out. It was always the case that the New World was meant to be something startling in human history. Puritan Ruritania or Empire of Liberty, America was a nation with a Western historical subtext and a widening audience for its development. The issue of the American characteristic, as Tocqueville saw, need have little to do with any particular care for America. James's interest in the international theme, however it happened to spring from his own circumstances and however original his treatment of it, was not provincial. It was one proper theme of a novel-writing age of nationalism and cosmopolitanism.

If *The Ambassadors* was not provincial, Strether's intellectual habit was—at least at the start—characteristically so. Strether did what the Puritans said people were meant to do. His self-consciousness resembles inaction, but it is a version of the scrutiny that New England was founded to promote in individuals. It is the project in which he was supposed to be engaged. In Mrs. Newsome's intense misgivings about his way of doing it hangs the ironic tale: which of the two of them had the conscientious habit wrong, and what of it? Strether's was conscientious labor of the most active sort. But can conscientiousness shorn of predetermined conclusion be depended upon? The fate of Strether's conscientiousness is to some extent the predicament of *The Ambassadors*.[2]

The story of the novel shows how the earlier New England American ways of thinking—the symbolizing, conscientious, allegorizing way of reading motives and meanings into actions and reasoning from this to the proper social arrangement—go awry. Strether's own fate and his observations of others' fates reveal the disintegration of that old Puritan habit, the belief that individual conscience can mirror the moral world. *The Ambassadors* catches, in relativist midpassage, the old habit changing into the modern one. The Puritans warned against conscientiousness without predetermined conclusions. Literary historian Perry Miller's fascination with those towering instances of Puritan conscientiousness run amok (like Jonathan Edwards) italicized the difficult balance with moral seriousness that the moral order needed to achieve; contemporary scholarship regards conscientiousness as a literary problem. Strether was living out the attenuation of that New England history of earnest idealism. In Paris, he gained a perspective on America. Paris became his gallery of American types, fish out of water turned into representative objects. The book opens with a comedy of cultural interpretation, the comedy of the "sacred rage."[3]

The story is simple enough, although the book is not. Strether arrives in England. He is on his way from Woollett, Massachusetts, to Paris at the behest of Mrs. Newsome, the principal lady of his city. She is a rich, high-minded widow who has joined Strether in literary endeavors and who is more or less engaged to marry him. Strether's errand in Paris is to fetch Mrs. Newsome's son, Chad, home. Chad is wanted for himself and also for the family business, which is in a way to expand. It is felt that Chad will be the proper male relation to direct this expansion, and he is preferred to his sister Sarah's husband, Jim Pocock. His mother also believes, as does all Woollett, that Chad remains in Paris because he has fallen under the spell of a woman with whom he is enjoying a wicked liaison. Strether is Mrs. Newsome's ambassador, representing her and Woollett, and the claims of country, family, business, and morality. He is to bring Chad to his senses; that is, to bring him home. The test of Strether's worthiness to marry Mrs. Newsome is his ability to bring her son home, so the embassy has serious consequences for him, too.

At the time of the novel, Strether is in his fifties. Long a widower, he also has buried a young son. He works at his literary job, editing the *Review*, which is a highbrow and somewhat obscure magazine. He dwells in the civilized—that is, the female and feminine—division of Woollett. He is not connected to its business, public or private. Strether had traveled to Europe on his honeymoon, and he retains a series of impressions that have turned from inspiration to reproach. He is ironic about himself, his life, Woollett, and almost everything. But his irony does not extend to the moral assumptions of his embassy. He agrees with Woollett that Chad ought to come home, that a man's place is in business, that a son's place is at home, and that Paris must be detaining Chad on account of a liaison that Strether regards as simply wrong.

Strether keeps most of his irony for himself. He takes a tone, rather than a course of action, about the values and customs that must amount to the disappointments of his own life. His immediate emotion upon disembarking in Europe is an unaccustomed feeling of freedom, especially from his countrymen. James says of him: "He was burdened, poor Strether—it had better be confessed at the outset—with the oddity of a double consciousness. There was detachment in his zeal and curiosity in his indifference" (*Ambassadors*, Book First, chap. 1). In Strether's charm, his inwardness, his irony, lurks a skittishness that wants control. He sets the conversational pace of the novel with a wonderful, idiosyncratic speech that is surely Jamesian but, in *The Ambassadors*, seems to come first and most decisively from Strether. He conducts everybody to the tempo of his own talk, with its sense of the characteristic, its disclaimer that he is saying what he is saying, the lively buoying of speech with tone, and its vigilant keeping of the self at bay. Strether seems only partially externalized; that is part of his charm. He does not live fully in his own feelings, so that his process of discovering what is going on *out there* is the process of discovering what is going on *in here*.

He has arranged to meet his old friend Waymarsh in Chester. "The American lawyer Waymarsh" hails from Milrose, Connecticut. He smacks of the public and economic success that America rewards and that Strether has failed to win. Waymarsh is in Europe, where the wife he does not live with lives on an enforced rest cure. He is to accompany Strether. Before this rendezvous with his old friend, Strether makes a new friend—Maria Gostrey, an American lady living in Paris who spends her time as a social friend to Americans abroad, a facilitator of the wealthy American need to see (and not to see) the Old World. She is a knowing and conscious expatriate whose business depends on her sharp awareness of the state of Americans and American society. She and Strether begin a flirtation, an acquaintance, a friendship, an interpretive alliance, with precipitous suddenness and, for him, an almost licentious freedom. Strether commandeers Miss Gostrey, and she appropriates him. To some extent a literary device, Maria Gostrey is "our man" in Paris.

Miss Gostrey and Strether begin almost at once to talk, and they will continue to talk throughout the novel. He tells her of his mission; she helps him with Waymarsh. In the way that she helps him with Waymarsh, we see her lifting some of the burden of home off Strether's shoulders. Or does he shed it like a snakeskin? Theirs is a conversational conspiracy. Much of Miss Gostrey's role is to keep the story before us. Strether needs someone to talk to about the other characters, someone to compare notes with about what happens to him.

Miss Gostrey's interludes with Strether afford sympathetic conversation for two Americans alienated from some aspects of their country and yet compelled to rethink them all the time. They breathe an atmosphere of intellectual freedom rooted in one of interpersonal freedom. Strether does not always honorably discharge this last. Some part of his freedom with Miss Gostrey is what he withholds from her. What they both know— which Mrs. Newsome and Madame de Vionnet (Chad's Parisian friend), for example, do not—makes them too close for romance but exactly not too close for talk. They are each, if not collectors, then surely appraisers of the American characteristic and are companions in a marvelous discussion of Americans in general. Their particular knowledge comes from being

American as well as from being critical of America; they are alienated observers seeking detachment. Their attraction succeeds and fails on account of their seeing one another clearly.

Waymarsh and Strether go on to Paris, where Strether takes his own sweet time calling on Chad Newsome. He acclimates himself to Paris, which is more than Waymarsh wants to do or wants Strether to do. The constant breeze of Strether's enjoyment wafts through the book. He sniffs it, remarks it, even seeks it. When Strether calls on Chad, he finds, instead, John Little Bilham, an expatriated artist chum of Chad's who charms Strether and begins to interest him in the possible complexity of Chad's situation. By the time Strether dramatically meets Chad in a box at the Comédie Française, he is prepared by his own melting response to Paris—and whatever it is inside himself that responds to being there—to be overwhelmed by what he takes to be the change in Chad. He and Miss Gostrey attribute this change to the influence of the woman in Chad's life.

Strether is led to believe and desires to believe that Chad's relationship is virtuous. By this, he means that he likes the resulting transformation in Chad and would prefer to believe the relationship to be tutorial and not sexually intimate. The more Strether knows of the people involved the more ingeniously he tries to arrange their relations in a tableau of virtue. He likes what he sees, so he supposes that it must be good. Chad's life is so beautiful to Strether's eye that he assumes that whatever brought him to this peak of sophistication and civilization must also be "wonderful"— which means good, virtuous, and not sexual. It is one of the chief assumptions of Strether's Woollett that the beautiful is sacred, virtuous, pure, and can be safely described by conventions (although it is said to be "higher" than the conventional). One of its ideals is that it does not offend sexual, not to mention social or capitalist, conventions.

Strether's automatic "Woollett-pilot" functions to protect him from threatening recognitions. It also fuels the novel's comic suspense because Strether must compare his own relations with Mrs. Newsome to those he supposes Chad to be having with Madame de Vionnet. His own freedoms with Miss Gostrey (and, later, with Madame de Vionnet) throw his intense and yet rigidly confined relations with Mrs. Newsome into clear relief. Strether uses his relations with Mrs. Newsome to set off his relations with other people. Like an erring husband, he needs the excitement of what he is escaping. Before seeing Chad, Strether's relations seem playfully eroticized, intimate, free, imagined, and within his own control.

At the sculptor Gloriani's garden party at the stylish center of Paris, Strether meets Madame de Vionnet and her adolescent daughter, who enchant him. His growing delight in them makes it impossible for him to believe that Madame de Vionnet and Chad are involved in any but a beautiful way, which still rules out what Woollett would call immoral. For a while, he plays with the possibility that Mademoiselle de Vionnet is meant by her mother for Chad—that she, in a way, is bringing them up for each another. Strether spends much of the book trying to figure out and yet trying not to put a name to the relationship of Chad and Madame de Vionnet. Everyone else knows and supposes Strether to know that they are lovers. Strether is beguiled by everyone's different attitudes into thinking that they, like him, are uncertain. In fact, they are only divided, one from another, by their reactions to Strether's understandings of what they all recognize goes without saying.

On the auspicious occasion of the garden party, Strether utters to Little Bilham, Chad's friend, the great soliloquy in which he reflects on his own disappointments and urges Bilham to live his own life at any cost: "It's a mistake not to." At this point, Strether commences to live what may or may not be his own life. It smacks of Chad's life. Chad is ready to return to Woollett. Strether, liking Chad and Paris so much better than anybody or anything at home, champions Madame de Vionnet's cause. Indeed, he writes to Mrs. Newsome to say he believes it would be better for Chad to stay in Paris: things are not what they had seemed.

All along, Strether has engaged in constant, voluminous correspondence with Mrs. Newsome. One of the novel's pleasures is James's leaving the letters they exchange within the grasp of the reader's imagination. On account of Waymarsh's probable secret warnings, Mrs. Newsome's alarm at what she takes to be Strether's defection from the network of allegiances whose ambassador he is causes her to cease communication with him. She sends her daughter to replace and to recover Strether, if possible, but certainly to carry out the primary business of reclaiming Chad. Accompanied by her husband and her sister-in-law, Mamie, whom Woollett intends for Chad, Sarah Pocock arrives in Paris.

Chad wines and dines Sarah and, indeed, shows her that fabulous Parisian luxe that so enchanted Strether, and in the very company that seduced him. She enjoys the splendor, or endures it, but she remains proof against Strether's view that Chad's translation to this sphere proves the beauty of his relationship to Madame de Vionnet, or even that he is any the better for it. Sarah Pocock knows a bad woman when she is forced to meet one. She also knows that Strether has betrayed his mission and her mother. She resists Paris. She garners Waymarsh in a truly virtuous relationship in which she shows how an American man is to be saved from and not surrendered to Europe. She demands that Strether release Chad, who, having made his readiness to return home clear, has pledged to do whatever Strether says. Strether bids him wait. Denouncing Strether, Sarah and her party go off on tour with Waymarsh in tow. Strether, now that he can be seen to have opposed Chad's return, releases him to go home.

Wandering in the outskirts of Paris, Strether encounters Chad and Madame de Vionnet on a romantic excursion and realizes that their relationship is sexual.[4] Shaken by this, and by what he himself has become so far from Woollett, Strether also sees that Chad is tired of Madame de Vionnet and perhaps unfaithful to her; he sees that Chad is not transformed in quite the way he had thought, that he is not unsuited to Woollett after all. He also realizes that the relationship on which this deceptive transformation was based is not so high-toned as he had supposed, hoped, or needed to believe. His identification with Chad, Little Bilham, and their Parisian world had lent him a kind of resigned ease about his own life that this final series of recognitions appears to shatter.

In a last, sad interview with Madame de Vionnet, with whom he has come to share a tender understanding, and in a rueful talk with Miss Gostrey, Strether reveals that he will return to America, "so as not to have gotten anything for himself." He renounces what he might have had in Paris, having consciously sacrificed both what he had and might have had in America. Strether seems at the book's close to have lost everything except his horrid eye for what makes him right, as Miss Gostrey puts it.

The central story of *The Ambassadors* is about Strether figuring out the situation in Paris. He spends the book trying to arrive at a conclusion that will fit the facts and the requirements of his conscience, his experience, and his employers—those irreconcilable elements of his embassy. He keeps writing letters home we never get to read. Much of the action of the book is contained in the speculative conversations whose conclusions the letters contain and that the next chapter's conversations destabilize.

Contemporary readers of hard-boiled detective stories, especially those along the lines of Raymond Chandler and Ross MacDonald, are more familiar with this cerebral kind of tale of trying to figure out, with mounting hysteria and intensity, what the hell is going on, and of not being able to leave well enough alone. Like Lambert Strether, Phillip Marlowe and Lew Archer spend their time trying to understand things so that the story they believe and tell will account for what is happening to them. The other people's stories they are hired to investigate are always transparently fake. The detective has to find out the answers for himself. Straightforward answers disappear in a farrago of detective-related happenstance. Answers must contend with prearranged notions of guilt or innocence, the detective's own somewhat battered conscience, his defensive irony about his own ideals, his need to protect them from "reality." His battering becomes the stigmata of his attempt to be an honest, detached observer. Answers cease to matter, if indeed they exist.

The key characteristic of the "private eye" is a conscientiousness as garrulously vented as Strether's, albeit in shorter sentences and simpler dialogue. A skirt gets someone into trouble—someone another dame, usually a lady, is trying to track down and maybe get rid of. There is always a woman in the case. It always turns out that the bad girl is not really bad, or at least that is what the detective thinks. The twists and turns of convention's judgments are as eerie and isolating in Strether's soft-boiled world as in the hard-boiled world.

Of course, Paris represents a different kind of exile from the domestic expatriation a Marlowe feels in Los Angeles or Bay City, but they are equally memorable fictional locales, symbolic and rich with a certain slant of shady history. Once we imagine Strether in this half-light, his activity becomes a little clearer. There are no murders in *The Ambassadors*, but there are little deaths. The action is slower and the investigator's confusion and irony are seen in more relief. And it takes a lot more—and a lot less (more on the surface, less below) to shake the private eye. But the activities are alike. The story keeps getting retold, and it takes the whole book for something to click into place. Usually, it's something everyone else knew and that is staring the private dick in the eye.

One longs in *The Ambassadors* for the familiar scene when Sherlock Holmes, Hercule Poirot, Miss Marple, Charlie Chan, or Nick Charles gathers the principals in a room to crack the case. The detective forces everyone to admit her or his degree of guilt, and the air clears. How one longs for the air to clear in James. Readers who dislike Henry James want the windows opened at once. This is essentially what William James was getting at when he criticized his brother's fiction.[5] The timing of how the suspense is broken is one way to tell genre from art. The longer you hold off from that scene, and the more ambivalent the revealing and the more ambiguous the revelation, the artier the story.

Art corresponds to something like the expectations the reader brings to the book and must surrender to it, in terms of philosophical disillusionment, in order to "get" the story. Genre really means the stories that a culture approves, the kind told around the campfire or other communal glowing heap, the kind that fit easily into Disneyland (see chapter 2), the kind that classroom, television, classic comic, or collectible versions redact effectively. The culture can approve certain kinds of disillusioning experiences, mostly to make sure that they do not in fact take root or get out of hand. The culture has a stake in the seething subtexts of such stories as well. They are meant to stay inarticulate.[6]

The Ambassadors tells an uncompromising tale of disillusionment. Nor is Strether's disillusion safe or fashionable, a malaise without remedy. It is specifically a disillusion with central aspects of American culture and with the terms on which an American is expected to live. Unlike the other late James, *The Ambassadors* is not sexually discouraging. Strether, in his way, is as attractive and dashing as Phillip Marlowe; their lost illusions are equally attractive. One secret of the sex appeal Strether shares with the detectives, or Bogart's Rick Blaine in *Casablanca*, is that the loss of illusions is understood to be the saving of the good. The adult attitude is that you lose your youth, you lose your illusions, you lose your virginity, you lose your ideals. This is regarded as a natural process; it entitles you to membership in the club that runs things. It is the deprivation that makes a "man."

This attitude may merely exchange one set of illusions for another. Strether's own touching interactions with young people in *The Ambassadors* suggest that the conventional connection between these elements of day-to-day truth, common sense, and the standing order may not be the true one. Strether is a possible Socrates, with subversive potential for the Woollett young. Had it been told, one of the funny stories in *The Ambassadors* might have been Mrs. Newsome's recognition of just how dangerous to her precious son her fiancé was. Even Jim Pocock, getting the details all wrong, catches on that Strether is a caution to a well-behaved American male, a caution and an inspiration. Poor Waymarsh flees his old friend's quiet stripping away of the layers of necessary deceit.[7]

The Ambassadors is a nonutopian comedy of male liberation. Like the Platonic dialogues, it contains philosophical and male drama that is erotic, funny, deep, and dangerous from the point of view of society. Strether is no Socrates, although he has his Platonic moments, and his Aristophanic ones, too. But he is not a philosopher and not a teacher, and he tends to be talking to himself even when talking with other people. Dialogue is not his forte, conversation and soliloquy are. Plato's warning to Crito is implicit in Strether's final decision to take everything on himself; this warning seems emblematic of his understanding of where, at the novel's close, he finds himself: "Take care, Crito, lest in agreeing to this you agree to something that you do not believe. For I am well aware that only a few people believe these things, or ever will believe them. And between those who believe and those who do not, there can be no common counsel. They can only have scorn for one another as they see one another's resolves" (*Crito*).

Strether begins to face the set of illusions that assures connections between sex, love, beauty, and goodness; there are also the illusions that inform the American understanding of culture. Strether begins to unravel, without wanting to, the whole fabric of high-toned, American, genteel deceit. He certainly comes to see that one's ideals are probably not the same as one's illusions, and that a loss of illusion may be the condition of preserving one's ideals. This recognition is the breakthrough in his critique of American culture. He comes to it reluctantly but, then, decisively, youthfully, and illusioned (but not hopelessly so), through a variety of erotic feelings.

In a much simpler way, the detective's cynicism, like Strether's irony, is a kind of cover-up for his inner idealism. Cynicism must be given up to feel freely and tenderly and to love the beautiful, the young, and oneself. One's beliefs might well require that one buck a relentless, hypocritical orthodoxy, but in the end ideals are attractive and heroic, as appropriate to men as to women, and gained in the fighting for and not the standing by.[8] You don't preserve ideals by not living. Not living is how you preserve illusions. Ideals and life are alike. To protect your ideals you must use them. James came to this, and his late works immortalize the many moods of this recognition. *The Ambassadors* ennobles even a belated recognition and soothes disappointment with generosity and love.

James had philosophical views. For all the appeal of its low glamour to modern intellectuals, the detective genre hard-boiled down to settings, attitudes, and assumptions. A culture calls a story that is problematic or beautifully endorsing "Art." One reason people get confused about Art is that it is capitalized to mean both what we cannot and what we must take for granted—the difficult and the comfortable. Sherlock Holmes and Agatha Christie's detectives do it all for the reader, entertainingly. The hard-boiled types do the work but deliver it in a lean style, throwing in street-smart philosophical talk, a kind of middlebrow disillusion in wise-guy language, a pie or a gun in the face of your parents' middle-class expectations. Readers think they are doing the detective work, finding something out on their own.

The Ambassadors makes the reader do most of the work. It examines essentially ordinary, albeit luxurious, lives. If you compare the way James describes things to the post-Hemingway enumeration of detail, it is striking how important setting is to both narrative approaches. Neither can manage the old-fashioned conventional setting. James's eye is a feeling, musing, speculating, symbolizing, proliferating, lest-something-be-lost-on-it eye. The private eye is a reporter. Deadpan enumeration may or may not furnish the world, but it is clear that it can only describe what life is like in it if everyone is equally familiar with the allegorical auras of the details. The detective story propounds a modern allegory. But Henry James did not write about what can be agreed upon. His solidly specified details are the occasion for real consideration.

Marlowe or Archer cannot ever quite carry off what we would like to happen in detective novels. For one thing, the story they tell is always untidily Gothic, never coming down to a finger-pointing "You did it." The events in their books yield no succinct truth or blame. Nor is Strether a Charlie Chan. There are scenes, when everybody is gathered in Sarah Pocock's hotel room and at Chad's place, when Strether might call a halt to the proceedings and straighten everything out, make a clean breast of it. But, of course, he cannot: the book is about his not being able to see, let alone say, things that way.

Strether treads a disillusioning path to truth. Guilt can be ascertained only after the very notion of guilt is somehow diminished, or distributed beforehand. Miss Marple and Charlie Chan, and even Mr. Holmes, show that the criminal is, up to a point, like other human beings, but that the crime is the point of departure of bad from good. We all have our faults, tell our little lies, have alibis and whereabouts instead of the blameless lives we claim, but criminals commit crimes. The modern detective tends to confuse the difference between good and bad, criminal and not. American detective fiction struggles with the sense that the world is a sewer; and guilt and innocence are explained, if only a little, by the way of the world instead of a difference in people.

Strether's is a proto-philosophical detective story. Its solution lies in the disillusionment of the private detective, whose code of honor requires that he somehow sacrifice to solve the mystery, to tell the story his way. Dashiell Hammett echoed *The Ambassadors* at the end of *The Maltese Falcon* when Sam Spade—like Strether, although admittedly more unpleasantly and in different terms—shocks his secretary Effie (his Miss Gostrey) with his more-than-horrid, his cold, eye for what made him right. The loyalties, the sexual energies, and the gender attitudes that genre encases are present for Strether, too. He prowls the leafy jungle of fear, desire, and terror that any breaking of the conventional surface reveals.

American detectives are characteristically presented with situations that blow up in the face of their investigations. They are catalytic in the guise of disinterested and ironic detachment. Burning with their own untended fires, like Strether, they get entangled in other people's lives. Strether is driven to unravel the story even when people come to him, as they always do to the private eye, to buy or beg or warn him off. "Get off the case now, Strether," Waymarsh, Miss Gostrey, Chad, Sarah tell him. "You won't like what you find out, you poor sap; it won't be good for your health. Get out of town. Go on back where you belong." He even refuses Chad's offer to go home with him (to clear up the case) because, of course, he is embroiled with Madame de Vionnet (a dame, and somebody else's dame at that), and that means he has to pursue the truth (the case, with any luck) at any cost.

Everyone in the book warns him off except the doe-eyed charmer, Madame de Vionnet, whose own uncertainties and a wistful attraction to Strether tempt her to use him as she does. She knows her warning will fall on his ears as a plea for help. The private eye has a code of honor that is only working well when some woman is using him. Strether makes the change midbook from Mrs. Newsome to Madame de Vionnet. So long as a woman is working him, however, he is himself. He emerges, as Miss Gostrey rather bitterly remarks, morally unscathed. That was the point— for him to be clean, to be right: and that means alone, back in American City, down some mean street or other.

THE STORIES OF *THE AMBASSADORS*

James did not reduce Madame de Vionnet to the generic elements a detective story needs any more than he made Strether into shoulders and a line of patter, Mrs. Newsome into a rough-tongued, castrating dragon, or

Chad into a weak, corrupt playboy. The Newsome drama is of a disintegrating American family, blood ties corrupted by prosperity and freedom. One of the stories in *The Ambassadors* is of a man's innocent victimization by women; it is more of a grown-up boy's story than it is the classic American rendition of high literature. *The Ambassadors* is not a boy's book, but it has those stories inside it.

One version of *The Ambassadors* might have had Strether telling the story over and over again and somehow just not getting it right because, for whatever reason, he could not face the fact that Chad and Madame de Vionnet were lovers. The obscure sexual energies of the novel put the relationship between Madame de Vionnet and Strether among the most poignant of all the ambivalent relationships in classic American fiction. It has the clinging, electric, fatal attraction of popular fiction and something of the ambivalent mythic power of Ernest Hemingway or F. Scott Fitzgerald. But their encounter is so delicately furnished, Madame de Vionnet is so refined a person, and her version of Brigid O'Shaughnessy's confession of her own lethal qualities is so subtle and civilized, that it seems that it is more than sex—that is, less—that is making Strether do things.

Strether's attraction gathers about her but is never quite to her. Her attractiveness is all bound up with Paris and the fact that she is the opposite of what Strether has had his fill of at home. In relation to her, Strether himself becomes the Chad that Woollett and he have concocted. That is why his relationship with her is so romantic; it has heights of allure because it strips him of everything. It is dangerous, yet nothing happens. In relation to her, he is bound to be misunderstood. Theirs is the beautiful and pure virtuous relation Strether has idealized. It frees him from Mrs. Newsome and keeps him close, but not too close, to Chad.

And where is the sex? Strether's need for something to limit the relationship gives his relations with women their edge. He is the classic American hero who won't. Drawn with unaccustomed delicacy and intense feeling, this study in avoidance struggles not to avoid. It is poised on the cusp of action and strains avoidance to its breaking point. Were it sublimation, cultural training, age, history, a conscience, any one thing alone that inhibits, Strether would surely break out; but it is all of these, fused into a portrait and formed into a character of probity and valor whose *won't* and *can't* defy what is available to him in Paris. There is so much more to his reluctance than there is to Chad's willingness that one fears the plunge for him.

The Ambassadors has the makings of all the classic American genres. James has Strether openly riffle and reject these as he tries to figure out his embassy. The American stories are here, baffled and recast. Strether is a hero who may act like an American but whose fleeting identity with American men is ironic and whose presence gives any genre a deflating, ironic twist. James refused the outdoorsy, violent pastorals of American fiction—the alleyways, fishing trips, whaling voyages, that get in the way of sociable human relations. It does not take place in Adventureland or in any other land. Strether's quest is in the heart of the heart of civilized life. He likes the women he is afraid of. He is a loving, charming, cultivated, deep, and decent man, Lincolnesque in his softer way.

Unlike most classic American fiction, *The Ambassadors* does not take place in Eden. "Eden" is the innocent notion that the novelist gives things their right names—as if things were new, as if things had right names, as if names had more than a little to do with things. Strether comes to see that sooner or later he will have to deal with things themselves, regardless of the names he gives them. *The Ambassadors* is not escapist, unlike the American cultural conventions it highlights from which Strether is on the lam. Insofar as the story itself is about staying on in Europe and not going home, *The Ambassadors* might have been written for Woollett's consumption as a tale of American men and women surrendering to the temptations and corruptions of European decadence or luxury.

The Ambassadors might also have commemorated an instance of female heroics. Mrs. Newsome's son Chad is waylaid on his tour of the Old World. He writes infrequent and evasive letters and shows all the signs of being entrapped by a dangerous intrigue with a femme fatale. Mrs. Newsome will not allow this. The trusted family friend is sent out to rescue the lad and instead writes home championing the son's new way of life. He is rumored to have picked up a stray American woman and finally appears to have fallen victim to the charms of the vamp.

The novel has the makings of a horror story—like *The Odyssey*, but seen from Penelope's point of view. The world is full of seductresses and enchantresses, home wreckers who prey on the essentially untrustworthy menfolk of decent women and who menace home, country, and capitalism with magical charms. Mrs. Newsome herself cannot go to the rescue; she has to run things at home and anyway is too "intense." She sends her heroic daughter, Sarah Pocock. Sarah arrives in Paris ready to do battle with Madame de Vionnet and to rescue her brother—and even Strether, if possible. James wrote this story wonderfully, but not from Sarah's point of view.

From Sarah's point of view, it is heroic. She resists any view of the situation but the home view. Leaving the reluctant Strether behind, shrewdly sensing he is a weak link in the Woollett chain, she lets him detach himself from the company of home. Better that Mrs. Newsome continue alone than with the likes of him; better that Chad return to attend his mother, a wife, sons and daughters, and a business; better that Strether end his life as a sacrifice to the things he was supposed to serve. All that this version requires is the recognition, which soap operas make all the time, that the proper point of view is that of the domesticated female.

It is the particular genius of the genre of women's books that their stories are told from that point of view, however simultaneously captive to the values of the standing order they may be. Women's books happen to women. Strether cannot be the hero of Sarah's book, *The Ambassadress*, in which she rescues her mother and brother from him. In Mrs. Newsome's book, *The Widow of Woollett*, the widow must give up Strether for family and business. She longs to see Europe with him, but she sends him off alone and he betrays her. Henry James made his first fame writing about Europe from Mamie's point of view in "Daisy Miller." The women's books James did not write show the hard truth of how females are marooned within the American domestic and capitalist order. Their menfolk can go off into the world, but they cannot.

From this vantage, one might see in Miss Gostrey's story a future Virago Classic: *An Expatriate Woman*. Maria's story, which is not told from Strether's point of view and is merely gleaned from James's novel, is one of an articulate and poignant expatriation. Think of her little Parisian house. There, in her net of gleaming things picked up here and there, gathered hither and yon from the wreck of her orderly life, one encounters this cheerful, seldom blinking woman who knows how to save herself and also how to be heroic. Think of what Maria's life with those friends and touring Americans must have been like. Strether disappointed her sorely. What a story was *l'affaire* Newsome, from Miss Gostrey's unmediated point of view! James gives her to us but only as Strether's convenience, hardly on her own terms. Her terms are sometimes close to his, perhaps, but *The Ambassadors* is not her story, any more than it is the dauntless Sarah Pocock's, the sacrificing Mrs. Newsome's, or even the bright Mamie's.

All those stories, and more, might have been recruited to the facts of the Newsome/Strether happenstance. They might have made successful novels and stories, plays and serials. Imagine the daytime serial: "Love in the Afternoon," with locations in Paris. Mrs. Newsome sends her fiancé off to find her erring son. She trusts her fiancé, but what is he doing in Paris with Maria Gostrey? How does Maria feel when he meets and falls in love with her old schoolmate, the beautiful and unhappily married Madame de Vionnet, with whom his future stepson has been sharing a life? Waymarsh is the perfect horse opera/soap opera man—moralistic and awkward. Picture him in the prized two-person close-up shot discussing Strether with Sarah Pocock, resentful in his bluff, prissy way: "How could he defend that woman to you, Miss Sarah, why when I think of it, a lady like you having to speak to the likes of that, well, it makes me downright . . ."

The less high-toned carryings on of the Woollett women and their menfolk might have made a prime-time mini-series (CBS, not PBS): "Woollett." The opening titles unfold in the mind's eye: "This is the story of a small New England town and its leading family." What cannot quite be shown in the soap or the James versions, we can see steaming on the screen. Young Chad, heir to a business, is in Paris with his aristocratic mistress, whose daughter pines for him but is destined for a prince. Strether, an American gentleman engaged to Mrs. Newsome, a rich widow and the power behind Woollett, is sent to bring the son home to take over his father's business. Conspiring with the American adventuress Maria Gostrey, Strether himself falls for Madame de Vionnet, heedless of the advice of his friend Waymarsh. Then, Sarah comes out to clear up the situation but seems to fall for Waymarsh. At the same time, and in what begins to seem like a ménage à trois, she effectively scotches Strether's suddenly downright sinister attempts to keep Chad in Paris. "Woollett" would be the Newsome saga as exposed to the prying curiosity, class envy, and hypocritical sanctimony of the popular taste. It would treat the aimlessness and boredom of the rich and mighty, in fancy dress and lewd tableaux, and their attendant lack of moral compass. Like the other versions of the subject matter of *The Ambassadors*, this would not fall far from the tree.

The Ambassadors also contains the stuff of which the canon is made. The classic American novels featured men—with those funny alternative energies to home, capitalism, violence, and democracy coursing feverishly through their veins—running away from women, trying to tell the good ones from the bad ones, or getting away from feminized civilization altogether. Such books might explain the characters and situation of *The Ambassadors* too.

The world of Paris that Strether reaches is also a hideout of runaway American men, far from the "widders" Douglass and Newsome. Europe was more of a territory than the American frontier after 1893. Would a sojourn in Paris turn runaways into renegades, as the West could? Waymarsh, the crybaby of the bunch, fears so. He must be dragged kicking and screaming through every step of the journey into Europe because he senses that each breakfast menu and every custom must be resisted if liberation is to be resisted. So closely does he clutch the apron strings that bind him that, when Sarah Pocock appears on the scene, he hugs her with an incautious spasm of relief that looks like it will land him in her sphere for life. Chad appears at first to be the gang leader but turns out to be a Tom Sawyer, compared to Strether's Huck Finn. Like Huck, Strether has a conscience, and his actions obey it. Little Bilham, Chad, Strether, and Waymarsh make a remarkable foursome of rogue American males stranded together in dear old Paris. Waymarsh is easily regained, and Chad has all along intended to return. Strether, having tried to keep all three with him, succeeds only in encouraging Little Bilham and in keeping Paris inside himself for the lonely rest of his days in internal exile.

Here flourish the makings of several "male weepers." A Laurel and Hardy movie makes the point. The two "boys" want to go to a Loyal Sons of the Desert Convention, but their wives nix that. So, they lie and say they are going on a cruise for reasons of health. The ship they are supposed to be sailing on sinks. Their wives think they've drowned. The very night they sneak home full of lies, their wives discover that they have been at the convention, after all. Assured of their safety, the women mean to make them sorry for their deceit. There is also a *Così Fan Tutte*-like side bet between the women as to whether the boys will be truthful. Mrs. Ollie knows they will not; Mrs. Stan thinks Stan will be.

The last scene of the picture shows the two-family house the couples share, a lower-middle-class Hay/Adams arrangement. On one side is Laurel, who, when confronted with the lie and his wife's gentle reminder that it is better to tell the truth, starts to cry. He tells his wife that he's sorry and won't lie anymore. He gets to recline on the sofa in a dressing gown and is served ginger ale by his gun-toting, good-looking, very tall wife, who is also scratching his head of standup hair the way he likes and telling him, see, Stanley, it pays to tell the truth. Stanley gets the point.

Next door, Ollie's hard-faced termagant of a wife does the slow burn. Disastrously, Ollie tries to face out the lie. Picture him twiddling his fingers and his tie and his hat, looking bashful, calling her sweet names as she starts to scream at him: "Don't 'Sugar' me." Soon, every dish and pan in the house is flying; the walls bulge and crash with the ruckus. Stanley strolls out to see what's up. The pampered and the punished look at each other. Ollie makes one of his lunges at Stan, and we see them for what we have always known them to be—prisoners of the war between the sexes in the women's camp, the home front.

At the end of *The Ambassadors*, Waymarsh peeks safely from Sarah's clutches at poor Strether out in the cold. The great political man, wandering Europe battered and confused by a bad marriage is, of course, just the one to turn coat and return to a good woman's side. Strether, unlike Waymarsh, jettisons his moral compass so he can lose the way and find his own. Chad enjoys his escapade. Like some early Herman Melville sailor having his breadfruit and eating it too, he welcomes rescue: no revolutionary, or even mutineer, Chad.

Of Little Bilham one hardly knows what to say. Bilham is, in Strether's book, Chingachgook to his Natty Bumppo, or perhaps a sly version of Ishmael. One cannot see even Henry James writing Little Bilham's book. It could not have been published in America for fifty years. Bilham becomes even more of a boon companion to Strether than Miss Gostrey. The sight of him prompts Strether to self-revelation and self-recognition. Nevertheless, the book must leave Bilham pretty much alone. There are two coming-out stories in *The Ambassadors*, but, unlike Strether's, which can be translated into individual moral terms that do not involve sexual preference, Bilham's must wait. His story anticipates and requires the genres of gay writing in the post-Stonewall period, books that entertain openly fulfilling solutions to energies *The Ambassadors* contains. To James's credit, however, Strether unconventionally encourages Bilham to stay in Paris and live his own unconventional life.

The story *The Ambassadors* ends up telling is not Strether's or anyone's male weeper. Once Strether makes his mind up about Chad, he changes his mind about Woollett and everything else in a desolately serious way. Like Huck, he says that he will go to Hell. Huck could light out for the territories; Strether must come in from the cold. He does not see American things from their mythical future but from their past. *The Ambassadors* is not those other wonderful books whose makings it contains. Strether's book refuses the generic. However much he chooses a kind of thinking rather than acting, Strether chooses unconventionally at the last. The point of the American conventional was exactly to prevent such choices, in fiction as in life.

In addition to the many versions of its story James chose not to have *The Ambassadors* tell, there are the versions he had already tried out. In one earlier book, James staged an encounter of expatriated sophistication with home-bred staunchness in a pastoral comedy. Had *The Europeans* been better, it would have been Shakespearean, with its crossed lovers and Arcadian setting. The problem with *The Europeans* is that the lovers are not so much star-crossed as culture-crossed.

By bringing the Baroness Munster and her brother Felix Young from their Bohemian splendor and necessity to a Woollett-like suburb of Boston to visit their American cousins, the Wentworths, James assembled some of the elements he later brought into such heightened play in *The Ambassadors*. But the Wentworths' America is as ill-defined and imprecise as their cousins' Europe. The Europeans in *The Europeans* are American, and that is part of its point; the possibility of respectable escape into cosmopolitanism, for certain temperaments like heroine Gertrude Wentworth's, is almost the whole point of the story.

In *The Ambassadors*, we know very well why Madame de Vionnet cannot live in Woollett. She cannot marry Chad because she is married already. It is part of her attraction for Chad and Strether that she is rooted in the best and most characteristic Paris. The problems she would present in Woollett are not like the rather vague unsettlings the Baroness's ennui causes the Wentworths' little commonwealth. The menace is implicit, and the comparison unexplored. The choices are curious. The Baroness returns to her native European exile. Gertrude and Felix design for themselves a streamlined expatriation without moral reproach. The novel begs the questions it raises, turning morality into setting: this kind of person gets to live here and that kind of person gets to live there. In a way, James's transatlantic fiction revives nature-versus-nurture writing that takes culture more seriously than Darwinist genres did.

The Europeans justifies and eases a certain expatriate choice. Some people travel. Other people had better stay home. After all, homes differ, as people do. James makes light of the New England strain by essentially saying, with a muffled "poor dear things" echoing somewhere, it does fine for the likes of most Wentworths and their friends. New England has a good and attractive set of local customs, but they will not really do for everyone; and when someone like Gertrude comes along, who is a sport in the family line, let her go off to find something more fit for her in Europe. The book does not take very seriously that which would judge her (or anyone similarly disposed toward expatriation). Native allegiance is a mild obstacle to be removed, a local custom to be appreciated. The book lowers the stakes of social comedy.

The Europeans reflects New England with the unearned irony of the rearview mirror. Driving away is not running away, in this view. You can look back and see what you think you are leaving behind, because when you look back in the mirror you do not see yourself. Unlike *The Ambassadors*, *The Europeans* does not take New England moralism seriously. It makes light of the damage it does, about which James seems more hopeful than he later came to be. It never entertains the possibility that the morality sticks to the ribs of the people it rears, that civilization might really turn out to be, as the Wentworths think, no laughing matter. Strether had to face this question in Paris, and it took *The Ambassadors* to answer it.

The grim Protestant moralism that flourishes among the Wentworths is harmless, restrictive, funny, charming, decent, and mild. Really. Above all, unlike Strether's, it is someone else's problem, not "one's" own. Reading *The Europeans* is like going back home again too soon after leaving home. It takes a sportive look at what you naively think you have survived and left behind. Everything is a little dull and rather good, nothing to be ashamed of as a place to have come from. But what is one to do when the furniture is not as good as the morals and, alas, is decidedly better than the conversation?

The big difference between the Europeans and the Americans is one of relative sophistication. James's comedy, like Anthony Trollope's, whose Barchester books it resembles, does not challenge notions of class or character. It turns out that Gertrude can be a Wentworth, that she and Felix can be happy together by recognizing that her character need not fear the morals of a wider world. Robert Acton and the Baroness are in the same awkward, difficult relation that one senses in Strether and Madame de Vionnet but, without their reasons to be indirectly involved, are lacking magnetic obstacle. Their interest for one another is not direct, let alone important. So with the rest of the book. The Jamesian drama of recognition set out to require that people learn about themselves, not talk about other people. Unlike Emerson, James doubted the possibility of finding out about oneself in America, since what there was to find out was not in the soul but in the culture. James resisted the thought that a person's real identity comes from inside. Among Europe's creature comforts, the luxury of a traditionalist notion of individuality—as opposed to the American, Emersonian idea—most attracted him. Part of the problem with *The Europeans* is its lack of erotic variety and heat. It may be that the truth about Massachusetts cannot be discovered there, that it does not contain the human truth about itself. This is the Tocquevillian claim. And if New England does not, no American place does. New England was, for James, as later for Santayana, the place to attack an American culture because it was in New England that civilization was understood to be, above all, a conscientious act of consciousness.

No matter that it is still bruited about that James was not a sexual writer. Find the sex and you find the book in Henry James—even if the sex is not had, the desire not owned, the object not identified, the love not made. The emotions and situations expressed may not be the ones that appear. Thus, in *The Portrait of a Lady*, sexual feeling informs partings, not matings. *The Bostonians* spends much improbably conservative cross-cultural invention trying to discourage the deepest sexual energies. The fight of a New England feminist (Olive Chancellor) and a Southern reactionary (Basil Ransom) for the soul of a mystical young girl (Verena Tarrant) gains force from its regional revenge subplot. Olive's stature as a character reflects in part how staunchly she bears, and how memorably our thought of her survives, James's betrayal and humiliation of her. Basil could never have administered by himself the punishment Olive endures. The fact that Olive wanted Verena was enough for Basil to want Verena for himself, and for him to count himself a hero for having rescued her from high-minded New England voodoo and its sinister human relations. In *The Bostonians*, James looses satiric control to genuine abuse. He joins Basil to punish Olive, and we know that is where the love and sex are. James fantasized Ransom's countering of Olive's desire for Verena with as hopeful an energy as he had imagined Olive with a pessimistic feeling. Basil reads like a "straight" alternative to a "crooked" desire. In Olive Chancellor, stifled and bereft at the end, naked as no other character is in James, we see what James might write when he was afraid.

The Bostonians dramatizes the Emersonian grip on New England and suggests how menacing self-recognition was to James. It is his most American Tocquevillian book and his least sympathetic exploration of the Emersonian and of New England. It offers a fictional justification for a person like James living elsewhere, based on deep feelings of alienation from the state of America's highest-minded society. Basil Ransom's views go further than Tocqueville's but are American Tocquevillian as well as Southern. They challenge the innovative personal possibilities democracy opens up for American individuals. The core of his reaction is to the changes in gender role and self-identification that Boston advances. Basil sees woman-identified women and men as the problem; they are to be mocked and resisted as the proof that American reformers are mountebanks and crackpots. James preferred his European freedom to American innovation and Emersonian self-identification. *The Europeans* had shown nothing so intense. The intensity that expresses or represses desire affected the Europe/America drama. However troubled the relation, James knew no other motive so important to life.

The question remains what the consequences are for characters whose joy comes from natures intensely grounded in and yet incompletely accounted for by the cultures of their *patriae*. When James came to write *The Ambassadors*, he had learned to pay these issues a graver attention. He had come to understand that America had spawned a characteristic social system as well as characters. James was writing about a civilized America in which men made money and women made morals and culture, and in which a mannish woman might find a place in society by managing domestic and social things and a womanish man (if, by womanish, one means a man who excels in the sphere of life allotted by the culture to women and is artistic, morally serious, and sensitive) might only with difficulty find his place. The problem with the men in *The Europeans* was that they might as well have been making money, for all their lack of dislocation. James suspected that American men and women did not like one another very well. In *The Europeans*, Gertrude and Felix marry for "liking" and live abroad. The rash thing to do in that Massachusetts was to marry according to the European custom. Gertrude and Felix shared a spontaneous compatibility, which is what made their marriage work, presuming that it did.

The Ambassadors is about a man who likes women, as did James himself. It is also about how America treats men who like women and whom women like back. What America expects of men is a theme of *The Ambassadors*. By taking Strether, a man who likes women, out of Woollett and setting him adrift in Paris, James could compare the relations that must inform civilization, as he preferred it, to the American inhospitality to those very relations. All the ways Woollett mistakes Parisian relations suggest the shape and fault of American civilization, especially its hypocritical idealism about what really counts in a life. James saw that the prevailing American genteel moralism was a degenerate morality, and he suspected it had to do with keeping the enterprise of American business culture going behind a veneer of professed ideals.

James founded an America in Paris composed of only the sorts of Americans he himself might know. The genteel classes and their sensitive instruments figure prodigiously. They form a class of people on whose nerves their civilization presses in any number of ways. They are people who are nervously and intellectually aware of their America. They are, in fact, Americanists, conscious specialists in their nationality, uneasy about their allegiance. Their America is remembered, gleaned, pieced together, corresponded to, and abstracted from immediacy. The ambassadorial metaphor facilitates interpretation. Europe is at the ideal American Tocquevillian distance for keen observation.

Paris transforms America into a choice. James makes the choice consequential. Even Woollett seems slightly removed from the American fray. It needs Chad back to captain its re-entry into the mainstream. Fearful of losing its young men to Paris, it may not realize that it will lose them to New York. Expatriation is raised not as a fictional convenience but as a life issue, as it was with James himself. When the characters meditate on their personal choices in this book, their musings cast the long shadow of their deciding whether to live in Europe or America, and as Americans or Europeans. The drama might be said to concern a family of Americans threatened by the expatriation of its men. Woollett is America, presided over by Mrs. Newsome, who needs two men in her life—one for her business and one for her ideals, a son and a lover. She sends her lover to retrieve her son, her culture man to rescue her business man, but the lover falls for the son and culture persuades business that Paris is where the things that truly matter are.

The absence of hierarchical institutions that define position and value in the United States had raised the stakes of interpretation. Culture, genteel culture in Woollett, had to establish value. The genteel culture assimilated the Jeffersonian harmonizing of disparate elements, forsaking the old–New England, fierce moral thoroughness. Emerson replaced Edwards in this world, and Woollett evinced paradigmatic Victorian domestication of Emersonian views. This Emerson sponsored the genteel world of nature, morals, art, and religion. Woollett also posited a "real" world, whose presumptive reality the real Emerson had challenged but the genteelly received, "Emersonian" Emerson accepted. Mrs. Newsome knew that the real and the ideal must be kept distinct. Gentility relaxed the self-reflexive Puritan morality, while keeping an eye on conduct. It believed ideals had their place. The moral fires that once burned in New England and America had become hearth fires, comfortably warming to people whose ancestors had trembled as they tended the flames. The relation of Americans to these fires of ancient American belief formed the interpretive drama of *The Ambassadors*.

THE "SACRED RAGE"

Early in their acquaintance in *The Ambassadors*, Strether and Maria Gostrey sound their first interpretive note of home. The subject is enjoyment, the mode flirtation—she with him.

> "You're doing something that you think not right."
> It so touched the place that he quite changed colour and his laugh grew almost awkward. "Am I enjoying it as much as *that*?"
> "You're not enjoying it, I think, so much as you ought."
> "I see"—he appeared thoughtfully to agree. "Great is my privilege."
> "Oh it's not your privilege! It has nothing to do with *me*. It has to do with yourself. Your failure's general."
> "Ah there you are!" he laughed. "It's the failure of Woollett. *That's* general."
> "The failure to enjoy," Miss Gostrey explained, "is what I mean."
> "Precisely. Woollett isn't sure it ought to enjoy. If it were it would. But it hasn't, poor thing," Strether continued, "any one to show it how. It's not like me. I have somebody." (Book First, chap. 1)

Strether conflates himself with his home, poor thing, and identifies his pleasure-suspecting superego with Woollett. He makes it clear that he is a captive rather than an adherent and is glad for Miss Gostrey's help in escaping. She tells Strether that she is a courier and makes the national connection in describing her vocation: "I bear on my back the huge load

of our national consciousness, or, in other words—for it comes to that—
of our nation itself." An American specialist in Americans—an Americanist—Maria Gostrey proves just what Strether needs, suffering as he is from
the American, the New England malady: "I'm always considering something else; something else, I mean, than the thing of the moment," Strether
tells her. "The obsession of the other thing is the terror. I'm considering at
present for instance something else than you."

This double consciousness took many forms in the American character. Calculation was its hardest and fastest form: conscientiousness, moral
earnestness, and suspicion of pleasure were some others. What is wrong
with him, says Strether, is that he cannot live in the moment. America
defines the moment as something to be seized for the future. Woollett disci-
plines the present moment with a high-minded, refining past and future,
with duties and meanings and elaborate rituals of consideration that have
the effect of rendering the moment free from any driving impulses, free
from itself. This may lead to restraint. It is bound to lead to hypocrisy since,
if the motives of actions be not good, high-minded, beautiful, and profit-
able, they must not be acknowledged. To the degree that someone's motives
are those defined by Woollett as errant, they must be disguised and denied.
At the same time, Woollett understands perfectly well that the moment is
always to be seized for serious material interest.

Archly, their conversation traces the movement of Mr. Strether's and
Miss Gostrey's flirtation—she pressing for the moment's feelings, he shy-
ing away; she reassuring him that she will show him the ropes, he worried
but aroused. Their duet ends with his arm geriatrically in her keeping, then
dropped as, somewhat separately, they approach the hotel. But let James
tell it:

> It was at all events perhaps lucky that they arrived in sufficiently sepa-
> rate fashion within range of the hotel-door. The young lady they had
> left in the glass cage watched as if she had come to await them on the
> threshold. At her side stood a person equally interested, by his atti-
> tude, in their return, and the effect of the sight of whom was instantly
> to determine for Strether another of those responsive arrests that we
> have had so repeatedly to note. He left it to Miss Gostrey to name, with
> the fine full bravado, as it almost struck him, of her "Mr. Waymarsh!"
> what was to have been, what—he more than ever felt as his short stare
> of suspended welcome took things in—would have been, but for her-

self, his doom. It was already upon him even at that distance—Mr. Waymarsh was for *his* part joyless. (*Ambassadors*, Book First, chap. 1)

With the appearance of the joyless Waymarsh, the plot thickens to its American consistency.

Waymarsh's presence gives the sunny sky of Strether's idyll before Paris a variety necessary to its pointed charm. His version of the American heavy weather does not storm, but it clouds the prospect a little. Waymarsh is a public man, a success in American arenas, and a little ridiculous sans habitat—a beast without his jungle. This first interview of the old friends establishes certain things. Waymarsh has not gotten the hang of Europe in three months. Strether is liking it already. Success, which Waymarsh has, is enviable and a little silly. Strether wishes he could complain as little of his lot as Waymarsh does of his marital misery—and that he had so grand an income. Waymarsh is an American success, that much is certain, and Strether a failure. Strether insists on both.

Strether can distinguish Milrose, Waymarsh's hometown, from Woollett. "It was not quite pointedly sceptical, but it seemed somehow a plea for the purest veracity, and it thereby affected our friend as the very voice of Milrose. He had long since made a mental distinction—though never in truth daring to betray it—between the voice of Milrose and the voice even of Woollett. It was the former, he felt, that was most in the real tradition" (*Ambassadors*, Book First, chap. 2). Strether means that Milrose has not prettified the old American, New England, republican, Puritan ways. It has refused such truck with sophistication as even Woollett has sought. The old friends discuss Europe and Strether's errand there. Strether's candor wobbles a little under Waymarsh's fierce gaze. The truth is that Woollett is fond of sophistication, maintains a compromised code of beauty, claims ideals that are not all about duty; beauty is included under the heading of, but is not defined by, duty. The genteel tradition sways Woollett, and the genteel tradition centers on what this moralism does to beauty. The sacred rage burns in Milrose, and the sacred rage is about what beauty does to moralism.

Woollett regards liking Europe as a convenient part of duty, as developing the capacity to withstand knowledgeably large, regular doses of traditional civilization at home and abroad; Milrose knows balefully better. Milrose tells harsh truths and refuses pleasure in its new guise as culture. Woollett domesticates the Emersonian heresy; Milrose knows backsliding when it sees it. Woollett wilts under the Milrose gaze, like a gambler who takes a risk his brother declines. Milrose plays no games of moral chance. And, under the conviction that what transpires under the Woollett auspices is by its venue purified of whatever taint it may have, Woollett has begun to gamble. It has an Arminian complacency about the cut of the deck and a sense that it may need to expand in order to prosper.

Woollett is as canny about prosperity as it is high about culture. Strether's errand is to compel Chad's participation in expansion and to realign the drives of prosperity for the disks of culture. Milrose is like a grandparent who can shame you and even make you feel antique guilts but is nothing like as scary as a parent who does not spare the rod in the here and now. Milrose's scruples and punishments are recalled through dear old Way-marsh. Woollett's require no recollection; the thought of Mrs. Newsome is enough to inspire her modern brand of terror.

Milrose can shame Woollett, as the New England past can shame a New England and American present and future. But Woollett holds the future, not Milrose. Milrose's public man has broken down, his wife will not live with him and keep him honest—his wife will not even live in America. Like Waymarsh, Milrose suffers from cognitive dissonance, a moralism in search of a landscape. Milrose cannot see how Europe can be enjoyed without being surrendered to. Waymarsh is in the active grip of that point of view. He is in Europe but resisting it.

Waymarsh's cure has been a mild antidote to America founded on a mild critique of what is wrong with it. Pretty places and remarkable old things should, according to the American gospel of culture, be able to modernize and soothe the tired American. Waymarsh shows it not working. He wants to go home. Strether will tuck his friend in, but he will not take him home. He is not about to take anyone home, no matter what he says about Chad. Then, Waymarsh, with a shrewdness born of Milrose's directness, asks why Strether is in Europe: Is he running away from Mrs. Newsome? Strether answers that he is not running away from her, that it is on Mrs. Newsome's business that he has come to Paris. The question hangs in the air.

Milrose has some power to make Strether candid according to the an-cient code, as Woollett has the power to make him conscientious according to the modern. They both harry him with New England second thoughts. Milrose is primitive, tribal, and true. Woollett is the matrix from which Strether must act—how things are now. Milrose is way in the back of his mind, if there at all. The better Strether likes Europe, the more he and Miss

Gostrey have to say to one another, and the less he has to say to Waymarsh. Miss Gostrey, like his therapist for a European talking cure, speaks the voice of the desires she divines in Strether. The sight of Strether's enjoyment recalls Waymarsh to his own duty of refusal. You have, in the proper Puritan community, to mind the other fellow's business. This is how you keep yourself in line.

Miss Gostrey, like Mrs. Newsome, proposes quite another allegiance. Miss Gostrey makes it clear that she does not have a very high opinion of any standard that would rank Waymarsh higher than Strether. Strether is not sure. On one hand, he agrees with her and thinks well of himself. On the other hand, his life experience as an American has made him very well aware that he does not possess the elements for success. Miss Gostrey corrects Strether's superego by refreshing his ego.

The Ambassadors is not particularly about success. Nor does it appear that how one responds to the things of Europe takes one's measure. But James does compare Europe to America in order to stretch Strether out of his American horizons. The first stage of Strether's embassy dramatizes the comedy of relativism. Europe uncovers his American point of view, the less-than-ingrained American habit that makes Strether think so apparently little of what he in fact prizes in himself. Miss Gostrey, who agrees with the "secret" Strether, finds him attractive and likes his cultivation, his irony, his sadness, his very unsuccessfulness. She admires him. She brings him out.

The question of the action is how to gain Strether for his inner self. America is understood to have required a set of attitudes that stunt and mock that self. Strether's American shell must therefore be cracked, his American skin must be shed, his American superego transcended. This struggle begins in England and its triangular parties are Waymarsh, Strether, and Miss Gostrey. Strether's irony, his double consciousness, is understood to express the division between his real feelings, wants, and possibilities (his "virtue," as he says) and the signals of Woollett and Milrose that keep him tuned into denial.

What makes this preliminary, however, is that Miss Gostrey cannot cure him of Mrs. Newsome. Their friendship tests the old New England, not the new New England. Miss Gostrey liberates Strether for his serious test. The energies of his feelings for Maria do not risk the terrible and real, the mystifying. Perhaps she is merely the contrivance James called her, the necessary machinery to bring Strether into being. With Maria, as with Little Bilham, Strether makes his philosophical progress. She, like Little Bilham, helps Strether see. But it is his tangled erotic attachments that make him renounce and grow and struggle and do—that let him be. The book's London interlude unleashes Strether's idealism, leaving him freer of the old New England conscience but more involved with what he takes to be Woollett's beliefs. The restraints of homegrown hypocrisy no longer hold him, and New England idealism soars once more.

His struggle is reflected even in store windows. Waymarsh likes the "merely useful," but Strether responds to the array of lovely things.

> Do what he might, in any case, his previous virtue was still there, and it seemed fairly to stare at him out of the windows of shops that were not as the shops of Woollett, fairly to make him want things that he shouldn't know what to do with. It was by the oddest, the least admissible of laws demoralising him now; and the way it boldly took was to make him want more wants. These first walks in Europe were in fact a kind of finely lurid intimation of what one might find at the end of that process. Had he come back after long years, in something already so like the evening of life, only to be exposed to it? (*Ambassadors*, Book First, chap. 3)

Shopping introduces lightly the moral issue on which Strether's embassy is to founder. Panic has already seized Waymarsh, although so far everything is all talk. It turns out that talk is what it is all about: what you talk about, how much you admit of what you want, how you say what you say. Whatever else Waymarsh is, he is no fool when it comes to scenting danger and, when feeling endangered, frantically trying to pick up the scent of home. And so, on this London shopping expedition, we see Waymarsh in flight.

"Something," Strether does not know just what, gets to Waymarsh as they stand contemplating an especially Old World street: "'He thinks us sophisticated, he thinks us worldly, he thinks us wicked, he thinks us all sorts of queer things,' Strether reflected; for wondrous were the vague quantities our friend had within a couple of short days acquired the habit of conveniently and conclusively lumping together." Waymarsh makes "a sudden grim dash" across the street, disappearing into a jeweler's shop, where he remains for some while. Miss Gostrey and Mr. Strether hash it over. They guess that Waymarsh has "struck for freedom," as Strether puts it. Waymarsh may buy out the whole shop, for somehow freedom and buying on a grand scale are connected. Neither Maria nor Strether can afford such freedom (*Ambassadors*, Book First, chap. 3).

They canvass the freedoms they can afford, the freedoms they take with one another and in talking about others. Strether contends that Waymarsh will never discuss him with Maria, implying that Waymarsh is too good. Maria replies that Waymarsh is too stupid. "There are not many like you and me," she says. Strether is struck by the thought of Waymarsh as stupid. He is a success, after all, especially as measured by money:

> "He makes it—to my belief. And I," said Strether, "though with a back quite as bent, have never made anything. I'm a perfectly equipped failure."
> He feared an instant she'd ask him if he meant he was poor; and he was glad she didn't, for he really didn't know to what the truth on this unpleasant point mightn't have prompted her. She only, however, confirmed his assertion. "Thank goodness you're a failure—it's why I so distinguish you! Anything else to-day is too hideous. Look about you—look at the successes. Would you *be* one, on your honor? Look, moreover," she continued, "at me." (*Ambassadors*, Book First, chap. 3)

Their lack of money, their nearness to it, and to what it can buy, afford them a perspective.

Miss Gostrey connects them as two failures. Strether appears unsure of her direction, gallant where she is matter-of-fact. Just before Waymarsh's return, Strether seals the bargain of their conversation. They will continue to talk freely and specially; that much he will give her, since she has already cost him, as he puts it, "Well, my past—in one great lump."

This leads to their deciding together to take Waymarsh as a joke—which means that Strether decides that the ancient voice of Milrose will no longer speak seriously to him or make him feel guilty. Without this decision, the rest of the story cannot happen. The pulls of Paris cannot stretch him until he has settled these vestigial tugs in London. He stills them with a blasphemous joke.

> If Waymarsh was sombre he was also indeed most sublime. He told them nothing, left his absence unexplained, and though they were convinced he had made some extraordinary purchase they were never to learn its nature. He only glowered grandly at the tops of the old gables. "It's the sacred rage," Strether had had further time to say; and this sacred rage was to become between them, for convenient com-

prehension, the description of one of his periodical necessities. It was Strether who eventually contended that it did make him better than they. But by that time Miss Gostrey was convinced that she didn't want to be better than Strether. (*Ambassadors*, Book First, chap. 3)

Strether has abandoned Waymarsh.

The Ambassadors does not find it convenient to tell the story of the abandonment of dear old Waymarsh, but this in fact happens in the course of Strether's stilling the voice of Milrose in his head. Waymarsh had seemed formidable for being a success but had been formidable only for being the voice of Milrose, that ancient form of New England on which Strether had patterned what he called his virtue. The sacred rage was both a sterner and a ruder creed than Woollett's, striking a different bargain with the world. In choosing to name it with a laugh, in choosing Miss Gostrey as his confidante over Waymarsh, in choosing ironic flirtation over ironclad friendship, Strether has also to make the ideological choices of the sophisticated, the worldly, the wicked, and the queer. He chooses the experience of Europe over the resistance to it, which is what Waymarsh would call choosing Europe over America. Siding with Maria Gostrey in a variety of ways, he also makes fun of Waymarsh, which is not very nice and, perhaps, not very smart.

It may be that, had James written Waymarsh's story, we should discover his hurt. As it is, we see his rage, which is comical. It is the power of the ancient gods of New England seemingly reduced to a private joke, something terrible diminished. It leaves Waymarsh to assert the terms of his success by buying things, probably *awful* things that would make Strether and Miss Gostrey shudder. Waymarsh's bad taste is the assertion of the insecure—the need to buy something whose primary aesthetic attribute is that it looks expensive. He must assert his sense of self, his cultural and personal identity, his American success, all of which he can feel shrinking in the picturesque light of these gabled, crooked alleys. Europe is kryptonite to this over-the-hill Christopher Newman. His material plunge must retrieve the thing that distinguishes him for being able to afford it. Vulgarity here means taking a shortcut to a very limited vocabulary of display.

There is nothing wrong with display, but the Milrose notion of American display in Europe is bound to result in aesthetic failure. Strether's treachery to Waymarsh is to let Europe make him and his old American values look ridiculous. The sacred rage cuts no ice here, however much it buys. And the buying shifts the balance of the creed. Strether and Miss Gostrey know how Europe can panic the likes of Waymarsh. Miss Gostrey soothes such panic for a living. They decide, as it were, to keep Waymarsh around for laughs and to put up with his "periodical necessities." This is merely a lark for Miss Gostrey, but it may be Strether's moment of hubris. He does not appear to see how much of the sting of the sacred rage has been removed for him—not by Miss Gostrey, with whom he merely shares his joke, but by Mrs. Newsome and Woollett, which have replaced Milrose. They burn with no sacred rage but with something that does more than glower. They had been weaning Strether from the sacred rage for years. At this moment, Strether may underestimate the ultimate cost of the freedom that allows him to make merry and light. Out of the frying pan . . . .

The joke about the sacred rage cuts several ways. It mocks the descent of the New England errand into sudden scurries of material excess. The voice of Milrose spoke of virtue in accents of shrewdness, and driving a hard bargain was always its moral method, as Henry James well knew. But the goods diminished if they were not heaped up anew each generation, which Henry James also knew. And the heaping up was work that required a great deal of adjustment. Waymarsh, suddenly revealed as the desperado of the sacred rage, seems out of place in the world from having been out of place at home. Waymarsh is looking for moorings and turns out to be ready to settle for some version of what Strether risks. If the joke begins with Waymarsh, a somewhat moth-eaten lion, roaring and Strether feeling his own strength, it will end with the sacred rage smoking at the Woollett hearth like an old cob pipe. The sacred rage signifies more than Waymarsh's necessities since he is looking for a home, his kind of country.

The sacred rage records the assimilation of the blunted Puritan judgmental habit into an imperial America. Edwards and Emerson had each revived self-scrutiny as a means of judging the bargain ideals cut with the material status quo, in any given generation. This introspection constituted the moral testing of the state of the faith in relation to the state of the times. Waymarsh needs someone to buy things for. Modern America required a sacred rage that did not question materialism too closely, that became a worldly conscience about the worldly, that would take art for faith on faith. In such a situation, Strether, still with that old New England double consciousness but without the sacred rage to support his moral seriousness, is dangerous and vulnerable.

As jokes do, this joke says something about the people who make it.

Strether begins, it turns out, by naming the sacred rage. It is his first identification, his beginning as an Adam-come-lately to the garden: "Those occasions on which Strether was, in association with the exile from Milrose, to see the sacred rage glimmer through would doubtless have their due periodicity; but our friend had meanwhile to find names for many other matters" (*Ambassadors*, Book Second, chap. 1). Thus, the second book of the novel begins by reminding us that the sacred rage was Strether's baptism in giving familiar things their new names, in seeing them in a new light, and in understanding them for what they are and not necessarily for what Mrs. Newsome, orthodoxy, or convention say they are. Like any serious interpretation, the sacred rage, which is an ironic interpretation of a formidable phenomenon, runs not only the risk of error but also the even more interesting risk of pride—of explaining what has ceased to loom as if it still endangered, of giving the superannuated make-believe life in interpretation. *The Ambassadors*, like life itself, will make Strether run the real risks of his interpretive folly.

The shared joke of the sacred rage ushers in a lull of false calm and enjoyment, which Strether needs to relax enough so that he can be seized truly by the situation he is meant to size up. The terms of Strether's errand make even skepticism on his part something of a dilution of his duty. For him to experience Paris, as he cannot help doing from the start, is a dereliction. He knows this but refuses to acknowledge it. Joking about the sacred rage tips the first domino of Woollett hypocrisy. Waymarsh symbolizes that with which Strether had credited Woollett all along.

Waymarsh's refusal not only comprehends a rejection of Europe, thinks Strether, but shows that simply making the American case plain to Chad (as in saying, for instance, "Stop this fooling around, son, and come home where you belong, or else!") is somehow crude and illiberal. It is a kind of liberal—or what we have come to understand as "liberal"—temporizing that Strether seems to launch, a willingness to understand the point of view of the other fellow, a sympathy with it extended to the point of real compromise in an adversarial situation. Of course, he faces the liberal dilemma, because there is a point at which the parties to the conflict in *The Ambassadors* will not accede to compromise. And one of those parties, Strether has still to learn—again, in liberal fashion—is Lambert Strether himself. In such situations, the liberal's willingness to compromise is seen as an unreliable loyalty to the interests he is representing. They understand his difference from them to mean that he has his own interests. He cannot

believe this of himself. And it is no accident that Strether's loyalty is putative and ambivalent. The less stonily loyal to Woollett he is in Paris, the less
passionately loyal to Mrs. Newsome he seems to her to be. The fate of their
romance gauges his other loyalties.

A second problem is that Strether professes to take both sides at their
word. The true liberal dilemma is the reliance on profession and intention.
Waymarsh is, through and through, what he says; his is the unironic voice
of Milrose. It is this voice that Strether rather grandly throws off and rather
meanly deprecates at the start. But it may be that he has not thrown off the
old habit, gained under the ancient Puritan sway, of taking people at their
word; he thinks consistency the measure of moral seriousness. This view
may constitute a problem when dealing with strangers, but it is a dilemma
when dealing with friends.

The sacred rage underscores how much American morality in its primitive phase depended on a simple connection between word and deed. Its
moralizing was the commotion of the often unsuccessful effort to keep that
connection straight. The worst that you could say (did not Hawthorne?)
about the old ways was that they led to varieties of hypocrisy that did
cruelty against the human heart and feelings in the name of an ideal of
love. Or as Emerson said, they made rules out of experience, answers out of
life's questions. It remained to be seen what the successor, genteel morality,
might do at its worst.

Behind all this stands the unspoken fact that Maria Gostrey acknowledges when she talks about Strether's sharing her own unsuccess: they share
the failure's knowledge of America. This frees their judgment of its chains.
Expatriation is a conspiracy of making the best of that failure by the lights
of it, which means taking a critical view of the possibility of success. Their
conversation canvasses with delicate defiance what Strether will not name
but what Woollett talks about all the time; it is the very thing Chad is being
called home to expand the manufacture and the marketing of.

Miss Gostrey goes to the heart (or for the throat) of Strether's particular situation. He edits the *Review* for Mrs. Newsome; for her, he came to
Paris. Miss Gostrey knows the details of his situation in Woollett. She's
"the very deuce," as Strether puts it, because she knows, for instance, how
Mrs. Newsome arranges her hair. What she sees, of course, is that Woollett
is a characteristic American situation and that Strether essentially is bound
there by being true to type. She sees that Mrs. Newsome is a "moral swell,"
that Strether is the biggest thing she can get hold of, and that the *Review*

is for him only because he is for her. Maria makes out the shape of his situation and senses its precariousness. She sees how Mrs. Newsome has arranged things.

Strether, at once ironic and confident, will not see his own vulnerability. Close with Mrs. Newsome before someone bigger comes along, Miss Gostrey warns him; do not trifle with the likes of her. Her acute advice fades in the light of their plain talk about his relations with Mrs. Newsome— truly plain talk about his selling his love to her. The exchange concerns Mrs. Newsome's backing of the *Review* and Strether:

> "I don't begin to have her faith. She provides," said Strether, "three-fourths of that. And she provides, as I've confided to you, *all* the money."
>
> It evoked somehow a vision of gold that held for a little Miss Gostrey's eyes, and she looked as if she heard the bright dollars shovelled in. "I hope then you make a good thing—"
>
> "I *never* made a good thing!" he at once returned.
>
> She just waited. "Don't you call it a good thing to be loved?"
>
> "Oh we're not loved. We're not even hated. We're only just sweetly ignored."
>
> She had another pause. "You don't trust me!" she once more repeated.
>
> "Don't I when I lift the last veil?—tell you the very secret of the prison-house?"
>
> Again she met his eyes, but to the result that after an instant her own turned away with impatience. "You don't sell? Oh, I'm glad of *that!*" After which however, and before he could protest, she was off again. "She's just a *moral* swell." (*Ambassadors*, Book Second, chap. 1)

He does not trust her. She sees things too straight and says things too outright. And, although Strether will allude to his condition, it is an ironically guarded reference to his imprisonment, not an open discussion of the situation.

Love and money, love and money. The periodic necessities of the sacred rage are simple in comparison. Strether will admit to being supported but not to being loved. Maria tries to tell him to be as realistic about what is going on as she knows Mrs. Newsome will be. She shows him, with her knowledge of Mrs. Newsome's hairstyle, how very detailed is her grasp of his situation. But Strether, who will joke about deals, will not admit to doing one. He is prepared to mock the sacred rage and shies from calling the genteel tradition the spade it is. The nexus of money and culture and love scares him. His self-sacrifice is ominous. Not only will he take on his embassy and the work of high cultural and moral idealism, but also he is prepared to vindicate his principles to the very limit of his capacity. He is determined to be straight.

Unlike Milrose and Woollett, Strether thinks there is more to life than America affords, and other views on matters of consequence. Milrose thinks there is no place like home. Woollett thinks you can get the best of the world on a visit and bring it home, and that the principal duty of the traveling American is to collect without surrendering. Milrose thinks this treasure is the worm in the American apple; Woollett thinks home could do with some plunder but panics at Chad's apparent defection, in part out of its lurking fear that Milrose may have been right. It holds its head up high and, after all, brings Chad home, and it even rescues Milrose's wandering Waymarsh without giving a rhetorical or an ideological or a material inch. Woollett is formidable, imperially so—James knew that about America. It had suffered sentimental loss. Mrs. Newsome and Strether had something fine: but business is business.

Woollett is the provincial capital of a moral imperium, an empire that must believe in the booty it decorates its walls with. The stuffed heads of high culture populated the American parlor as thickly as the prizes of blood sport. Men who went in for culture and less savage hunts confused and troubled the norm. Woollett encouraged Chad's grand tour but was merciless about his expatriate way of life because it grasped the practical implications of his desertion—hence its moral import. Strether separated the moral from the interested. His irony stemmed from his sense of the small influence of the moral. He was ironic about his own helpless, moral seriousness. Taking the moral at its word—that it was something higher than the everyday, a separate sphere from the commercial—he decided that Paris had improved Chad by the parlor standards that Woollett professed. He missed the whole point, of course. Strether found a relationship in which a virtuous lady had, to his eye, improved an American gentleman. This is what was supposed to be going on all the time in genteel America. Indeed, it was his and Mrs. Newsome's ideal. But, in supposing as he did, Strether outraged the very center of feminine power: women's moral hold, their absolute domestic grip, and their implicit connection with the material order on which they depended. No matter what they said about themselves, they knew all along that in Paris, in the real world, such relations were never virtuous.

Poor Strether missed the point, but Woollett never did. Woollett had to expand the material and generational base. You cannot have a future without your young men. To fool with that fact, even in the name of fine things like moral distinctions and art and even love, undermines the social order. Strether's softness on the key question of imperial America doomed his attempt to use its highest sentiments against it, to soften the workings of its material and moral judgments. The sacred rage was less confusing. The sacred rage simply frowned on extramarital relations, as on so much else. The genteel tradition permitted the idealization of what was illicit, its "virtuous possibility," as if to cleanse it.[9] The witticism about the sacred rage conceals a kind of lament for an age of American noble savagery, after all. It certainly would have been easier for Strether to deal with the sacred rage than what he had to deal with.

Joking about the sacred rage readies Strether for Chad. Strether miscalculated Woollett, mistaking its modernity for his own mildness. Woollett, he might as well be assuring Miss Gostrey, does not suffer from the sacred rage. The subject is how blameless Woollett expects young men to be.

> "But you strike there a curious fact—the fact that Woollett too accommodates itself to the spirit of the age and the increasing mildness of manners. Everything changes, and I hold that our situation precisely marks a date. We *should* prefer them blameless, but we have to make the best of them as we find them. Since the spirit of the age and the increasing mildness send them so much more to Paris—"
>
> "You've to take them back as they come. When they *do* come. *Bon*!" Once more she embraced it all, but she had a moment of thought. "Poor Chad!"
>
> "Ah," said Strether cheerfully. "Mamie will save him!" (*Ambassadors*, Book Second, chap. 1)

Liberal Strether regards the mildness of the age as having necessitated certain changes. Woollett, he believes, no longer expects its young men to be blameless—to burn, that is, with the sacred rage, here reduced to a not comprehensive demand of chastity. The notion of the constant self-conscious resistance to pleasure, of being morally on your own hook and responsible for your character, and the connection between a plain, self-denying, duty-bound, and blameless good life is seen as outmoded, mildly regretted, mildly replaced Yankee custom.

The wider world beckons, and Woollett can change with the times. A little experience is not, after all, a bad thing. Woollett knows that the secret to settling a man is not his own virtue, as the sacred rage asserts, but the love of a good American woman—Mamie Pocock, in this case. Here is sound Woollett doctrine in a liberal mouth. Note how Strether puts things; historical changes take the burden off this moral change. He takes a tone of tolerant accommodation without seeming to realize that Woollett's accommodation is very particular, grudging, and clear-eyed. Woollett has its own reasons for wishing to reform Yankee orthodoxy, whose suspicion hampers luxury and confines power, and whose caution seems superstitious. Woollett intends to enjoy the age on its own terms, which means for Woollett, by Woollett, and in Woollett (unless Woollett should decide to relocate nearer New York). Miss Gostrey knows that Chad is to be pitied because he will have to go back there and become one of their successes.

Strether credits Woollett with a tolerant cosmopolitanism that it shows no signs of possessing. His dilemma is the liberal's dilemma. In the cause of a new relation between self and convention, one strays from the authentic pull of culture. Strether identifies American modernization with his own internal liberation. Strether's identification was the same as the moment when Henry Adams identified himself with an older order, as would George Santayana. Lambert Strether may be doing it in Paris, but, nevertheless, he is consulting his own individuality. This potential American Tocquevillian has wandered into the Emersonian. Strether seems about to free himself from the horizons of genteel orthodoxy. Woollett goes from orthodoxy to orthodoxy, from the isolationist sacred rage to the internationalist genteel tradition, organizing people on renegotiated terms, not freeing them.

Lambert Strether reads some letters from Mrs. Newsome while sitting on a penny chair in the Luxembourg Gardens. He thinks about his life. He feels a troubled surprise to find himself at such a distance from her—and seeing her, as it were, so distinctly, to find out that absence really does make his heart grow.

> His friend wrote admirably, and her tone was even more in her style than in her voice—he might almost, for the hour, have had to come this distance to get its full carrying quality; yet the plenitude of his

consciousness of difference consorted perfectly with the deepened intensity of the connection. It was the difference, the difference of being just where he was and *as* he was, that formed the escape—this difference was so much greater than he had dreamed it would be; and what he finally sat there turning over was the strange logic of his finding himself so free. He felt it in a manner his duty to think out his state, to approve the process, and when he came in fact to trace the steps and add up the items they sufficiently accounted for the sum. He had never expected—that was the truth of it—again to find himself young, and all the years and other things it had taken to make him so were exactly his present arithmetic. He had to make sure of them to put his scruple to rest. (*Ambassadors*, Book Second, chap. 2)

To find himself young. Strether wanders back down memory lane with this feeling of youth. This remarkable internal soliloquy of recollection deserves pairing with his monologue in Gloriani's garden. For, here, Strether reviews his own situation and his life. He reads Mrs. Newsome's letters in that spirit of detachment that shows him already, as he says, free from what she clearly regards as a binding commitment. Sitting there, in the Luxembourg Gardens, Strether feels free and young and regards his escape. Something has happened to separate him from Woollett and to make him a freer agent than Mrs. Newsome had sent out.

Strether reexperiences his exhaustion when he reached Europe. He was so worn out that "what he had wanted most was some idea that would simplify, and nothing would do this so much as the fact that he was done for and finished." That solution had proved transitory, a necessary, sedative bromide. To think about what a failure he was, how little he had to show for his life, would doom him. "Everything he wanted was comprised moreover in a single boon—the common unattainable art of taking things as they came. He appeared to himself to have given his best years to an active appreciation of the way they didn't come; but perhaps—as they would seemingly here be things quite other—this long ache might at last drop to rest." To take things as they came would mean to let the accumulated view of his life go. This would mean, in effect, to dissolve his connections with the view of his life that made it a failure—with American views, Woollett's views, and, ah, Mrs. Newsome's views.

Strether recollects his failure with a somewhat less insistent scenario in mind. He resents Mrs. Newsome's planting him on the cover of their *Re-*

view because he then owes his small eminence to her patronage. She has bought him cheap. Strether is just beginning to put two and two together. He still thinks he and Mrs. Newsome share their high ideals, and he does not suspect her devotion. He thinks she makes him ridiculous because she is ingenuous; he thinks she relies on his judgment and his opinion; he thinks she made him her ambassador because of her confidence in him. This trust goes a long way with Strether. The exploited are often confused by their exploiter's apparent dependence on them. "He had incurred the ridicule of having to have his explanation explained. He was Lambert Strether because he was on the cover, whereas it should have been, for anything like glory, that he was on the cover because he was Lambert Strether. He would have done anything for Mrs. Newsome, have been still more ridiculous—as he might, for that matter, have occasion to be yet; which came to saying that this acceptance of fate was all he had to show at fifty-five" (*Ambassadors*, Book Second, chap. 2). Strether does not know that he is angry, let alone how angry. He keeps thinking the choice is between youth, escape, and a sense of living life as it comes and his past, Mrs. Newsome, being ridiculous (which seems to mean marrying her), his old life, and Woollett.

Strether remembers his honeymoon trip to Paris. "It had been a bold dash, for which they had taken money set apart for necessities, but kept sacred at the moment in a hundred ways, and in none more so than by this private pledge of his own to treat the occasion as a relation formed with the higher culture and see that, as they said at Woollett, it should bear a good harvest" (*Ambassadors*, Book Second, chap. 2).Strether's own sacred "something" glows dimly through the years of his deprivation. Woollett has to do with the loss. His bargain with Mrs. Newsome will somehow seal it. This business with Chad is the test of it. Strether's thoughts turn to Chad and his mission. He thinks about Chad's history in Paris. His reconstruction of Chad's time is all mixed up with his own experience as a young married man in Paris. Strether had been a young American in Paris in a virtuous relation, determined to be improved by a sacred relation to the higher culture. He returned to America, where he failed at everything he tried and lost everything he cared about. Strether fantasizes Chad's life and fantasizes Chad—as if Chad were Strether, as if Strether might have been Chad. One wonders if Strether really believes that the best thing to do for Chad is to return him to Woollett, where his relation to that higher culture will suffer the American fate. Once Strether begins to identify with Chad, however gingerly at first, does he not wonder if he can bring him back alive? Mrs. Newsome is Spartan in her demand for her son's return. But Strether shows how already committed he is to another view of Chad's humanity. He wants to understand how it happened.

> He had wanted to put himself in relation, and he would be hanged if he were *not* in relation. . . . He wasn't there for his own profit—not, that is, the direct; he was there on some chance of feeling the brush of the wing of the stray spirit of youth. He felt it in fact, he had it beside him. . . . He reconstructed a possible groping Chad of three or four years before, a Chad who had, after all, simply—for that was the only way to see it—been too vulgar for his privilege. Surely it *was* a privilege to have been young and happy just there. Well, the best thing Strether knew of him was that he had had such a dream. (*Ambassadors*, Book Second, chap. 2)

The best thing Strether knows of Chad is that he is a potentially luckier Strether: only, Strether had not had Strether on his side.

Strether is ushered into Chad's new world by the delightful Little Bilham, about whom Strether's first impression stands. Seeing him from a distance on Chad's balcony, "Strether wondered at first if he were perhaps Chad altered, and then saw that this was asking too much of an alteration." Just how much to ask of an alteration nicely states Strether's problem with Chad Newsome. Chad's set-up enchants Strether; Little Bilham, who himself casts a kind of sympathetic glow over Chad's arrangements, charms him. About Little Bilham little is really said. Telling Waymarsh about his adventures, Strether tries describing the "little artist man" as someone "notoriously not from Boston" and who does not return home "because he likes it over here." Waymarsh, of course, answers gruffly that Bilham ought to be ashamed of himself. Why should Strether bother with Little Bilham? Strether answers, " 'Perhaps I do think so myself—though I don't quite yet admit it. I'm not a bit sure—it's again one of the things I want to find out. I liked him and *can* you like people—? But no matter.' He pulled himself up. 'There's no doubt I want you to come down on me and squash me' " (*Ambassadors*, Book Third, chap. 1). Indeed.

Waymarsh shows he is Strether's friend by telling him to quit: "I mean your nosing around. Quit the whole job. Let them stew in their juice. You're being used for a thing you're not fit for. People don't take a fine tooth comb to groom a horse." He gets Strether to say outright that Chad is needed for the business and that, if he does not get Chad back, Mrs. Newsome will end the engagement. Waymarsh understands his friend, who says, as if in defense against the mercenary charge, that he is freely taking his chance of "the possibility, the danger of being influenced in a sense counter to Mrs. Newsome's own feelings." That is, his nosing around is a kind of moral test for himself. He runs the risk to prove his own probity before accepting what he still seems to think he wants. Waymarsh recognizes the scrupulous con game when he hears it and calls his bluff. Strether is a "humbug": "Yes, you ask me for protection and then you won't take it." Waymarsh and Miss Gostrey see Strether engaged on something that will spoil the Strether each one loves. In funny harmony, each advises him to quit it.

Strether does not put Waymarsh off in quite the same way as he does Miss Gostrey. Sensing an imminent parting of their ways, he acknowledges that he has gone beyond satisfaction with what Waymarsh is satisfied knowing. Strether takes Mrs. Newsome to be giving him enough rope to hog-tie Chad or hang himself, and he means to use it. He has to size things up for himself because he already, internally, has become convinced that there is more to his quest than her errand.

Strether agrees with Paris, and with the antic Parisian of Chad's circle, Miss Barrace, that Waymarsh is an American primitive. Miss Barrace says, "Oh your friend's a type, the grand old American—what shall one call it? The Hebrew prophet, Ezekiel, Jeremiah, who used when I was a little girl in the Rue Montaigne to come to see my father and who was usually the American Minister to the Tuileries or some other court. I haven't seen one of these ever so many years; the sight of it warms my poor old chilled heart; this specimen is wonderful; in the right quarter, you know, he'll have a *succès fou*" (*Ambassadors*, Book Third, chap. 1). Strether must begin to realize that Paris values him as well, shares his view of home, and regards him as a success because of his qualities and perceptions. Mrs. Newsome will redeem his failure because she prizes him. She will print his name on the cover as if he were a success because success is so important a convention to her. And he tests her appreciation for him by insisting on going about things in Paris his own way. He is showing Mrs. Newsome what he would be like and he is showing himself how she would take it if he were. It is a prenuptial trial of sorts.

The sympathetic company of Chad's circle is not all peaches and cream to Strether. They try his moral patience, taking for granted things that he cannot even speak to Mrs. Newsome. "This he was well aware was a dreadful necessity; but such was the stern logic, he could only gather, of a relation to the irregular life." Its enjoyment by Chad's circle was "the insidious, the delicate marvel." As Strether enjoys Chad's surrogate hospitality in his own absence, he himself comes into relation to the irregular life and finds that it sits well upon him, too. After Miss Gostrey meets Little Bilham—"Oh he's all right—he's one of *us!*"—Strether reflects on how fully he understood what she meant by that and "took it as still another sign that he had got his job in hand."

He complacently assumes Miss Gostrey to mean "that they were intense Americans together." Of Little Bilham, however, Strether comes to think this significant series of things: "The amiable youth then looked out, as it had first struck Strether, at a world in respect to which he hadn't a prejudice. The one our friend most instantly missed was the usual one in favor of an occupation accepted. Little Bilham had an occupation, but it was only an occupation declined; and it was by his general exemption from alarm, anxiety or remorse on this score that the impression of his serenity was made" (*Ambassadors*, Book Third, chap. 2). Strether might be looking in his glass, but irony is not the exemption that leads to serenity.

To rid oneself of the settled double consciousness on which irony is founded is to face up to a choice, to unbalance the perspective of the double consciousness. Strether had gained his irony in an old battle—the battle Woollett had won from Milrose. He required a fresh alternative to Woollett. He arrived at one that replaced his conscience with his native feelings, his responses to discoveries like Paris, his unprejudiced look round, and his new self in a new world. The Old World is new to Strether; it makes him young again. Strether works by seeing himself through others, by identification and fellow feeling. Little Bilham is an important acquisition. Having caught a glimpse of himself in the little artist man, Strether may now meet Chad.

THE SECRET HEARTS OF *THE AMBASSADORS*

Strether catches up with Chad in a box at the theater. Chad is different from what he expected, and Strether is crazy about him—head-over-heels crazy, heart over head.

Our friend was to go over it afterwards again and again—he was going over it much of the time that they were together, and they were together constantly for three or four days: the note had been so strongly struck during that first half hour that everything happening since was comparatively a minor development. The fact was that his perception of the young man's identity—so absolutely checked for a minute—had been quite one of the sensations that count in life; he certainly had never known one that had acted, as he might have said, with more of a crowded rush. And the rush, though both vague and multitudinous, had lasted a long time, protected, as it were, yet at the same time aggravated, by the circumstances of its coinciding with a stretch of decorous silence. They couldn't talk without disturbing the spectators in the part of the balcony just below them; and it, for that matter, came to Strether—being a thing of the sort that did come to him—that these were the accidents of a high civilisation; the imposed tribute to propriety, the frequent exposure to conditions, usually brilliant, in which relief has to await its time. Relief was never quite near at hand for kings, queens, comedians and other such people, and though you might be yourself not exactly one of those, you could yet, in leading the life of high pressure, guess a little how they sometimes felt. It was truly the life of high pressure that Strether had seemed to feel himself lead while he sat there, close to Chad, during the long tension of the act. He was in presence of a fact that occupied his whole mind, that occupied for the half-hour his senses themselves all together; but he couldn't without inconvenience show anything—which moreover might count really as luck. What he might have shown, had he shown at all, was exactly the kind of emotion—the emotion of bewilderment— that he had proposed to himself from the first, whatever should occur, to show least. The phenomenon that had suddenly sat down there with him was a phenomenon of change so complete that his imagination, which had worked so beforehand, felt itself, in the connexion, without margin or allowance. It had faced every contingency but that Chad should not *be* Chad, and this was what it now had to face with a mere strained smile and an uncomfortable flush. (*Ambassadors*, Book Third, chap. 2)

The emotion Strether cannot show is not exactly bewilderment, although he is surely bewitched, bothered, and bewildered. This is *the* moment of feeling in *The Ambassadors*. And the feeling is Strether's overwhelming attraction to Chad.

Henry James knew what Strether was feeling. James had been in love with a young sculptor, Hendrik Andersen, whom he had met in Rome in 1899—the year of personal renewal that Leon Edel marks as James's own emotional source for Strether's second spring. James met the indifferently talented but very good-looking sculptor in Rome, took a fancy to him, and wooed him in a friendship that resulted in tremendous feeling, passion, and love on James's part. Edel concludes that we cannot be sure what passed between them at their several meetings during the remainder of James's life, but that Andersen inspired in James feelings "akin to love," by which Edel probably means *love*.[10]

The letters James wrote to Andersen reflect the many moods and the intimate language of love. Edel notes the physicality of their imagery. However understood and expressed, Strether's feeling for Chad—like James's—is of an intense and direct order. It is a response to his beauty and presence, which he then attributes to Chad's change, his way of life, his ease, and the many qualities that he, like James, can discern in the beloved to explain his own inordinate attachment. James had already given Strether his out by making Chad the object of his errand.

The enumeration that somehow ties the beloved down, or maybe that diverts the feeling into more navigable channels, is what imagination gives back to—or defends itself with—from passion. To explain the inexplicable and control the uncontrollable, it must use the weapons from one sphere to win a losing fight in another. Strether keeps finding and giving reasons for his intensity about Chad. The reasons have a life of their own in *The Ambassadors*. They have to do with the plot. They explain why Strether stays on in Paris near Chad. And they explain, from the inside out, why Strether must keep Chad in Paris, in the setting where he so appreciates him. Strether's feelings for Chad do not disturb the heterosexual surface and working out of the novel's plot. James borrowed from his own life to animate his character, although there is no sense in which Strether can see this about himself, nor can James quite say it about him. The deep source of the convincing freeing of Strether's feelings that makes the book the singular book it is was James's recognition of his own feelings as positive and his decision to give them encouraging, if not altogether literal, expression in his most winning male character since (significantly) Ralph Touchett in *The Portrait of a Lady*.

Edel's account of the James-Andersen friendship holds that Andersen and James had different purposes. Andersen was flattered by the eminent author's good opinion of his work and himself and thought James's friendship would prove useful to him in the great world. James seems to have felt, in addition to his passion, a sense of emotional reawakening because of that passion. The letters suggest that, although Andersen caused James pain and frustration, James's feelings for him also freed his art. The love was welcome for the sudden impetus it gave to his work and to his style. Andersen may have been a frustrating object for the man and an embarrassment to the artist in the man, but for the writer he seems to have opened the most wonderful inside door of all: to the most personal and assertive, least compromising, finally Jamesian James. The famous Max Beerbohm caricature pictures James kneeling down outside a door at a country house, looking with his glass at the mixed pairs of shoes outside. His passion for Andersen brought James back to his own door and emboldened him at last to enter.

Edel says that James saw himself in Andersen, that Andersen was a mirror to his younger self. He was an object not only of desire but also of vicarious, as well as direct, identification. We know that Andersen was had by James's consciousness, much as Chad was ravished by Strether's. *The Ambassadors* recounts the transfigured love story. Edel also suggests that James's idyll at Lamb House with Andersen consoled James: "Forgotten for the moment was the pride of reputation, the envy of the best-sellers, the weight of the world. He lived for a small, a cherished idyll, of happy summer months." So, for Strether, is Paris an idyll during which he keeps the discouragement of his American failure at bay while he changes. Strether resists the temptation of a kind of American success (marrying into money) and goes again about his own business in his own fashion. Chad is at the heart of Strether's Parisian interlude, as Andersen was at the heart of James's personal regrouping.

James celebrated his renewal with his late masterpieces, and he glowed with love and longing whenever Andersen reappeared in his life. He saw through the sculptor and loved him, as one does, even after the imperfect real person takes off the mask of the perfect beloved. He no longer attributed to him the special qualities he had once needed his late life's passion to have. James dealt with Andersen as a special friend, a contact who always inspired intense and poignant feelings. James resumed being James, refreshed and readied.

Strether's experiences distill James's. They are not mired in ordinary futures and disappointments. *The Ambassadors* shows the traces of James's own life, but the novel is better than the biography. Chad gives Strether the great gift of unrequited passion—the intense experience of one's own heart. In Strether, as in James, life and art no longer war. Strether need no longer see the beautiful as unrelated to, burdened with, scandalized by, or innocent of, the possible. It is, perhaps, his fuller recognition of these feelings and his unprejudiced delight in them that he comes into in *The Ambassadors*; he experiences a kind of self-forgiveness and belated recognition of his own charm and possibility, one he seems content or determined to enjoy in solitude.

Strether's love is less open but more fulfilled than James's could have been. His passion for Chad is recognizably different from his feelings for Mrs. Newsome, Maria Gostrey, Little Bilham, and Madame de Vionnet but does not monopolize his emotional, or even his erotic, repertoire. The consummation of his erotic feelings remains in doubt. James is generous enough with the feelings—the passage thrills with them—that it is superfluous to second-guess his plotting of them. There remains, however, a discrepancy between how James must accommodate this attraction to the rest of the novel and what Strether says and does about it.

The long moment of his recognition of this other, that moment of important sensation, is the stuff of obsessive, enraptured love. It is the crowded rush of his feelings, the suspended time, the tension of just sitting next to Chad, and Chad's utter domination of his consciousness. He had known and been thinking about Chad but had seen him in a new light, as if for the first time. The means by which James brings Chad to life stir Strether to his very soul, almost shattering him with the surprising force of a guerrilla attack from his insides. And the very world must absorb the aftershocks of Strether's feelings. He was not prepared to cope with these emotions. Chad's unwarranted possession of Strether's heart authenticates the action, gives Strether his caring sincerity.

This passage provides the clue to the secret heart of the rest of the book, and it really is secret. Strether's unacknowledged grappling with his feelings for Chad shadows his involvement in the plot. He feels he must reconcile the Chad who appears to him in the box with the real Chad. Strether was prepared to meet a Chad who was an idealized and fortunate young Strether not up to the luck of his privilege, but Chad's glossy beauty and savoir faire quite overtake Strether's cautious fantasy and seem to give it life. Through the action of the novel, but also when Strether's heart allows it, Chad becomes Chad again, improved but no longer luminous. This means Strether has had to let go.

Strether experiences his own renewal vicariously, by feeling more of Chad's life, through his more acute consciousness of it, than Chad does.

At a certain point, he no longer needs an idealized Chad, no longer needs Chad in Paris to live his own life, no longer needs to borrow from Chad the occasion for feeling. What is attractive to Chad about Strether is this intense and flattering consciousness Strether has of what seems to have become for Chad a somewhat stale, although agreeable and attractive, life. It turns out that Strether and Chad have met in a corridor outside Woollett—Chad returning, Strether just leaving. Chad uses Strether to ease his return. Strether somehow makes this possible, but also he shows Chad the understanding and transitional sympathy that make it possible for even so hardened a character to see himself home.

Strether's attraction to Chad is not saving, but it is liberating. Chad does better by Strether than Mrs. Newsome does. Chad's Woollett would keep Strether around on better terms, although the price it would exact of seeing everything straight is high: there would be no genteel idealism, no hiding out in parlors from the truths of life or capitalism, and a relation to the irregular, perhaps, but not to the higher culture. For Chad gives Strether the object, the situation, the circle—a world, really—within which to recover his own feelings and his true self. It offers fair return for Strether's devotion.

The Ambassadors may tell the story of a crush. Strether's infatuation with Chad animates the surface of the novel, so that what we read seems true and even sufficient. But the passion that lurks beneath its surface makes *The Ambassadors* the marvel that it is. Motive does not neatly motivate. Feelings overwhelm action, and consideration and thought and conversation use up unspent energy. The passion finds many wonderful and realistic shapes. Strether's interest in Chad; his endearing participation in Chad's life at his own pace; his sympathetic involvement with Madame de Vionnet; and his intense, romantic, and sentimental reinvolvement with young people, almost as if he were one of them himself, express the passion that grips Strether's heart. The more sinuous expressions of that passion—his threesome with Chad and Madame de Vionnet; the odd, sweet, intimate relation he comes to have with her; his proprietary feelings about her liaison with Chad; the way he defends them with reluctant but determined integrity, willing not only to lose all for their sake but to look the fool—betoken the curious dance of self and other in that ménage. What is so ineffably realistic and moving is James's portrait of Strether involved with other human beings for their own sake. Intense passion fuels and intense feelings undergo the unconsummated action that rewards incomplete possibility.

Strether's heightened awareness of Paris, of people, of light, and of life is his reward. It is, he feels, what is left to him of life. At Gloriani's party, he is so aware of the glamour and distinction about him that he needs less intense doses of it to satisfy him than those who are more robust or jaded do. His awareness of celebrity satisfies his appetite for it. Perhaps it is so with passion. He savors the meal prescribed for the refined palate of the old. His appetite is not young, although his zest is real and his enjoyment fresh. It is important and characteristic that his last encounter with Chad and Madame de Vionnet comes after his solitary aesthetic stroll, during which the beauty of life and what art notices of it fuse again in him. On his country ramble, Strether has the experience that New England genteel culture in its fear of other things keeps denying by making a practice, a ritual, and a superstition of art. So, when he does see the lovers, he sees them at last for what they are, however shocking, because he can see things the way they are and be himself the way he is. Strether's recovery of his native self is the accomplishment of the translation into fiction of James's being out to himself in his relationship with Hendrik Andersen.

Strether may, after all, wish for no more than this. He certainly transcends his passion, so unbecoming to his principles, for those Newsomes. He learns not to idealize Mrs. Newsome or Chad. He learns what brutalities they are capable of yet appears to be forgiving and abiding in his affections for them, without wanting to live among them in Woollett. He seems to choose Maria Gostrey, Madame de Vionnet, and Little Bilham over Mrs. Newsome, Chad, and Waymarsh. He then leaves them behind in Paris to return on his own to America. And, when he goes home, he does not go empty-handed, after all.

The mere strained smile and uncomfortable flush Strether shows is mute testimony to how private his feelings are. Yet we know them, and probably Chad senses them. And we are faced with the task of recognizing that the feelings that stir Strether are not the ones that the novel treats. He spends the novel living Chad's life along with, and sometimes instead of, his own. His deepest empathy for Madame de Vionnet results from his own understanding of what she must be going through for love of Chad. There is a deep division in Strether between his own feelings and how they shadow the events of his life, which are vicarious. James's secret heart throbs with Strether's inner and outer life and makes a novel that tells the adventure story, intense with feeling, of consciousness.

One senses that James's working through of his own feelings projected and transfigured Strether's getting over Chad. Two letters James wrote encourage this reading. To Jocelyn Perse, he wrote of Strether's "vague resemblance" to himself, which combines with Strether's concoction from a remark of William Dean Howells to make one feel that Strether's starting ground may be Howells, but his range is James's own.[11] A 1912 letter to gay novelist Hugh Walpole says something important in an interesting way:

> It's charming to me to hear that *The Ambassadors* have again engaged and still beguile you; it *is* probably a very *packed* production, with a good deal of one thing within another; I remember sitting on it, when I wrote it, with that intending weight and presence with which you probably often sit in these days on your trunk to make the lid close and *all* your trousers and boots go in. I remember putting in a good deal about Chad and Strether, or Strether and Chad, rather; and am not sure that I quite understand what in that connection you miss—I mean in the way of what *could* be there. The whole thing is of course, to intensity, a picture of relations—and among them is, though not on the first line, the relation of Strether to Chad. The relation of Chad to Strether is a limited and according to my method only implied and in-dicated thing, sufficiently there; but Strether's to Chad consists above all in a charmed and yearning and wondering sense, a dimly envious sense, of all Chad's young living and easily-taken *other* relations; other not only than the one to him, but than the one to Madame de Vionnet and whoever else; this very sense, and the sense of Chad, generally, is a part, a large part, of poor dear Strether's discipline, development, adventure and general history.[12]

James knew what his own book was about and what he was trying to do; his stammering falling-off from that statement shows how his art took him only as far as his understanding of life did. What is extraordinary is the icon of feeling and sensibility and understanding to which James's resting place of hesitation brought him in Strether.

For Strether did not falter. His sweet, curious, suggestive, happy, virtu-ous relationship with Little Bilham shows how little he faltered. An artist, an expatriate, about as unfit for the American future as Chad is fit, Little Bilham seems gay to a late-twentieth-century reader, and to himself, and is probably as gay as James could write him. Strether goes as far as he can—he tells Bilham to live his life as he sees fit, in the safe place of Paris. He trusts his own feelings without irony to Bilham, who is like him and not like Chad.

The true readers of *The Ambassadors* are more like Bilham than Chad. Strether's new creed, including especially his "Don't-you-do-as-I-did" rule, is a way of coming out. His life would have been better had he done what it was that he did not do. The wrong reasons held him back from having his life. This inflects the story in terms of what drives it but does not precisely figure in it. Strether's feelings for Chad make him reflect on what of his own life he has failed to live. Understanding those feelings and what they bring him to makes *The Ambassadors* the singularly moving book it is. If Strether had not become himself because of his Parisian adventure, then his would have been an ironic but disheartening revision of Isabel Archer's renunciation. But he has become himself—because Henry James had become himself. Lambert Strether found and urged on Little Bilham James's mature vision of the Emersonian that had "failed" Isabel Archer. "Live all you can: it's a mistake not to. It doesn't matter what you do in particular, so long as you have had your life. If you haven't had that, what have you had?" In the choice between nature and convention, James chose his own nature and had Strether choose his.

The Ambassadors has more to it than sacred rage and secret heart. Strether's distancing of himself from the sacred rage, and his subsequent fall, make the action of the novel possible and plausible. He takes sides against Woollett and with the cause of what, it turns out, he had all along thought Woollett believed in. Unlike the friends he prefers, Strether clings to his ideals; this makes them stand the test of reality. His friends understand this about him.

He seems to have come to a sense of self that makes him implicitly critical of America rather than cynical, like his American Parisian friends. Everyone in *The Ambassadors* has views about America. Strether exhausts them and arrives at an understanding all his own. He seems to have decided at the book's end that it is part of his recovery of himself to go home. He reclaims his natural habit to admit—indeed, to insist—that, such as he is, he is American enough to live there. There is something remarkably keen about Strether. He anticipates the characters of modern American novels, who find America a strange habitat. They acclimate themselves to their country by modulating, incorporating, or using a critical view or self-conscious awareness of themselves in it. These post-Stretherian heroes do not tame America the wilderness but encounter America the civilization.

In his great soliloquy in Gloriani's garden, Strether shows himself ready to do battle with Woollett and the genteel tradition (Santayana was to call it "the Woollett sort of compromise") and articulates what is at stake in that contest. He is alive again, with his resistance overcome, his nerves and senses atingle, and he is about to meet his fate. Madame de Vionnet is more Strether's fate and his match than Chad because, finally, Strether prefers her to Woollett. He attributes to her, and in general to people, too much beauty, too many scruples, too much consciousness, too much meaning. He does not take seriously enough the *value* placed on beauty by the culture. He does not recognize that the price that places things beyond his reach is meant to bring them within the grasp of people who value things by pricing them, who do not value what they cannot own, and for whom owning is the limit case of appreciation.

Strether puts naive credence in the professed value-system of his culture. That is why he is a favorite of the ladies, a luxury. He is a principled, aesthetically advanced man, whom, like their religion of art and their high moral swelling, they can afford. But, in crisis, luxuries go first. Strether jokes about being a "failure" because, as Miss Gostrey realizes, he does not think that being a "failure" is failing, exactly. He is shattered when Sarah shows him that he is a superfluous luxury. He had believed himself safe in speaking to Woollett from its highest ground. Strether learned that what he thought was his trump card, Woollett's professed ideals, was really the joker. Pleading Madame de Vionnet's case to Woollett becomes pleading his own. What Strether wants from Chad for Madame de Vionnet is also what he would have wanted for himself: loyalty to the difficulty of the finest things.

The garden party at Gloriani's must have been something to see: Strether, standing in that perfect garden amidst that splendid throng, sacred rage gone. Madame de Vionnet should be an alien type to Strether, but she strikes him as charming upon their first meeting. How naturally he compares her to Mrs. Newsome and Sarah, how immediately he feels her "common humanity." In that instant, Strether belongs to what Woollett had denied him: his experience of things. He sinks upon a bench, full of impressions, knowing that this is but a respite in what will be a time crowded with the incident of impressions.

Bilham appears. They dawdle, and, refusing more introductions, Strether says it is too late for him. Bilham gallantly replies, "Better late than never," to which Strether returns sharply, "Better early than late!"

This note indeed the next thing overflowed for Strether into a quiet stream of demonstration that as soon as he had let himself go he felt as the real relief. It had consciously gathered to a head, but the reservoir had filled sooner than he knew, and his companion's touch was to make the waters spread. There were some things that had to come in time if they were to come at all. If they didn't come in time they were lost for ever. It was the general sense of them that had overwhelmed him with its long slow rush. (*Ambassadors*, Book Fifth, chap. 2)

What overwhelms Strether is the impression, gained through Chad's life, of what his own might have been. He seems to see that it was unnecessary hesitation, caution, and false consciousness that kept him from his own youth. There is a certain poignancy (and a figurative current of sexual release) that he utters this speech at Bilham's gentle touch and to Bilham. The relation of Strether and Bilham is sweet, curious, suggestive, virtuous, and inconsistent.

The Ambassadors must be about Strether and Chad but is also about Strether and Bilham. Their relation requires a repudiation of Woollett, to which what you do in particular matters more than anything, and which seems to mount a constant argument against living your life—unless your life happens to be the life Woollett means for you, to which end material and moral resources are bent. If living life is somehow accepting experience as it comes to you, it is contra Woollett.

Strether regrets everything and nothing in particular. This amounts to more than a regret for the passing of youth, although there is the comedy of that in it. Clearly, Strether feels Chad's youth is wasted on him. Strether is uncannily a child, a pure heart. Youth moves him, and he is moved to say so. He ends up championing what he was meant to argue Chad out of. This is his "All right, I'll go to Hell" moment, whether he quite knows it or not, because it shall not be in him to argue Chad out of his life, their life. He will feel Chad's return as a betrayal and Bilham's staying on as a vindication. And, so, Strether urges Bilham to have his own life, as a way of declaring his regret and making it the cause for his liberality to youth.

There are two ways to deal with a consciousness of one's own regrets. The venerable way is to accept life and to give grudging approval to wild-oats-sowing, with a chuckling recollection of one's own salad days. Woollett improves on the sacred rage, as Strether says, by allowing her young men their time before settling down. Strether sees how punitive that can be, punitive and repressive and wrongheaded. Instead of the conventional wisdom, which gives a certain leeway to youth so long as it will be taken back reliably by early middle age, he says the opposite—live all you can. If you cannot, you cannot. But try. Don't live it up while you may, but have the life you feel inside you, since that's all there is to life. And the implicit radicalism, relativism, and generosity of this sentiment animate the passage. It is a great moment in the history of American imagination.

Ahab does not give Starbuck this sort of hope. But the countertradition of clear-eyed generosity and encouragement, of Jefferson, Emerson, and Eleanor Roosevelt, among others, shares this odd moment with Strether. He takes his stand for the rising generation, on the basis of the disappointments of the old—not against them on the basis of their parents' resentment that they get their try at life, too. Strether's message of encouragement is one good reason for him to go home. His message seems to be that, since life will disappoint some hopes, it is all the more reason to have the hopes and the life that will be disappointed.

That Strether speaks his piece to Bilham is not only dramatically apt. He would not say it to Chad, who knows it instinctively, anyway. It is Little Bilham's life, after all, that, more than Chad's, resembles the one Strether might have lived—one conducted with that real shrugging off of conventional *shoulds* that Strether finally feels. Of course, unlike Bilham, Strether has his own moral imperatives, his conscience, which is one of his treasures and which identifies him. He is a grave and weighty character whose rush of feeling here does not lighten him. Rather, it frees him. We do not know if Bilham gets a conscience in the end. Indeed, it is not certain that Strether recommends having one. He may recommend to Bilham something his own conscience keeps him from attempting. A large part of Strether's *right* is his own history.

Strether makes the philosophical leap to the nature of things that marks his essential New England seriousness. It is not America he throws off, after all; it is America he vindicates. The conscience is American equipment, the compass for the old moral wilderness. An American needs to know what freedom is, not merely to enjoy it, here or there. But one's life gets lived, like it or not; it is only later that one sees it as somehow destined, if not predestined. What one learns about the nature of life, then, is unfortunate, precocious wisdom, bad socialization. Life deserves to be lived unburdened with what experience of it has taught other people. Strether sounds Emersonian here, in the accents of the original, not the genteel, Emerson—as if he has peeled away the Woollett layer on the domestication of that New England radical's break with the New England past.

> What one loses one loses; make no mistake about that. The affair— I mean the affair of life—couldn't, no doubt, have been different for me; for it's at best a tin mould, either fluted and embossed, with ornamental excrescences, or else smooth and dreadfully plain, into which, a helpless jelly, one's consciousness is poured—so that one "takes" the form, as the great cook says, and is more or less compactly held by it: one lives in fine as one can. Still, one has the illusion of freedom; therefore don't be, like me, without the memory of that illusion. I was either, at the right time, too stupid or too intelligent to have it; I don't quite know which. Of course at present I'm a case of reaction against the mistake; and the voice of reaction should, no doubt, always be taken with an allowance. (*Ambassadors*, Book Fifth, chap. 2)

Would that the voice of reaction really sounded like Strether. His image surpasses Jack Burden's "great twitch" or Henry Adams's Darwinist and mechanical fancies. Strether sees past his own life history to his onetime future. The illusion of freedom may be all the freedom there is, but that is the great gift, he says. You cannot help your life, he seems to say, so do not add to its accidental or determined quality another layer of interpretive trouble. Inherited wisdom about how to live life may just be an attempt, for good or bad reasons, to prevent you from living it in your own way. This life, Strether says, is all you get.

The sacred rage recognized what he said about life but chose to fill it out with conscience and deity and predestination and character, understandings that somehow bind us causally to the worst that life has in store for us, as if it were any help. The sacred rage was at least fixed to a consistent position. It had a kind of primitive patriarchal glory, as Waymarsh did until Woollett got hold of him. Woollett relies on character and class, the verities of the capitalist order, and the comforts of art to get one through a purposefully narrowed experience of life, of which security seems to be the goal. It compromises the provincial severity of the sacred rage to get more of the world's goods.

Strether's awful, funny image of consciousness taking the shape of a fluted or plain mold suggests more than Strether does. Ancient New England said the shape taken was determined by God; modern New England had views about character. The Woollett line on everything is that it knows ahead of time what it will feel and what something is worth, so that neither art nor principle, and certainly not love, can interfere with the business of life. It likes the shape its consciousness takes and, indeed, claims credit for it. Woollett spares no feeling for those whose lives give their consciousness a different shape. Strether's borrowing from the great cook is at once more random and more truly demanding than either. Destiny is random because jelly is helpless. Destiny is demanding because life requires adjustment, taking alien shape because of its sad truth about the hopeless difference between what we are like inside and how we have to seem outside.

Such tone and language appear to diminish the stakes of the fit between the individual and convention. The illusion of human freedom was a common thought of the day. Historians have pointed out that the determinist message conveyed the substance of home truths in up-to-date ways. Strether's advice is to act as if you were free and take responsibility for your own life. He strikes a not unprecedented compromise between the contradictory elements of life and arrives at a presently familiar ground. His views obviate Woollett's role. The community no longer speaks loudest to the conscience. Strether's experience throws the harm Woollett does into clear relief. It surely does subvert the authorities that stand in the way of the likes of a Bilham's, or a future Strether's, living all they can.

Living all you can makes a relativist statement about the human condition. To arrive there, Strether must throw off the retarding orthodoxies by which he has been living his little of his own life. It is a necessary moment of self-revelation for Strether. In it, the rest of the novel is foretold. James carefully describes Strether's ideological divestiture to make the peace he makes. The end of the orthodox is the beginning of Strether's adventure. In order to bring him to it, James liberates him, from the inside out. *The Ambassadors* leaves Strether liberated from most of what he seems to have had or liked—his prospects, his home, Paris, his new friends, his old friends—all alone on his way back to America. Chad is, as Strether admits to Maria Gostrey, his father's son.

Strether may have identified with Chad, but not as his father's son. He says of Chad that he is "formed to please," which Strether knows firsthand and which Madame de Vionnet, who formed him, will know to her sorrow. And of Mrs. Newsome, he says, "She's the same. She's more than ever the same. But I do what I didn't before—I *see* her." Why go home? Home to what? Miss Gostrey offers him a haven of perfect understanding. He understands, but he does not want perfect understanding. He must go, "to be right." Neither Chad nor Madame de Vionnet can resist Strether's sharp eye for what makes him right. His conscientiousness is very attractive. The sacred rage may have been reduced to spending sprees and the genteel tradition exposed as the prop it is, but Strether carries through the plain old American habit of conscience. Madame de Vionnet once had asked Strether why he could not trust himself. At last, he does.

In Strether's final scene with Waymarsh, the Milrose wayfarer comes to Strether as Sarah's cavalier, in her imperious behalf, to announce their departure. And, after a while, after Waymarsh has lied to Strether for Sarah and has done her bidding, he talks about the trip; maybe he ought not to go: "It was the conscience of Milrose, in the very voice of Milrose, but oh it was feeble and flat! Strether suddenly felt quite ashamed for him; he breathed a greater boldness. '*Let* yourself, on the contrary, go—in all agreeable directions. These are precious hours—at our age they mayn't recur. Don't have it to say to yourself at Milrose, next winter, that you hadn't courage for them.' And then as his comrade queerly stared: 'Live up to Mrs. Pocock'" (*Ambassadors*, Book Tenth, chap. 2). This is not "Live all you can."

Strether frees Bilham into the air; puts Waymarsh into a cage; leaves Chad to his predatory eminences; but Strether himself flies away home. The book's lesson lies between "Live all you can" and this sad advice to poor Waymarsh, who has forfeited his right to the sacred rage, to do what Strether has declined to do. Waymarsh has joined the Woollett people whose relation to the world is one of plunder and whose relation to their own heritage is one of inevitable betrayal. The sacred rage at least resisted the world because it recognized and resisted immorality. It was narrow but not hypocritical; it did not deny other people what it enjoyed. Waymarsh gives in and goes back to live as American men do with women. Chad winks conspiratorially, his mouth full of too much protesting that he knows how to take from women without giving himself up. Strether goes home freed from illusion about the present, and his ideals become the second nature he has decided to prefer.

Why did James tell *The Ambassadors* as he did? The story he wanted to tell was not susceptible to the plainer style and conventional compass of the genres. Strether concentrated his whole life in the gain and loss of his embassy to Paris. A series of things brought him to a long moment of intense spiritual renewal. He crossed over to the country of feeling on his own errand. His intense experience of his own feelings—for that is what reunited his double consciousness—changed him. The trouble with any other way of telling this story is that all the available genres and points of view stop short of Strether's strenuous learning experience. He carries back to America what his experience has taught him about himself. Since he had been a creature of the New England version of the American regime, morally speaking at least, his feelings have brought him to a view of America.[13]

The Ambassadors is a nonutopian comedy of male liberation, after all. The captive ranks have swelled with Waymarsh, Jim Pocock, and Chad Newsome, who apparently is intending to return into captivity. Little Bilham is staying on in Paris, confirmed in his exile rather than warned off it. Strether has somehow decided to live on his own. Again, funnily like the hard-boiled detective or the cowboy, he seems to think that domestic entanglement endangers his essential moral nature, his ideals. However much one may feel that his deepest erotic pulls lie elsewhere, the book shows him convincingly attached by and to a trio of remarkable women who offer him a panoply of possible terms on which to settle. His refusal of Miss Gostrey's perfect understanding may have to do with his passions being otherwise engaged, but he also seems to believe that his conscience requires solitary tending. What is so sad elsewhere in James, in Strether is not.

Like all of James's work, *The Ambassadors* discourages hopes that the relations in life can institutionalize more than the relations of life. Having relations is not discouraged, but they do not transform—they happen. More and more, people have had to learn what James knew: the conventions of society tend to fail the privileged as well as the poor and the unusual. For poor people, this failure occurs quintessentially at the moment when cant about hard work and character prove helpless against the realities of the economic system. It is a dire material failure. The modern literary tradition has been responsive to this situation in deed and in critical requirement.[14]

The problem James posed to his devoted mid-twentieth-century readers was that many of them worried about the implications of their intense taste for James for their intense political commitments. F. O. Matthiessen and F. W. Dupee, for instance, wrote wonderfully about James but never could quite reconcile what they took to be his politics and their own. One reason they wrote so well about James is that their ambivalence about his politics warred to a kind of stalemate with their deep feeling for his books. It kept their notions of literature safe from the brutalities common in their—and in anyone's—engaged politics. It also kept their readings of James from the attempt to catch the measure of the luxurious world he lived in and chronicled. They did not long for the world of the "Master" or dissolve the hard edges of his books where they presented problems or issues for the world. Lionel Trilling presents a different case. He read James politically, in the broadest sense, as an instance of another important critique of American moral liberalism and of easy political or moral engagement.

The James revival seems to have encouraged a stilled absorption in his genius, which became a way of saying how little else one found absorbing and stilling in the bustle of contemporary America. The seemingly apolitical and asexual nature of James's fiction, its shushing of the gender verities, and its demanding style gave its readers a kind of borrowed distinction. The image of James that wafts from even the dullest criticism has not dispelled one's sense of him as the most advanced genteel American artist, our real claim on high-culture civilization.

Dominant readings are never all wrong. James probably does protect many a civilized moment from the ravages of a blunt and hurried society. His writing requires and rewards concentration, and the better one can read, the better one can read James. His books reward education, knowledge, taste, subtlety, irony, maturity, cultivation, rereading, and even, one feels, disappointment. The self-conscious habit flourishes in reading James. He would have welcomed his growing posthumous reading public. He would have thought that the more readers Henry James had, the better America was getting to be.

There is an alternative and almost a challenge to America in James. But, inevitably, there is in his wake a kind of plush, contented manipulation of James as a cultural symbol, as shorthand for what his books require and what reading them suggests about a person. This cachet stems in part from his life and circle; he was the darling of a snobbish and self-styled superior crowd. It also comes from the books. James fashioned an alternate language for people as well as for writers, and it is as distinctive a slang as tough guys speak. Its particular virtue is that it is very different from life; it is about the moment-to-moment awareness of it. Heightened, noticing, sensitive, and protected, it calls on all the feelings that ordinary modern life abuses or invalidates or has no time for but gives them free rein in a place where they are valued as the crucial instruments of life. It privileges many of the things that American life barely tolerates and certainly has no notion or means of helping to flourish. His fiction offers a place where it is safe to indulge these intense awarenesses and feelings. The delicacy, the irony, the fineness of perception in James's writing can be the epigrammatic distinction of a safe, genteel, and even spiteful privilege. The Jamesian risks the cozy and the too literary.

Reading James might be an emblem of a too-early acceptance that life was not going to be, in Strether's sense, lived. This is how people in Woollett might have come to read James. *The Ambassadors* may be difficult, highly stylized, idiosyncratic, and ironic, but it is not complacent or unpolitical. It is about the structure of culture, its hypocrisies, and its victims. James always needs rescuing from the parlor because his truths are not the truths of which street revolutions are made. They do not serve the large categories of activism or political currency. But James is as natural a taste for the committed critic of America as for the committed student of literature.

The 1930s were not in the habit of looking at the issues James raised with the same intensity of political scrutiny that we deploy. They had Marx and Freud, fresh. They worried about the working class and the id. The politics of family, the subtle effects of class, the culture of materialism, and the issues of gender and sexual preference were not on their agenda. The Great Depression symbolized the common bonds of economic experience the critic could have with the proletariat. Today, abundance, privilege, the flourishing of the self, and the relation of American good fortune to the rest of the world do figure in intellectual life. James is a writer whose materials and whose instincts speak to the shared level of privilege, education, sensitivity, comparative leisure, and material advantage that demographically define a substantial educated American reading class. James anticipated that class, and his writing anticipated its politics and consciousness.

Being a "paleface," James was suspect within the context of American letters. He was a presumably unmanly, bloodless type on the wrong side of what American Studies defined as the basic disagreements in American culture. He was "English," not "American," Old World rather than New World, civilized rather than mythic. He either had the wrong view or had no interest in what the "American-Century" critics were defining as American issues. He was also suspect as a homosexual. Literary critics have a stake in maintaining the literary closet. The political character of the canon has to do with English professors' fear of being called "sissy" and the consequent homophobia as well as with misogyny and antidemocratic cultural politics. American literature professors have had a hard enough time with the suspect practicality and masculinity of their own work. The critical tradition preferred to worship James's obscure hurts, to elide his own preferences, to emphasize the disappointment of his message and the art of his writing. Art rewards disappointment in life.

James garnered readers, but his reputation for having no politics clung to him. And "unpolitical" meant not liberal, not Left, antidemocratic, critical of mass culture, and even more critical of reform and revolution. It is now a commonplace that injustices of the class system do not always occur along class lines, that things happen within classes and families that deserve a politics to vindicate them. People suffer from the injustices of family and gender and sexual tyrannies. Conventions tyrannize the privileged and educated in ways the old Left would not accommodate or recognize. The Left was ashamed of its own sufferings unless they occurred in the broad categories on which the revolution was to be waged.

James's perceptive understanding of the American order is not far away from readers who have experienced the hurts or frustrations of the degree to which the compromise between the ideal and the real, between art and material culture, and among high, middle, and low obtain here. The upper-middle-class American cultural orthodoxy propounds understandings of sexual, economic, aesthetic, and moral life that do not necessarily serve the inside needs of the people in whom they are inculcated. Strether's experience speaks to the feelings of dislocation from the inside out. *The Ambassadors* details the friction between convention in culture and nature in people. It is about the waylaying of human beings after their material wants are supplied. How do you liberate the prosperous or the dependent from a society that does pretty well by them? How do you begin to recognize and live with the nature of the society from within? And how does art ever stay alive in anyone but the artist, the person who devotes a life to it?

The Ambassadors is a comedy of male liberation because Strether pioneers the escape from the trap that America sets for men, from the "success" of business, or the domestic captivity of the elegant failure; human work and man's work need reconciling. He begins as a failure and ends liberated from success. The book records his piercing of the ideology that imprisons him. Woollett's ideology hinders his self-realization, so he discards it. Europe is where Strether sides with what he believes in, although he also has to see how misleading his attraction to what he believes in is. The erotic, which leads him to what he believes, is no more disinterested than the motives that lead Woollett to what it professes. Woollett claims to believe in certain high ideals. Strether's experience as Mrs. Newsome's ambassador is that she is in possession of ideals and claims a relation to the higher culture, but that her conduct on serious matters dares none of the risk those ideals entail.

Strether is not the kind of man America trusts. The erotic currents of *The Ambassadors* give his unfitness a more than intellectual or tonal explanation. He is too well-liked by women; he likes women too well. He can resist them in dangerous ways, too. Strether reverses the American male way with women. The book suggests how, deep in his nature, he may be alienated from the compelling motives that would make him play the American game. The book does not advance a claim that Strether is what America needs or that he should be running things. Chad will be better at America's work, now that he has got used to the sophistication of the world; the morning of the American century will need a more experienced brand of centurion. Strether emerges tempered in his complacency but strengthened in his ideals. But his ideals have required of him that he recognize them as a discipline, a set of unshared conventions that make him leery of material connection with the culture around him.

Plato's warning words to Crito will do for Strether: Take care, Strether, lest in agreeing to this you agree to something that you do not believe. For I am well aware that only a few people believe these things, or ever will believe them. And between those who believe and those who do not, there can be no common counsel. They can only have scorn for one another, as they see one another's resolves. Because of what Strether would have had for himself if he could, his saying he could not have anything for himself may be plausible. He still thinks he cannot have what he wants, but he has learned to value what he does have. He cannot have anything for himself, not because he is a Puritan—he has given up the sacred rage—but because he sees that having things for oneself corrupts; it is self-interest as the American mainspring, as the world understands it, that he seems to stand out against. By superior lights, there is no such thing as enlightened self-interest, as the American Tocquevillian counsels. There is only the Emersonian decision to have your own life from the inside out.

After all his mockery of the sacred rage, Strether sadly bids it farewell in Waymarsh. He recovers a dim ironic light of the sacred rage in his own heart when his eye for what makes him right assures him that he would rather not live with qualms. A good conscience is what he wants. He does not burn with the sacred rage. He has cleaned the lamp. He is not burning guilt any more. He lights it because he wants to live by light and maybe by its warmth. He has reconciled conscience with desire, made good on his ideals, and decided to live all he can according to his lights. He thinks the risk you should take is with, not against, people's inclinations. That is the good cheer in the sadness of the ending.

Strether is like William Dean Howells, after all, or Oliver Wendell Holmes, Jr., or other natural American aristocrats. They came to feel their distance from the doings and even the feelings of their country as a part of their attachment to it. The democracy became sacred to them as much because it did not follow them as because it might. It tested them and bound them in consequence. The adaptation of Puritanism to democracy is to let democracy be the conscience, to let one's knowledge of its errors go unclouded by one's allegiance to it, but to let one's allegiance to it be the principle of right that dominates in all but the direst of circumstances. It is a doctrine that satisfies conscience and loyalty. It gives one allegiance.

Henry James created in Lambert Strether an instance of the achievement of a perspective on American civilization that is not blinded by it or to it. Strether sees things for what they are. But, unlike his fellow Americanists in Paris—Miss Gostrey and Little Bilham, and unlike Henry James—his interpretive foray makes him come round to home again. His allegiance to America may be that he is too old to live somewhere else. But that is where most people find themselves when they know what is really wrong with their country. Good interpretation takes the place of innocence and youth. It recognizes that, to refuse the homeland's hypocrisy, one need not refuse the homeland. By accepting its stated ideals as your conscience, by using them as a guide in your criticism of other people and, in the last resort, in your own conscience, you can temper your inevitable feelings of alienation with a sense of duty and, perhaps, ultimately, of belonging. Strether does not talk of democracy, but his going home reads this way. The real joke about the sacred rage is on Strether. He will be burning with something like it, after all.

Henry James did go home for a visit. He wrote about what he saw in *The American Scene*, a book about his travels in the United States. It is a remarkable book in which Jamesian sensibility and prose confront American material reality. The result is a standoff; Jamesian sentences try to enclose the "scene" but finally disclose the Master's indwelling. In his fiction, that inside world of James mirrors in exciting and revealing ways an outside world it invents as it alludes to it. In this last travel book, we feel James's discomfort, his acuteness, his brilliance, but really his alienation. *The American Scene* is a success story. It justifies Henry James's choice of expatriation. But it is not a very happy book to contemplate, from the point of view of what Strether had waiting for him at home. If, that is, Strether is like Henry James and will live there as James might have. If, however, Strether is more like William James or William Dean Howells, one might look to *The Varieties of Religious Experience* or *A Hazard of New Fortunes* to imagine what Strether will experience in the United States. And that is a more cheerful prospect.

There is an obligatory quality to the admiration Americanists express for *The American Scene*. Listen to Irving Howe inventing the "ideal reader" for this book:

> He would be a man very much of the contemporary moment, yet willing to spend some months in savoring the pages of this book, two or three an evening, a half-hour at a time, without impatience, haste or anxiety. There is no story to worry about, no uncertainty as to how "it will all come out." There is no message of instant redemption which if only we heed will transform us, for a day or two, tomorrow morning. No, *The American Scene*, for all its brave recognitions of change, is a conservative book. In motivation, if not always perspective, it is often elegiac, a journey of the imagination backward in time, where all is fixed and irrevocable, beyond the blur of fashion. Toward the present James marches boldly; he grasps it, embraces it, repulses it; but always he is most deeply engaged by the memory of an earlier America.[15]

The book is Tocquevillian, a disengaged look at a country left behind, among the most attractive of such encounters. James achieved cosmopolitanism. Strether, on the other hand, rejected that cosmopolitanism, and his gesture went beyond what James himself could encompass, which is why Strether stands so tall among American heroes.

Early in his American travels, Henry James visited New Hampshire after apple-picking time. He found himself happily "in some lonely confined space, that was yet at the same time both wide and bright" and remarked the beauty of the scene, "furnished by its own good taste; its bosky ring shut it in, the two or three gaps of the old forgotten enclosure made symmetrical doors, the sweet old stones had the surface of grey velvet, and the scattered wild apples were like figures in the carpet."

> It might be an ado about trifles—and half the poetry, roundabout, the poetry in solution in the air, was doubtless but the alertness of the

touch of autumn, the imprisoned painter, the Bohemian with a rusty
jacket, who had already broken out with palette and brush; yet the way
the colour begins in those days to be dabbed, the way, here and there,
for a start, a solitary maple on a woodside flames in single scarlet, recalls nothing so much as the daughter of a noble house dressed for a
fancy-ball, with the whole family gathered round to admire her before
she goes. One speaks, at the same time, of the orchards; but there are
properly no orchards where half the countryside shows, all Septem-
ber, the easiest, most familiar sacrifice to Pomona. The apple-tree, in
New England, plays the part of the olive in Italy, charges itself with
the effect of detail, for the most part otherwise too scantly produced,
and, engaged in this charming care, becomes infinitely decorative and
delicate. . . . The apples are everywhere and every interval, every old
clearing, an orchard; they have "run-down" from neglect and shrunken
from cheapness—you pick them up from under your feet but to bite
into them, for fellowship, and throw them away; but as you catch
their young brightness in the blue air, where they suggest strings of
strange-coloured pearls tangled in the knotted boughs, as you note
their manner of swarming for a brief and wasted gaiety, they seem to
ask to be praised only by the cheerful shepherd and the oaten pipe.[16]

A few years later, Robert Frost surveyed the same scene.

After Apple-Picking

My long two-pointed ladder's sticking through a tree
Toward heaven still,
And there's a barrel that I didn't fill
Beside it, and there may be two or three
Apples I didn't pick upon some bough.
But I am done with apple-picking now.
Essence of winter sleep is on the night,
The scent of apples: I am drowsing off.
I cannot rub the strangeness from my sight
I got from looking through a pane of glass
I skimmed this morning from the drinking trough
And held against the world of hoary grass.
It melted, and I let it fall and break.

But I was well
Upon my way to sleep before it fell,
And I could tell
What form my dreaming was about to take.
Magnified apples appear and disappear,
Stem end and blossom end,
And every fleck of russet showing clear.
My instep arch not only keeps the ache,
It keeps the pressure of a ladder-round.
I feel the ladder sway as the boughs bend.
And I keep hearing from the cellar bin
The rumbling sound
Of load on load of apples coming in.
For I have had too much
Of apple-picking: I am overtired
Of the great harvest I myself desired.
There were ten thousand thousand fruit to touch,
Cherish in hand, lift down, and not let fall.
For all
That struck the earth,
No matter if not bruised or spiked with stubble,
Went surely to the cider-apple heap
As of no worth.
One can see what will trouble
This sleep of mine, whatever sleep it is.
Were he not gone,
The woodchuck could say whether it's like his
Long sleep, as I describe its coming on,
Or just some human sleep.[17]

One sets a scene the other inhabits and, perhaps, Lambert Strether ended up inhabiting what Henry James set.

Henry James felt other allegiances at the end more keenly than his American ones. But *The Ambassadors* suggests that James understood the terms on which one could live in America, little as he liked them. He saw this more clearly than Henry Adams, for instance, whom he advised to cheer up. Strether suggests that it is possible to be clear-sighted without being hateful, to love the future even though you live mostly by the flickering lights of the past. Donald Justice has taken James's visit to the United States as the occasion for a sonnet. Like the currents of feeling in the journal passage it echoes, the poem shows how James's feelings led him to envision American places he could not quite see:

Henry James at the Pacific
—Coronado Beach, California, March 1905

In a hotel room by the sea, the Master
Sits brooding on the continent he has crossed.
Not that he foresees immediate disaster,
Only a sort of freshness being lost—
Or should he go on calling it Innocence?
The sad-faced monsters of the plains are gone;
Wall Street controls the wilderness. There's an immense
Novel in all this waiting to be done,
But not, not—sadly enough—by him. His talents,
Such as they may be, want an older theme,
One rather more civilized than this, on balance.
For him now always the consoling dream
Is just the mild dear light of Lamb House falling
Beautifully down the pages of his calling.[18]

The greatness of *The Ambassadors* rests on many things. The tender generosity with which James sends Strether home to America is an especially telling, clear, and consoling message about what he understood of the democratic condition.

CHAPTER FOUR

GEORGE SANTAYANA AND THE GENTEEL TRADITION

GEORGE SANTAYANA

George Santayana made himself anything but plain in his writings. Even when he was memorably, aphoristically direct, he toyed with the contrary, the piquing, the enigmatic, the confounding. He even got in the habit of regarding his own obscurity as the emblem of his integrity, as his boast. It remains hard to get a grip on him because he meant it to be impossible to lay a glove on him.

Santayana is better remembered for what he had to say than for anything particular about him or his long life (1863–1952). He was born in Spain to Spanish parents who lived in the middle echelons of Spanish imperial life in the Philippines. Santayana's mother was the widow of a Boston scion of the Anglo/New England merchant prince Sturgis family. She left the five-year-old George with his Spanish father in Spain to return to Boston to raise George's three Sturgis half-siblings. At the age of nine, George joined her in America, where he was educated in the best Boston manner and experienced what was to be his lifelong position as an insider/outsider—welcome by virtue of his claim and his talents within the precincts of societies to which he could never feel that he really by right belonged. Santayana's salad days came as a Harvard undergraduate, where he drew, wrote poetry, discovered the study of philosophy, made warm friendships, and settled on the tone he was to take through life.

He stayed on at Harvard to study with William James, Josiah Royce, and others in that golden age of American academic philosophizing. He distinguished himself in his studies, and from his teachers in his attitude toward them. He early began to sound his characteristic note of joyous disdain of ordinary philosophical practice. He stayed on at Harvard after earning his degree, rising to the rank of professor and enjoying a great success with a particular following. The confidential report of the redoubtable, modernizing President Eliot concerning Santayana's promotion to assistant professor in 1897 suggests the problem Santayana posed to his conventional fellows, a problem he himself understood as a challenge: "The withdrawn, contemplative man who takes no part in the everyday work of the institution, or of the world, seems to me a person of very uncertain value. He does not dig ditches, or lay bricks, or write school-books, his product is not of the ordinary, useful, though humble kind. What will it be? It may be something of the highest utility; but, on the other hand, it may be something futile, or even harmful because unnatural and untimely."[1] Harvard came to value him, but Santayana's career was marked by those key terms, "unnatural and untimely." At forty-eight, having come into an inheritance, Santayana resigned his professorship and left America. He spent the next half of his life wandering in Europe and ended up living in his famous refuge with the Blue Nuns in Rome.

Santayana wrote poetry until, as he said, his muse deserted him—one senses it was his candor that deserted his muse. He wrote many books about the history of philosophy and subjects of philosophical inquiry and literary criticism. He developed and perfected, in his view, a philosophical system in several big books written over many years. He was also, memorably, an essayist, whose observations about America (*Character and Opinion in the United States* and *The Genteel Tradition in American Philosophy*), Germany (*Egotism in German Philosophy*), and England (*Soliloquies in England*) are classics of modern national observation. He even had an American literary success in the late 1930s with his novel *The Last Puritan* and finally became, with *Persons and Places*, one of the century's most interesting autobiographers. All of his books bear the unmistakable stamp of his witty, formal, and beautiful English prose and abound with his remarks, which are keenly observed and gracefully phrased, original and provocative, and truly memorable gleanings from whatever the subject at hand brought to his extraordinary mind.

In his own day, Santayana had many admirers and readers, although the assurance and insolence with which he sought his own way irritated his more earnest philosophical fellows. His contempt for their science, their systems, their care, their colleges, their schools, their politics, their logic, and their pretensions made him at best uneasily regarded by the run of them. He made sure that no one ever mistook him for one of them. He made fun of them. Having decided that difference was his natural lot, Santayana turned this to his advantage. He claimed to consider every topic outside the conventions of its regular consideration, including the conventional philosophic. At the very moment when philosophy was questioning its own sources of power and generalization—"What do we mean when we say this?"—Santayana seized with maddening confidence the very ground his fellows scrupulously abandoned. He restored the delightful to philosophy in a time when it had ceased to be something someone might want to do in the regular course of a civilized life, on a sunny day, in a beautiful place, in good company, with a light heart, confident in being the better for the pleasure of it.

Santayana preferred to live on his own, associating with friends, attractive men, talented, cultivated, curious, and wealthy people, and predominantly expatriated Americans, migrating rather than nesting. His understanding of the philosophical life borrowed from the peripatetic and the gentlemanly. He divided his time, as he did his mild allegiances, between the Latin and the northern countries. He lived most happily in Spain and Italy, but he was most absorbed by America and England—absorbed and attracted, rebuffed and rebuffing.

His sojourns and acculturation in England and New England unfitted him for life in Spain, giving him an unnatural perspective on his *patria*. The perspective that his *patria*, in turn, created for him in the lands of his adoption was critically important. He really did see things and take a tone about America, and perhaps also about England, that few have equaled. He came to America and England, to modern life, from a medieval setting in Avila, which was the backwater of an imperial backwater where his best chance at getting on would have been to join the Spanish establishment.

He saw through his father's dogmatic Enlightenment liberalism at the same time that he was prevented by his emigration and his nature from taking up the conventional Spanish life in Oedipally automatic reaction.

He was thrown from his mother's narrow perch into the commercial and cultural capital of a new imperium without being able to make its cause his own—America, after all, had won its imperial spurs from Spain while Santayana was in early middle age. He was an unconvinced Roman Catholic, nevertheless finding himself in a situation where his Spanish nativity and identity as a Catholic were always more defining of him to others than to himself. Within the life of the Sturgis clan, he was the secondary relation of poor relations. Circumstances and cool temperaments kept him at a distance within his own family. To be on the fringe, even of the center, was his fate.

Santayana spent his formative intellectual years as a foreign student in a New England that was branching out and dying out. The old New England fierceness that had made so much of American commerce and culture was being supplanted by the large energies, capitalist rather than commercial, democratic rather than genteel, that the world has come to know so well. Santayana was placed, almost uniquely, to regret ancient traditions without sentimentalizing them, to criticize modern conditions without refusing to live in them. His loyalties were diluted as well as divided, and he was alienated in one way or another from them all. He came early to a powerfully defensive insight into whatever might lay claim to him. He refused to fantasize, as did Henry Adams or Walter Pater, the substitution of some past for the present. Neither the present nor the past struck Santayana as susceptible of improvement. The laughter in his books is seldom compromised by huffiness or sentimentality, nor, it must be owned, by passion.

Santayana's upbringing holds a clue to his distinctive attitudes. *Persons and Places* recounts the origins of his cosmopolitan detachment in his odd childhood. He was alienated within his family, finding early a stubborn sense of his natural individuality as a condition of separation, isolation, and difference. Santayana's tone about his family is of a piece with his other writing. The more intimate the subject, the cooler his depiction. His portraits of his father, his mother, and his sister Susanna are remarkable for their chilly appraisal and their rendering of truly mixed emotion. One senses in *Persons and Places* the anger that fuels the detachment, energizes the accomplishment, protects the child, and distinguishes the man.

Reading Santayana, one has little sense of change or development. He was an old youngster and a youthful ancient. His letters and writings, as a young man, have sometimes the feeling of premature wisdom, beyond precocity; how could anyone so young have known what he knew? As an old man, he retained a freshness of response that survived his failing physical powers and kept him to the end fascinating to and interested in whatever there was that was new to him—which he also knew was not new under the sun. That his detachment was his protection was something he understood. That it was founded in his childhood he also knew. That it harbored his resentments, that it nurtured his hurts, that it replaced participation and avenged him on the world, he would not allow; for Santayana claimed that the world or what hurt him in it did not touch him, that it did not matter to him.

In accounting for his peculiar perspective, Santayana did not address his homosexuality. His autobiography is not coy about his attraction to men. His most recent biographer, John McCormick, concludes that Santayana was homosexual, but for sound social and personal reasons was unwilling to risk what was in his day at best a precarious preference to live. To that repression McCormick attributes the distant tone of Santayana's writing, especially his poetry:

> One conclusion about his early experience of sexual passion, whether consummated or not, is that he became frightened of the power of sexuality, and that Spanish canniness and the classical invocation to "Know Thyself" led him away from sexual luxury. By the time he composed his paragraphs on "Rational Authority" in *Dominations and Powers*, he could refer to sexual inversion, "which must tend to die out in each case, nevertheless reappears occasionally," as a custom perhaps suited to human nature because it had "not yet proved fatal to all who adopted it." His slow, steady, Epicurean withdrawal from America between roughly 1893 to 1912 . . . may indicate not coldness and distaste, but the reverse: warmth, the will to involvement which society and inner wisdom both discouraged. How else relate the worldliness, the humanity, and the sympathy of the informal Santayana to the courtly, formal, almost chilly Santayana of most of the published work? [2]

McCormick's restraint matches Santayana's own reticence and endorses his apparent sexual renunciation. But the autobiography makes clear that the matter was not so simple. Friendship—Santayana's with the men in his life—is the theme that runs throughout the book. Santayana stopped writing poetry because of what he dared not reveal. *The Last Puritan* comes alive in the clearly sexual excitement of the relation between Oliver Alden and his father's ship captain, Lord Jim. That relationship in turn moves through the range of feeling from sexual captivation to the disappointments of a frustrated, albeit unacknowledged and unconsummated, love affair to an ambivalent, sentimental friendship—present in life in Santayana's enduring relationship with the second Earl Russell, the great passion of his adult life, a story guardedly told and only somewhat revealed in the autobiography. Santayana's tone toward Howard Sturgis and the homosexual ménage and milieu at Queen's Acre reveals even more directly his own ambivalence toward homosexuality. And his several explanations for not being married and, finally, for leaving America—indeed, for his whole emotionally detached life, require this element to make their sad and interesting sense.

Santayana lived in a closet, and *Persons and Places* is a fascinating book, in part, for how elaborately he constructs for us the glass house in which he must have lived. The narrowing of emotional response, the self-protective detachment in his personal relations, and the persistent animus Santayana felt toward the worlds he inhabited and the people he met suggest that he was not so calm in renouncing his sexual nature. It is not to say that he should have chosen differently to say that reading *Persons and Places* makes one understand all too clearly why people nowadays come out of their closets. And the evidence that the world suspected something "unnatural" in Santayana, as President Eliot did, suggests the tense interplay between his desires and a world he must protect himself from, an interplay that cut deeper than his philosophizing. The cost to Santayana of this suppression of his own nature is reflected in his writing, which is so critically gripping but, when raised to the level of positive system, too often cloudy and hard to grasp. One is never sure what he is arguing for: surely not belief, surely not unbelief, surely not passion, surely not the absence of passion.

It does not disparage Santayana to see in him the genius of the closet: a life dedicated to seeing everything outside himself clearly, in order to protect what he thought would have exposed him to hounding persecution and oppression. Much of the insight one prizes in his writings comes from what must have been a necessary alertness to everything, a defensive awareness of the hypocrisy of the conventional world, of the ordinary things that posed special obstacles to him. He saw through things that, at the same time, he did not mean to disturb and made a career out of distancing, seeing them at arm's length. The perspective he affords on the conventional remains one of the chief benefits of reading Santayana. But he paid a price for this distance, and one encounters it in his refusal to trust the world. It was his host, as he liked to say, but not, apparently, his home.

What he liked about America were the athletes and the college life—the life of young men before business and family life and age compromised what he loved in them and removed them, it must be said, from his particular power over them, from their availability to him for the perhaps sexless but certainly sexual friendships he had with some of them. One senses in his fascinating descriptions of American and English men a personal attraction founded on an attraction to and revulsion from the civilizations themselves. He left Harvard and America in part because of the impossibility of joining with his students as he had with his fellow students, and also because he could neither win nor accept acceptance on the terms available to him. In a like manner, he would not settle in England. And, surely, he chose rightly. America and England must have pained him. Although they seemed to welcome him, they denied him what he desired from them. They must always be at cross-purposes with him. And his writings about both civilizations reflect his appreciative desire and his keenly felt exclusion—exclusion on the score of a difference less assimilable than foreign nationality or religion or even temperament. His detached assessment allowed him to transcend what he had to renounce, to mend his broken heart through dispassionate, superior judgment. Observing well is the best revenge.

Surely this sense of exclusion suggests an explanation for the tenor of Santayana's anti-Semitism. He criticized the ancient Hebrew traditions but blamed the cosmopolitan Jew for abandoning or compromising them. He resented with a snobbish fury the pretensions of anyone who thought they could master the tone of the ruling elite or the dominant culture. And he deployed all his own knowledge of that culture, a thorough and thoroughly ambivalent knowledge, at once aspiring and defensive, in denying such pretenders the possibility of successful assimilation. His difficult relationship with Bernard Berenson is very much to this point. Toward a Jew, Santayana could act out the condescending upper-class prejudice and its snide exclusivity. In this mean, if genteel, prejudice, Santayana might experience a feeling of belonging founded on the jealous, obsessive feeling that others shouldn't be allowed to get away with what he, so much better entitled to belonging, had to renounce. Surely they were what was wrong with the modern world. He saw himself as refusing assimilation and pretended to be in the same boat as those who attempted it. There was in all of this double reverse snobbery, displaced identification, and, alas, recognizable homophobia as well.

In discussing his own uprootedness, he writes, "But a *déraciné*, a man who has been torn up by the roots, cannot be replanted and should never propagate his kind." This is why the likes of Santayana should never marry. "I have been involuntarily uprooted. I accept the intellectual advantages of that position, with its social and moral disqualifications. And I refuse to be annexed, to be abolished, or to be grafted onto any plant of a different species."[3] On the one hand, Santayana did accept his situation, made the best and the most of it, and, indeed, let it inspire him. But his uprootedness was not susceptible of the kind of regrafting available to others because it was not cultural. It went to the core of his nature. His noble refusal to betray it and his understandable decision never fully to venture it made him resentful of those who had an opportunity denied him. If his anti-Semitism was an expression of his class and milieu, it was also the unnatural consequence of his closet.

At thirty-five, Santayana experienced what he called his "Metanoia," his life crisis. The autobiographical narrative about this in the chapter called "A Change of Heart" movingly skirts the precipice of his dilemma. It is a brilliant feat of self-understanding that, in effect, returned Santayana to his early sense of what he must give up in order to live. The almost-spoken almost gets said as he concludes about love in this line from the second sequence of his sonnets: "A perfect love is founded on despair."

> This paradox is condensed and rhetorical; to get at the truth in it we must expand it a little and ward off certain misunderstandings. It is not love simply, but only *perfect* love, that includes despair. Love in itself includes hope, or at least a desire to preserve the object of it, to enshrine and defend it. And in regard to the object even perfect love retains this solicitude. It is only in regard to the lover, as a poor human being, that hope must be cut off, plucked up by the roots, if love is ever to become pure, happy, and immortal. The *perfect* lover must renounce pursuit and the hope of possession. His person and life must, in his own eyes, fall altogether out of the picture.[4]

Santayana's closet required his absolute independence, his refusal to be re-grafted, and his equally absolute need to "fall altogether out of the picture."

Santayana's influence among philosophers has not equaled his literary reputation. He wanted readers, not students, and got them. William James, John Dewey, and Bertrand Russell, among others, acknowledged him with a wary esteem and paid him a cautious attention. He himself was always an issue in considering his system. Indeed, he anticipated the personalizing of his philosophy by his critics by insisting upon it himself. The theory of essences that capped his system is difficult to summarize. It has been more commonly understood as an adumbration of attitudes to take in the present toward the history of philosophy than as a philosophic working through of subjects and phenomena. Santayana identified most strongly with the Greeks and with Spinoza, but his allegiance even to his most admired predecessors was qualified.

He likened himself to Spinoza and, where another might "read" Spinoza and criticize him, Santayana removed the criticism from the study of Spinoza to an assertion about the world. His independence was astonishing and arrogant and remains attractive. Reading Santayana, one feels it is possible to fashion from the philosophic traditions of the West an individual philosophic apprehension of life itself. It is in definition of terms that Santayana does his little trick, or performs his little miracle, depending on your point of view. The extraordinary confidence and grace of his expression was his advantage in the game of definitional control. He moved from criticism of terms to bland assertion with an automatic shift into the highest and most poetic gear of his prose, carrying one with him or leaving one behind. Santayana used words so well that he succeeded in making his system appear to work. It was always grounded securely in his insights and took flight in the glory of his style and the appeal of his self-styling.

One is struck with his books' trenchant and perspicuous understanding of the faults and limits of the conventional and historical understandings he discusses. *Egotism in German Philosophy* devastates conventional romanticism more surely than it replaces it with Santayana's own kind of romanticism. There is nothing like the power in his own system that there is in his criticisms. He was too aware, perhaps, of too many worlds to believe in the abstractions from just one. Santayana seemed to know how difficult a place the world is, how capable of yielding pleasure but insusceptible of improvement. At twenty-four, he wrote to his friend Henry Ward Abbot, taking up Abbot's remarks about living life "from the point of view of the grave." "The point of view of the grave is not to be attained by you or me every time we happen not to want anything in particular. It is not gained except by renunciation. Pleasure must first cease to attract and pain to repel, and this, you will confess, is no easy matter. But meantime, I beg of you, let us remember that the joke of things is one at our expense. It is very funny, but it is exceedingly unpleasant."[5] Indeed, Santayana denied himself much that gave most human beings pleasure and pain.

Santayana not only refused to make a religion of religion but also refused to make one of art, philosophy, human relations, family, love, nation-state, or pleasure. He refused any thoroughgoing passion or perspective outside of his narrowed, renunciatory view. He retained an intense and beguiling responsiveness, but it was a responsiveness stripped of transforming or utopian partisanship. He had his prejudices and his tastes, his anti-Semitism, his flirtations with fascism, his selfishness and desire for comfort, and his pervasive and insistent and personal antidemocratic bias, which became the companion organizing principle with his theory of essences.

One consequence of Santayana's individuality is that his thoughts do not sound right except in his own words. He exemplified individuality but was competitive with others' individuality. *Persons and Places* thrills with his elegant fault-finding. It is as if even the people he loved in his life were fish. He separates their flesh from their bones with delicate precision, and much of the time we really see the skeleton in the fish. But this does not give us an understanding of how fish swim or live in the water. Similarly, his praise of philosophical objects is less memorable than his sharp separation of the skeleton of human error from the appealing flesh of belief and commitment. His own writing suffers from his incapacity for glorious assertion. You don't assemble a fish from its parts.

Of course, Santayana's readers would not accept this view. They make a convincing collective argument that Santayana deserves to be read and taken seriously. And he continues to attract readers who love and profit from his writing. He is the champion in the curious battle some intellectuals always wage with their own times. In such battles, the truly different are often proper heroes to the conventionally dissatisfied. However, they remain unaware of how their champions are deeply different at their own risk. Santayana inspires a kinship of attitude toward modern civilization. His own example, and his sense that modern society itself was what the inspired individual must resist, explains much of his attraction to so many of the best minds of his times and so many of its most gifted poets— including Ezra Pound, Wallace Stevens, Robert Lowell, Edmund Wilson, Lionel Trilling, Perry Miller, and Gore Vidal. Santayana was important because he really did understand the modern age; he was no stick-in-the-mud traditionalist. He read Freud, Eliot, Faulkner, and Lowell with zest and perceptiveness. He was a philosopher whose work and whose example made a place for the ancient vocations of philosophy and poetry in the unwelcoming modern world.

His resistance to the incursions of democracy seems to form the core of his appeal. Thus one does not mind his admirers' embarrassed, apologetic accounts of his anti-Semitism or his admiration for fascism because they are really saying, hoping, that one need not share those views to read and admire Santayana. The question may remain, however, of how to read Santayana without sharing his antidemocratic bias. That bias constitutes a major ground of his appeal. And what is the effect of an individuality founded on a detachment so narrowing of human choice and community? It is worth noting that Santayana got his full measure of represented experience. He understood Whitman as well as Dante. But he refused participation in life for his own special reasons, and we should be cautious in accepting his renunciation without considering its human sources, along with its philosophical justifications.

Santayana thought of himself as detached in some Greek philosophic sense from the ordinary claims of life and thus uniquely able to comment upon them, unbounded by the horizons ordinary attachments create. We may be persuaded that he was detached; but we may note with what unceasing animus his detachment proceeded and remark that the energy of his detachment is every bit as interesting as the calm he claimed for it. In its complexity, it was quite the key to his life and work that he thought it— but not necessarily to our own. Santayana is timely again. But we should recall, as his words enlist us to his cause, what that cause was. Santayana was a man of letters in this worst of worlds.

Santayana's reactions to attempts to characterize his thinking amounted to a refrain of, "No, that isn't what I mean." It stung him to be characterized as a dualist, a pragmatist, a naturalist, or to be lumped in any of the summary categories that make convenient the organization of intellectual life. He meant his work to obviate and undermine the existing categories in philosophy, perhaps with the ancillary purpose of making it impossible to label him. Santayana did not hide himself—quite the contrary—but his philosophy subverted the possibility of anyone's calling him like they saw him, although he prided himself on "calling a spade a spade," as he once actually put it. Santayana was a defensive expert on categories and the uses to which cultures put them.

In Santayana, mind is real. Much more than Henry James, Santayana privileged mental experience. He propounded an antiacademic understanding; but his was a philosophy in which the human being has no essential connection with the gods or fate or even nature, that is not apprehended, unromantically, in the sensing and knowing, rather than by the sensual or the doing. Yet Santayana felt the need to disavow even those, like the "new realists" who at least began with the key Santayanan perception. The absoluteness of Santayana's feeling for his own individuality distinguished him. Agreement and discipleship held the same danger for him as criticism, a danger that seems to have been even more threatening than attack. He expected criticism and appears to have enjoyed countering and dismissing it, playing cat-and-mouse with his critics, colleagues, and readers.

Criticism made Santayana surer of his own work because it made him, one imagines, surer of himself. He was bound and meant to incur criticism; he anticipated it and by his philosophical vocation forced it into an arena of his own choosing—and used the weapons and rules he had mastered. Agreement, friendly categorization, or alignment made him nervous, perhaps felt like annexation. Santayana generally knew where people would disagree with him and what to say in response. He had not—no one can have—an equally effective predictive grasp of what people would do to him, as he saw it, by agreeing with him. It takes daunting labor to repudiate the friendly, distorting uses to which one's words are put. In addition, Santayana's resolutions were so delicately made from contradiction—not so much cemented in place as accelerated by the rushing momentum of his own prose—that his champions could not equal his skill. Inevitably, the airborne in his arguments is the first thing to go. Since Santayana was more juggler than mason, that took a crucial toll.

One feels, reading him, that his fear was that friendly association would engulf him. His autobiography is relentless in treating his friends and enemies with equal irony and reserve, as having the same potential to do his individuality mischief. He must remind everyone, even in retrospect, of the limits of their claims on him, his feelings, his loyalties, and his good opinion. It is everybody else that Santayana's philosophy distances—everything and everybody else.

In the conclusion of his famous address on "The Genteel Tradition in American Philosophy," Santayana echoed Tocqueville's earlier feelings in the American woods. In telling a California audience how he supposed they must feel about nature, he revealed his own proud predicament:

> When you escape, as you love to do, to your forests and your Sierras, I am sure again that you do not feel you made them, or that they were made for you. They have grown, as you have grown, only more

massively and more slowly. In their non-human beauty and peace they stir the sub-human depths and the super-human possibilities of your own spirit. It is no transcendental logic that they teach; and they give no sign of any deliberate morality seated in the world. It is rather the vanity and superficiality of all logic, the needlessness of argument, the finitude of morals, the strength of time, the fertility of matter, the variety, the unspeakable variety, of possible life. Everything is measurable and conditioned, indefinitely repeated, yet in repetition, twisted somewhat from its old form. Everywhere is beauty and nowhere permanence, everywhere an incipient harmony nowhere an intention, nor a responsibility, nor a plan. . . . From what, indeed, does the society of nature liberate you, that you find it so sweet? . . . [Primeval solitudes] suspend your forced sense of your own importance not merely as individuals, but even as men. They allow you, in one happy moment, at once to play and to worship, to take yourselves simply, humbly, for what you are, and to salute the wild, indifferent, noncensorious infinity of nature. You are admonished that what you can do avails little materially, and in the end nothing. At the same time, through wonder and pleasure, you are taught speculation. You learn what you are really fitted to do, and where lie your natural dignity and joy, namely, in representing many things, without being them, and in letting your imagination, through sympathy, celebrate and echo their life. Because the peculiarity of man is that his machinery for reaction on external things has involved an imaginative transcript of these things, which is preserved and suspended in his fancy; and the interest and beauty of this inward landscape, rather than any fortunes that may await his body in the outer world, constitute his proper happiness. By their mind, its scope, quality, and temper, we estimate men, for by the mind only do we exist as men, and are more than so many storage-batteries for material energy. Let us therefore be frankly human. Let us be content to live in the mind.[6]

This surprising version of "The American Scholar," this echo of Whitman, promises an expansion founded on a shrinking. That was the famous detachment.

Where, in Santayana, book-learning leaves off and life-learning begins is hard to tell. Instinctively, from the core of his being, he felt that identification for him meant belittlement. The categorization of "George Santayana" must signify the assimilation or the execration of his specialness, which was both superior and different. His thinking exposed the categorical as reductive. Whatever the philosophy of essences fails to do, it succeeds in resisting reduction. It evaporates rather than boils down.

Santayana's hypersensitivity to the bludgeoning impact of category made him an extraordinary reader of culture. It animated and furnished his observations about America. No deep-seated loyalties hindered his seeing through to what cultures might do to individuals. Santayana did not believe in more than individual action about most things most of the time and was skeptical of even individual action. His attraction to fascism, like that of many people with like beliefs, probably reflected a latent wish to do something about what he knew about civilization. His views generally suggested to him individual withdrawal rather than class action. Santayana escaped as soon as possible both the ground of his frustration, which felt like persecution, and the temptation toward actions for which he might have been held liable.

It is a curious characteristic of the closet that it exposes one to persecution on the grounds of style, to avoid prosecution for an imputed behavior the style only somewhat represents. The style becomes the man—his vulnerability and his defense. But in Santayana's work, especially in his essays (which were in a sense agents he dispatched to secure the best terms possible for him in the world), Santayana explored some of what he had to learn about his culture to survive and, beyond that, to thrive.

Anyone's insides are an important element of how they see the world and what they do about it. The peculiar experience of a racial, gender, economic, religious, temperamental, sexual, or some other "minority" in a culture is revealing about that culture. The process by which cultures marginalize certain human aspects and set them off from others makes the term "minority" describe, especially, those who do not have access to equal power and selfhood in a society. In a democracy, the majority names and sustains itself, in part, by stigmatizing a minority. That definition fixes on some leading characteristic and an attributive assortment of secondary characteristics that stereotype the "minority" in order to justify its separation and stigmatization. It is for this reason that all American minorities at one time or another have been considered to have the same set of despised and/ or menacing demonological characteristics.[7] The mixing up of these cultural projections, the purpose of which is to protect a majority group from the genuine or characteristic traits of the particular group being defined, results in the truth and falsehoods of our cultural stereotyping. Cultures send messages that benefit some more than others and that privilege certain kinds of people, certain sorts of behavior, and certain strains of virtue. A defining element of American culture has been the systematic enforcement of white male and heterosexual privilege.

Gay and lesbian studies are presently transforming what a necessary accommodation with an oppressive system was thought to require. The perspective on the conventional world that helped keep body and soul together in the grip of oppression—the culture of survival, that is, for gays, the closet—has expanded and contracted into an active and open critique meant to support action, not to protect identity. The perspective of the closet has aspects that are unhelpful in situations of change and unfashionable in moments of high public assertion. This perspective was an unacknowledged force on American society, both in the development and the criticism of its formal culture. Because the culture made it almost impossible for the homosexual to live openly, he or she was required to learn "American" as an alien, or second, language. Coded and secret like the African American language, it was not culturally separate in the same way. It had less of its own to give away and less to return to, little independent ethnicity, and only unpredictable sharing of what there was, beyond isolated hardship, to be shared.[8]

Homosexuals had to discover that their native culture was not their own language and could not be trusted as an instrument of desire or assertion. The translation of the felt language of desire into a cultural language of love and custom was something homosexuals understood by doing without. The closet fostered interpretive skills because it necessitated using an alien language to express, to hide, to act out, to resist, to protect, and to revile one's feelings. Being a human being in the closet is like being a human being in the water. You can sink, tread water, float, swim—perhaps swim better than anyone—but water is not your native element. The best you can do is to survive an alien current with an artificial motion.

This created an almost instantly double awareness. The closet was the scene of that doubleness, the place where it was sometimes discarded, sometimes tormented, and sometimes forged into a keen, edgy perspective on the conventional life. It was the very language of American culture that the homosexual had to understand, doubly deeply, to survive. To get what they wanted, or to learn to live safely without, lesbians and gay men had to speak it convincingly, which often meant knowing how to make an impression of "straightness." Expressive activity might reward homosexual survival skills; the arenas of culture, art, and scholarship might offer the homosexual a haven.

Santayana's closet was crucial to his Americanist writings because it enabled him to go as far as he did in seeing through to the moralist heart of American intellectual convention without wishing to change it—or join it. That has always been the mystery and the attraction of Santayana's detachment—how deeply does one dare to see without wishing to take on the responsibility of changing what is seen through? It is an advantageous position for those who would claim democratic protection without wishing to extend it, and who would stay the course of liberal democracy at a certain point. Santayana's closet was a part of his insight and a clue to the extremity of his detachment, not the whole of it. His was not the only kind of closet. And his closet was only one element in the forging of his life's work.[9]

There was no single gay understanding of American culture but only the equivalent of a shared perspective from which it was variously seen. The perspective from the closet was what it was like, not merely to think, as so many artists and writers did, that one could not bear to live in America but to know, as Santayana and probably Henry James did, that one really could not. For a self-conscious, intellectually cosmopolitan, socially ambitious, and even for a closeted or sexually inactive gay man, life in America was inevitably thwarting. This might nurture the fervent commitment to change the society or to leave it, to ignore it or, paradoxically, to join it. Nevertheless, the homosexual's inside difference always made the fact of a conventionalized American culture palpable, something that required thinking about. Cultural interpretation was an indispensable homosexual survival skill, whether for the purpose of safe satisfaction of desires, self-protection, concealment, independence, accommodation, social change, expatriation, or the illusion of control. In the lesbian and gay man, self-awareness and cultural awareness were simultaneous and inextricable issues, whatever the result.

The cultural awareness that the closet helped to energize was not restricted to gay or personal issues. It was an element in a worldview. America remained inclement even for a celibate Santayana. The climate was moralistic, conventional, heterosexual, gender-oppressive, homophobic, and boring. High culture critiques of democratic culture shared the opinion that America was boring. Heterosexual and homosexual boredom are not always the same thing, although the alliance between highbrow women and closeted gay men, an enduring relationship in American genteel culture, may have some of its roots in sexual boredom and the frustration with what convention allows one to achieve in its sanctioned private arrangements. Art is meant to be more stimulating than commerce. It is one aspect of the lasting interest of his American writings that Santayana saw that the American genteel was really boring, boring as only the reverent, repressive, and sexually prudish can be. At the same time, beyond a certain point, he did not engage in what in America he recognized was not boring: business, sports, militance. He saw through too much, felt himself too much tempted and disappointed, and disdained too much.

Unlike Henry James, Santayana was neither artist nor felt American. As we have seen, James gave in art what he withheld in life, but Santayana remained angry and detached. His particular perspective had very much to do with his experience of something akin to the American artist's plight. Most of the writers who were drawn to Santayana's work could not, like him, leave America for good. The analysis strikes a deep chord in the person who feels at odds with his place and time because of Santayana's real at-oddness with his.

Santayana himself had many sources of alienation, including his remarkable individual genius. But his authenticating personal isolation dared not speak its name. Apparently, the philosopher said later to his amanuensis Daniel Cory that when he was at Harvard he must have been "what people nowadays call 'homosexual.'"[10] This retrospective half-candor explains how he felt at Harvard. It was also in a sense true. He was and clearly made the choice no longer to be homosexual. "America tried to make me a homosexual." He had to give them both up. Detachment required a different setting. Unwilling to hide his nature, unwilling fully to risk it or to risk the category to which other people might reduce it, Santayana turned away from something in himself. To the end of his days, he saw himself not in Spain but in America, at Harvard. He did not feel rejected by Spain but by America. He did not wish to punish Spain but America. In his autobiography, he gives a touchy account of his reception by English colleagues on the occasion of his visit there with an idea of settling. He took umbrage at a hint of rejection, seemed to have felt as if this would be but a repeat of his problem at Harvard, and left, never to return.

In Santayana's writing, what so moves a certain kind of person is how coolly he dispatched his terrible hurt.[11] The point is not to claim everything as a consequence of Santayana's libidinal preferences. But the powerful consequences of the pervasive, and as yet substantially unchallenged, repression of those ordinary, if unconventional, inclinations require emphasis. In Santayana's case, as in so many others, they had many happy results in his work, and some less happy. In Santayana's American writings, the closet made him a proper hero to those who needed an independent perspective on American culture.

The appeal of Santayana's analysis has had to do with its capacity to teach others how to separate themselves from an America they felt they could not endure. That is where his sexual nature comes in. It does not reduce the variety of Santayana's life and work to one aspect of his biography to point out how the homosexual might symbolize the more general situation of the artistically marooned in American culture. This cultural function was seldom acknowledged and deserves declaration. The gay endured, among other things, that firsthand deprivation within American civilization that to many artists and writers read like their own feelings of neglected identity, challenged masculinity or femininity, and isolation. The closet served the culture well: it hid its gays. Its artistic and intellectual productions gave the culturally alienated a profound secondhand experience of alienation. This experience was easier to use to identify with art and learning and the higher values of civilization than for acknowledging the self-identification of the gay or lesbian person.

The divided impulses of this situation in a man of exceptional talent and individuality describe the contradictory momentum of Santayana's thinking on most subjects, his fleet resolutions, the aesthetic trueness and the evanescence of his theory of essences, apart from what it stimulates in responsive readers. Santayana understood how willful and narrow the orthodox cultural claim about the natural always is. He differed happily from bitter nostalgists like Henry Adams. He had no patience for those whom disillusion surprised. Little stirred Santayana to irritation more dependably than categorization and the hopeful order in the universe such categories implied. He opposed both convention's grip and the delusion of change. Let him call himself what he might; he disliked it when other people called him anything at all.

The closet helps explain how Santayana knew some of what he knew. Thinking about it helps rescue some of the gallant authenticity of a critique of American civilization that loses some of its force when we take his own detached tone too seriously. There was more than payback going on; it was a facing down of the enemy that few men of letters ever dare. It is high time that what was hard for Santayana is as respected as what he made easier for his readers.

THE GENTEEL TRADITION

Santayana's observations of American civilization form a part of the American self-critical canon, in company with Tocqueville and Lord Bryce. They have influenced students of America from Van Wyck Brooks to Vernon Louis Parrington to Perry Miller, Lionel Trilling, and the American Studies movement. His happy phrase "genteel tradition" symbolizes Santayana's place as a founding Americanist. He coined it and, later, realized its worth and minted it. It remains, as Trilling said, an inescapable concept in the history of American letters and, we might add, an inevitable one as well.

Santayana's attitude toward American civilization amounted to more than his comments about it. Even after leaving Harvard, he retained his connections with the cream of the American cosmopolitan, intellectual, and artistic worlds until his death. He was a distant relation to American high culture and a magnetizing pole for a line of American writers and artists. His own status as an Americanist rests on his intimate connection with America as an alien resident, as it would have been if Tocqueville had had to make a life in Boston during thirty-five years.

Classic American literary figures question their "Americanness" to the brink of repudiation. The writer is the different one in the family. The writer is also the true American, the only child, and the rightful heir whose special difference marks the drifting of the others away from their proper heritage. And, of course, almost all the memorable American figures of letters claim both their distance and their belonging, sometimes in phases and stages, sometimes at the same time. Sometimes, like Henry James, they go abroad to assert their nativity. Sometimes, like William Faulkner, they stay home to discover their universality. But the dual relation to America, as changeling and as heir, frames the American literary career.

Santayana dwelt in that polarized field. He was not an American, and yet he was. America was his subject, his subtext, his youth, his curse. No matter where he lived, he kept American company and generally depended upon American wealth and readers and friends. And, of course, he had more scores to settle with America and Americans than with anywhere or anyone else. Santayana's American writings attracted readers because they were sharply insightful about the dilemma of American civilization as it felt to a certain sort of American. Even more than Tocqueville, but in some notably similar ways, Santayana discerned how it might feel to be a cosmopolitan, ambitiously artistic, ultimately modernist American of highly developed imagination and intellect and with the artist's or intellectual's needs. What made Santayana especially helpful was that, unlike Tocqueville, he understood that the cultural problems for the American were elaborate, orthodox, and bulkily discouraging. There were plenty of subjects, but the established institutions, he seemed to see, would not allow them. The American Tocquevillian might as easily be modernist as traditionalist. America could be faulted for its too earnest and its insufficient traditionalism, as well as for its too timid or too locomotive modernism.

Above all, Santayana's vaunted detachment from American life was the more impressive because he led so much of his life there. His residency led him to understand how his eager reader feels. Still, the aura of difference and detachment clings to Santayana. He wrapped himself in it, like the cape that attracted so much attention when he was teaching at Harvard. Not to care so much about the heartland, the American, about what America had done to one—was doing to one, might do to one—comprised the ambition to which Santayana's detachment appealed in his most important readers. It is uncanny how the authenticating grievances he had against America passed for a disinterested observation because, of course, that is what his readers needed for their own partisan feelings to seem philosophic and detached.

The American Tocquevillian must believe that what he feels about America is not about what it has done to him, but what it would do if he let it. The embarrassing grievance is translated into a much more elegant conditional sphere. The hurt that motivates his insight seeks distance, claims detachment, and visits retribution in the guise of analysis. It seeks a change in one's own estate, as if in the cause of shared Western ideals. Santayana proved especially helpful because his insights about American genteel culture and democracy shared so much grievance and were not simply native. His personal history authenticated his being of a wider world than the American world.

Santayana took the opportunity of leaving America to have his public say about it in his 1911 lecture, "The Genteel Tradition in American Philosophy." As scholars have pointed out, however, Santayana essayed the project on at least one previous occasion. His light verse, "Young Sammy's First

Wild Oats," read before the Harvard literary group, the Signet, in 1900, "represents the first version of Santayana's theory of the genteel tradition to see print." [12] It also reveals his underlying views of democracy more clearly than prudence would generally allow. That is the interest of this not very interesting literary episode.

In this poem about the Spanish-American war, Santayana tellingly directed his criticism at the anti-imperialist American intellectuals.[13] The notion came to him when he was trying to figure out his position about the imperial conflict between his two homelands. His decision not to mourn the defeat of Spain, his identification with the wild-oats-sowing of young America, and his direction of his irony toward the liberal anti-imperialists—who hoped still to keep American strength unimperial and honest in terms of its founding lights—are significant. As always, Santayana reserved his special scorn for those who had the energy of hopeful convictions—especially William James. It is no accident that Santayana's thinking about America circled around his teacher and colleague, William James. His subtle warfare with his mentor framed his quarrel with America.

"Young Sammy's First Wild Oats" recounts a conversation between old Deacon Plaster and pastor Doctor Wise. The Deacon is worried about young Sammy's (America's) carryings on, which stand for the American war with Spain, Sammy's picking up of Puerto Rico and the Philippines, and the protection of Cuba. Deacon Plaster wants moralistically to condemn young Sammy's adventures. Doctor Wise allows as how he would lie low and, "lying low and safe from harm / Shoot at poachers from the hedges / if they ventured within range / just round out my acre's edges / grow and grow, but never change." But he goes on to say that such prudent uses of full-blooded youth cannot be expected from the likes of Sammy. But the transplanting of the culture of moralism to a climate of liberty has resulted in a hot-blooded fervor that cannot be restrained with old pieties. We cannot blame Sammy but must rather blame ourselves.

> Can we blame them? Rather blame us,—
> us, who uttered idle things.
> Our false prophecies shall shame us,
> and our weak imaginings.
>
> Liberty! delicious sound!
> The world loved it, and is free.

But what's freedom? To be bound
by a chance majority.

Few are rich and many poor,
though all minds show one dull hue.
Equality we don't secure,
mediocrity we do.

The pastor then gives an early version of Santayana's views of American culture, in which energy and the finer things are at comic and destructive cross-purposes.

He's not Uncle Sam, the father,
that prim, pompous, honest man,
Yankee, or Virginian, rather:
Sammy's an American—

Lavish, clever, loud, and pushing,
loving bargains, loving strife,
Kind, rude, fearless-eyed, unblushing,
not yet settled down in life.

Send him forth; the world will mellow
his bluff youth, or nothing can.
Nature made the hearty fellow,
Life will make the gentleman.

And if Cousin Sam is callow,
it was we who did the harm,
Letting his young soul lie fallow—
the one waste spot in the farm—

Trained by sordid inventories
to scorn all he couldn't buy,
Puffed with miserable glories
Shouted at an empty sky,

Fooled with cant of a past era,

> droned 'twixt dreamy lid and lid,
> Till his God was a chimera
> and the living God was hid.[14]

Shades of, among other things, the sacred rage.

This would have made a much more amusing novel than *The Last Puritan*. The later genteel tradition argument amounts to a strategic selection from the attitudes the poem presents. The antidemocratic clarity of the stanza about mediocrity fades in the later American writings into the woodwork of the implied. The poem is rhymed Tocquevillianism. And it says things Santayana chose not to say to Americans directly, things he understandably, but certainly, withheld. He rather talked to Americans as Doctor Wise might have talked to Young Sammy, in a patronizing and avuncular vein. He sided with the energy against the morals.

In 1900 Santayana sounded interested in Sammy's good opinion, not Deacon Plaster's, protecting himself from the hot-blooded vitality he can appreciate and identify with but not join. Later, this sympathetic siding with Sammy seems sensible. Here, however, we must own that there is a positive delight in saying that the soul of this young hotblood, this version of his Harvard athlete type, is American. His delighted condescension expresses the Old World view of America as the adolescent empire whose own youth must seem unique to her, whereas it is a passing stage of the life of the national, imperial self. The American founders seriously considered this classical view of empire. They regarded their own work as having significantly altered its dictates. Santayana's refusal of the idea of America as an exception to the history of the world marks his view of the civilization.

Santayana's people manned the outposts of Spanish and American colonial and commercial enterprise. Santayana himself was part of the American empire in its first international phase since the eighteenth century, when Americans like Jefferson and Franklin were part of the enlightened empire of French reason. Santayana admits in *Persons and Places* how American, albeit expatriate, his world remained; he was a free citizen of the American world. And he developed a wonderful way of accepting American protection without accepting any serious claim on him in return. He liked living outside her borders but inside her sphere.

Santayana must have been a model for some of his admirers because he got to be in the vague scope of the American century without having to be in America at all. He knew very clearly which imperial ideologies would compete with America to dominate the world. He flirted with the fascist and hated the communist. Because he wanted the world made safe for himself, he ventured to prefer fascism to democracy when it looked as if Mussolini might be making the world safe for philosophy. But Santayana was too canny to accept from any regime more than temporary environmental haven. His writings advise thinkers to take cover where they must, to accept protection where they find it, but to accept no strings and to bite the hand that feeds them, should it try to pet them.

"Young Sammy's First Wild Oats" tried on the patronizing attitude for size. Santayana identified with the wisdom and the ways of the world in order to belittle by condescension the America he felt around him. He ridiculed the moralistic competitors to his own tutelage of the American youngster. Chafing at the notion of tutorial duty, he mocked their earnestness and exposed duty's core of superegoistic control. Oliver Alden, *The Last Puritan*, wasted away because his morals corrupted his enjoyments. It might be better for Sammy to stay put and resent offense within the borders of the nation, but that was not possible. One must not, Santayana always believed, confuse philosophy with morals.

Santayana liked young America, at a distance. His effort between 1900 and 1911, when he was ready to leave, was to find the means of living elsewhere and arriving at a view by which he might reject what he was glad to leave and find some relation to what he would miss. At Harvard, Santayana was still interested in the admiration and acquaintance of a certain kind of American youth. He was working out the attitude toward America that would make him someone whom aspiring American geniuses would always seek out—the uncle whose views of their home would help them make their own peace with it but would not make the mistake of thinking he could or even wanted to woo them away from it. He had to protect himself with a distant patronizing air toward the young he liked and whose protection and interest he continued to enjoy. He saved his venom not for their fathers but for their keepers: their professors and would-be reformers. Santayana was always drawn to those Americans in whom he recognized genius. He welcomed their company on the periphery of what he knew was a hard place for genius of his own sort to thrive. But, even in 1900, Santayana knew enough to distance himself from what attracted him in America and contented himself to praise and defend it, on occasion, in writing.

In *The Ambassadors*, Lambert Strether seems to be in a relation to Chad Newsome that resembles Santayana's to Young Sammy. That is, he takes the side of the young American against the constraining and hypocritical moralizing of the elders. He and Santayana share a sympathy with and attraction to the young, although Santayana was never so heedless or so romantic as Strether. Santayana's tone, however, differs fundamentally from Strether's. Strether learned from his feeling for Chad, experienced a wider world, and liberated himself from the narrowness and hypocrisy of the genteel tradition. Santayana freed himself of America by seeing through the genteel tradition and steering clear of involvement. Santayana patronized the young American and, having no plan of seduction, forbore trying to reform him. It is the way of the world, he said, that empires rise and fall. He had his fun with the old moralism that would impose itself on the expansive energies of America but refused involvement. His every-dog-has-his-day relativism about historical development expressed the futility of participation. There is nothing to be done about anything. By "living all you can," Strether and Santayana meant something very different, indeed.

Santayana did recognize in Henry James a fellow student of the genteel tradition. In the course of his discussion of William James, Santayana remarks:

> He and his brother Henry were as tightly swaddled in the genteel tradition as any infant geniuses could be, for they were born in Cambridge, and in a Swedenborgian household. Yet they burst those bands almost entirely. The ways in which the two brothers freed themselves, however, are interestingly different. Mr. Henry James has done it by adopting the point of view of the outer worlds, and by turning the genteel American tradition, as he turns everything else, into a subject-matter for analysis.

> For him it is a curious habit of mind, intimately comprehended, to be compared with other habits of mind, also well known to him. Thus he has overcome the genteel tradition in the classic way, by understanding it.[15]

Santayana read Henry James well. They shared ground and understanding. What attracted them in America failed to attract them to America. They shared also, if differently, the presence in their lives of Henry's older brother. By the time of the above-quoted remarks on Henry James, the genteel tradition, in Santayana's view, was not only moralistic but desiccated. But, in his youthful poem, the tradition of New England zealotry and freedom, as well as its decline, was still making the mischief. Deacon Plaster is a reductive straw man for the views of that most remarkable combination of old New England fervor and modern liberalism—William James. James would have stood in the way of American imperialism if he could. And he did stand in the way of Santayana's insistence on America's moral decline into genteel moralism.

Santayana was not coy about his troubles with William James.[16] He admired him, but James made him uncomfortable. As a student, he struck a note of condescension to James that persisted long after the senior man's death. In *Persons and Places*, the condescension read like a defense against James rather than against his philosophy. He described the conversation about the Spanish war that precipitated "Young Sammy's First Wild Oats" in the course of an account of his relations with James. James opposed imperialism, Santayana said,

because he held a false moralistic view of history, attributing events to the conscious motives and free will of individuals; whereas individuals, especially in governments, are creatures of circumstance and slaves to vested interests. These interests may be more or less noble, romantic, or sordid, but they inevitably entangle and subjugate men of action. The leaders couldn't act or maintain themselves at the head of affairs if they didn't serve the impulses at work in the mass, or in some part of it. Catastrophes come when some dominant institution, swollen like a soap-bubble and still standing without foundations, suddenly crumbles at the touch of what may seem a word or an idea, but is really some stronger material force. This force is partly that of changing circumstances, partly that of changing passions; but passions are themselves physical impulses, maturing in their season, and often epidemic, like contagious diseases. James, who was a physician and a pragmatist, might have been expected to perceive this, and did perceive it at moments; yet the over-ruling tradition in him was literary and theological, and he cried disconsolately that he had lost his country, when his country, just beginning to play its part in the history of the world, appeared to ignore an ideal that he had innocently expected would always guide it, because this ideal had been eloquently expressed in the Declaration of Independence. But the Declaration of Independence was a piece of literature, a salad of illusions. Admiration for the noble savage, for the ancient Romans (whose republic was founded on slavery and war), mixed with the quietistic maxims of the Sermon on the Mount, may inspire a Rousseau but it cannot guide a government. The American Colonies were rehearsing independence and were ready for it; that was what gave the declaration of their independence time- liness and political weight. In 1898 the United States were rehearsing domination over tropical America and were ready to organise and to legalise it; it served their commercial and military interests and their imaginative passions. Such antecedents and such facilities made inter- vention sooner or later inevitable. Domination was the implicit aim, whatever might be the language or even the thoughts of individuals. William James had not lost his country; his country was in good health and just reaching the age of puberty. He had merely lost his way in physiological history. (pp. 403–4)

Santayana concluded with the remark that James's anti-imperialism was not the result of sympathy with Santayana's homeland or with "anything in history that interests and delights me. On the contrary, it was an expression of principles entirely opposed to mine; much more so than the impulses of young, ambitious, enterprising America. These impulses may ignore or even insult all that I most prize, but they please me nevertheless for their honest enthusiasm and vitality."[17] Or so Santayana said.

This passage shows, if it is necessary to show, how shrewd and able an Americanist Santayana was. Here, before Charles Beard, was what Beard never quite had the nerve to say. But within the powerful unsentimental in- terpretation of the American founding, a wonderful passage in itself, there is something less godlike in perspective at work. Santayana's views leave two legitimate choices. On the one hand, the proper American can be vig- orous and play out the imperial or the national course. That is the way for the ordinary person, who can play the game but fails to understand what game it really is. The only other alternative is to see what Santayana sees and to detach oneself from the patriotic.

Santayana's caustic characterization of William James and the waspish insistence on their complete lack of true sympathy indicates how funda- mental was his opposition to James's view of America and, especially, to his principled attachment to the Declaration of Independence. This view vexed Santayana because he thought that James ought to have seen through all that. James's feeling of belonging to a country, his belief that one can be a participant as well as a philosopher, goaded Santayana into something like anger. Santayana despised James's engaged, unillusioned optimism. His nearly seventy years of reactions to James suggest that it was William James, above all, who was a problem for Santayana.

James believed that the horizons of American national life need not, by definition, be risen above. He took the Declaration of Independence, the notion of freedom of action, and the notion of the will as difficult but feasible guides to living in the moment. His opposition to imperialism in the context of his commitment to the democratic individualism of American regime baffled and provoked Santayana. If James was right in his Jeffersonian conviction that it was possible for the philosophic individual to participate in the American regime to specific and good effect, then Santayana's justification for his own withdrawal was not justified by more than personal reasons.

William James became for Santayana not an avatar of the genteel tradition but the natural aristocratic test case of working through the division in America between energy and culture. Santayana believed the attempt was futile. At the core of his detachment and the critique founded on it rests a fundamental conviction that what is valuable in the history of civilization is not practicable within American democracy. If the America he found uninhabitably resistant to improvement could be improved or made habitable, then Santayana was wrong, and his own situation reduced unacceptably to the merely personal.

It is one thing to leave a country because you do not like living there, and Santayana had right and reason enough for that. But the Americanist Santayana, who continues to have such a claim on American self-understanding, was not saying that. Santayana's notions of the genteel tradition asserted that nobody like Santayana could live in a place like America. He understood the likes of Santayana to stand for the artistically and philosophically gifted and inclined. To hold Santayana's view of America is to do something to the possibility of living there. Thus, in the argument with America lies Santayana's quarrel with William James.

This quarrel is cast as an argument with that class of American intellectuals, the Jeffersonian natural aristocrats, who are won to the cause of democracy despite its burdens—as opposed to the class of Tocquevillians, who are defined by their motivating disappointment with democracy's effect on civilization as they cherish it. It is the most important distinction in American intellectual life. It proposes, as Jefferson supposed it would, the persistent terms on which knowledge may gain power in America.

"The Genteel Tradition in American Philosophy" states Santayana's argument. Delivered on 25 August 1911, before the Philosophical Union at the University of California at Berkeley, the lecture was not about American philosophy but, as has often been noted, about the intellectual tradition in America. Although Santayana returned to the subject, he never surpassed this lecture. The occasion was his most dramatic public moment: elegant Harvard philosopher pauses at western extent of great nation he is about to leave to unburden himself of lifelong views of national mind. It was his "American Scholar." In occasion, in address, and in the rhetorical acrobatics, this discourse resembles Emerson's call to mental arms—resembles it and is ambitious to supplant it. Santayana's parting gift to America—as ambivalent as his feelings about his experience of it were—was a manifesto, an apple of cultural discord, a brilliant set of terms for the understanding of American civilization.

The terms have become familiar. Santayana began by saying that, no matter what anybody says, America *does* have an intellectual tradition. America always had a sophisticated philosophical habit. "The country was new, but the race was tried, chastened, and full of solemn memories. It was an old wine in new bottles; and America did not have to wait for its present universities, with their departments of academic philosophy, in order to possess a living philosophy,—to have a distinct vision of the universe and definite convictions about human destiny." America is a "young country with an old mentality," with "an old head on young shoulders. The wisdom is a little thin and verbal, not aware of its full meaning and grounds; and physical and emotional growth may be stunted by it, or even deranged." The alternative to this stunted precocity was strongly drawn. "Or when the child is too vigorous for that, he will develop a fresh mentality of his own, out of his observations and actual instincts; and this fresh mentality will interfere with the traditional mentality, and tend to reduce it to something perfunctory, conventional, and perhaps secretly despised." Who would you rather be, Ichabod Crane or Huck Finn? [18]

The curious image of the blighted precocity of the child, with his too-wise head lolling on his shoulders, contrasted with the vigor of the self-inventing youth, could stand for the difference between Santayana and William James. Certainly Santayana was a wise child, wise with ancient wisdom, precocious, and victimized as well as liberated by that precocity. Just as certainly, the energetic alternative strikes the note of William James.

But that alternative, presumably, was not what Santayana had in mind. To announce his point Santayana sounded an Emersonian chord:

> A philosophy is not genuine unless it inspires and expresses the life of those who cherish it. I do not think the hereditary philosophy of America has done much to atrophy the natural activities of the inhabitants; the wise child has not missed the joys of youth or of manhood; but what has happened is that the hereditary philosophy has grown stale, and that the academic philosophy afterwards developed has caught the stale odor from it. America is not simply, as I said a moment ago, a young country with an old mentality: it is a country with two mentalities, one a survival of the beliefs and standards of the fathers, the other an expression of the instincts, practice, and discoveries of the younger generations.[19]

It is not hard to imagine from these illuminating, elegant passages how Santayana's words might fall on American ears. They flattered an immense, self-conscious self-consequence and subtly caressed the old American conceit of being something young and new in the tired, old world. He played on the natural rebelliousness any rising generation feels toward the inherited wisdom of the fathers and, shamelessly, on the intellectual lack of self-confidence in Americans. He gave to the Californian the primacy of the frontier. And his particular formulation of the Emerson-like injunction that philosophy must express one's own life is irresistible, not least in moderating what was always scary in the Emersonian *I*.

Santayana's flattery projected intelligently what the American audience wanted to feel about itself. His charm perhaps beguiled his audience into missing the mischief-making unction of his condescension. America the boy wonder of the universe emerges a belittled, patronized figure. Santayana's bravado on this occasion may have been safe because of the academic circumstances and his imminent departure for Europe, but, nevertheless, his was a brave, insolent, funny, and daring undertaking. There was an unmistakable Socratic siding with the sons against the fathers in these passages. And, not surprisingly, Santayana proceeded to make common cause with Glaucan and Ademantan young America against the New England Thrasymachean and Polemarchean elders.

Santayana drew a famous panorama of the state of American culture:

The truth is that the one-half of the American mind, that not occupied intensely in practical affairs, has remained, I will not say high-
and-dry, but slightly becalmed; it has floated gently in the backwater,
while, alongside, in invention and industry and social organization the
other half of the mind was leaping down a sort of Niagara Rapids.
This division may be found symbolized in American architecture: a
neat reproduction of the colonial mansion—with some modern comforts introduced surreptitiously—stands beside the sky-scraper. The
American Will inhabits the sky-scraper; the American Intellect inhabits the colonial mansion. The one is the sphere of the American man;
the other, at least predominantly, of the American woman. The one is
all aggressive enterprise; the other is all genteel tradition.[20]

There is so much in this series of images, and it has had so much influence, that it deserves a moment's pause. Consider it, and then try to think
of a view of American civilization that does not seem to share in what it
articulates.

Notice Santayana's shrewd comprehension in the eternal terms of dualism. These were the terms he chose for understanding American civilization. He divided American culture between the higher and the lower, high
culture and enterprise, art and business, the masculine and the feminine,
the vital and the desiccated, the modern and the traditional, the crude
and the refined, the skyscraper and the colonial mansion. These divisions
express the essential duality that is one of the favorite shapes cultural self-
understanding among the human species takes.

As a contrast to Santayana's architectural trope to make his interpretive
point, consider Henry James's discussion of the skyscraper and its American
implication in *The American Scene*:

The reflecting surfaces, of the ironic, of the epic order, suspended in
the New York atmosphere, have yet to show symptoms of shining out,
and the monstrous phenomena themselves, meanwhile, strike me as
having, with their immense momentum, got the start, got ahead of,
in proper parlance, any possibility of poetic, of dramatic capture. That
conviction came to me most perhaps while I gazed across at the special
sky-scraper that overhangs poor old Trinity to the north—a south face
as high and wide as the mountain-wall that drops the Alpine avalanche,
from time to time, upon the village, and the village spire, at its foot; the

interest of this case being above all, as I learned, to my stupefaction, in the fact that the very creators of the extinguisher are the churchwardens themselves, or at least the trustees of the church property. What was the case but magnificent for pitiless ferocity?—that inexorable law of the growing invisibility of churches, their everywhere reduced or abolished *presence*, which is nine-tenths of their virtue, receiving thus, at such hands, its supreme consecration. This consecration was positively the greater that just then, as I have said, the vast money-making structure quite horribly, quite romantically justified itself, looming through the weather with an insolent cliff-like sublimity. The weather, for all that experience, mixes intimately with the fulness of my impression; speaking not least, for instance, of the way "the state of the streets" and the assault of the turbid air seemed all one with the look, the tramp, the whole quality and *allure*, the consummate monotonous commonness, of the pushing male crowd, moving in its dense mass—with the confusion carried to chaos for any intelligence, any perception; a welter of objects and sounds in which relief, detachment, dignity, meaning, perished utterly and lost all rights. It appeared, the muddy medium, all one with every other element and note as well, all the signs of the heaped industrial battle-field, all the sounds and silences, grim, pushing, trudging silences too, of the universal will to move—to move, move, move, as an end in itself, an appetite at any price.[21]

Santayana's dualism expresses what he and Henry James both knew about the American scene—what Henry Adams also knew—and what it felt like to know it. But it assumes a distance in order to remove the seer from the seen. It creates detachment through interpretation.

To be important, cultural distinction must be grounded in the myth-making of the persisting mysteries and divisions in human life. This truism needs repetition because so much of the appeal to the Santayanan distinction resulted from his uncanny skill in making the issues of American civilization evident in basic, mythic terms. The sophisticated and powerful reasoners who followed him with ever more comprehensive and interesting sets of terms for American self-understanding did not register that even the recognizable rendering of a national character in dualistic terms partakes of mythmaking and, indeed, risks creating the myths it would study even as it studies mythmaking. The history of American cultural interpretation

since Santayana has in some measure to seize for the native agony in Manichaean fervor that which Santayana offered in the slightly malicious irony
of worldly dualism.

Consider what we have gotten used to saying about American cultural
history, as if we were telling it in the quaint or exotic language of the mystic,
the soothsayer, or the sage:

> In American culture in the late nineteenth century, there was a parting
> of the Ways between the House of Wood and the House of Steel. The
> House of Wood lay in the Way of the Woman. It was the Old Way,
> and when the old ones were buried, their spirits haunted their daugh-
> ters who lived in the House of Wood and raised the children and took
> counsel with the priests of the ancient faith. The men were fighters
> and hunters. They left the House of Wood when they became men
> and they went the Way of the Man. They built the Houses of Steel.
> They slept with the women in the House of Wood, where they left
> their children. They spent their waking time in the House of Steel and
> left the Old Ways to their women. The Old Ways became the Way of
> the Women, for women and children and the Old priests. Sometimes
> the Women would tempt a man-child to follow the Way of the Woman
> and become a priest of the Old Way, and he would dwell with them.
> And the Men would pay for the priests and make them teach their chil-
> dren, but they would always take them, once taught, with them to the
> House of Steel and teach them the New Ways, the ways of men. And
> there began to be new priests, the priests of the Way of the Men.

But that is getting ahead of the story.

Originally, Santayana appears not to have intended the phrase "genteel
tradition" to go so sweepingly beyond the apt into the deep. He realized that it was a happy phrase and, in time, reclaimed it as his own with
special flourish. What made the phrase so apt was its precise naming; it
named something that suddenly needed naming, and in a way that could
be grasped and used. What Santayana called the genteel tradition had not
really wanted separate naming before, so pervasive had it been in American
cultural enterprise. Just as Strether and Miss Gostrey recorded a passing of
orthodoxy in their jokes about the sacred rage, so Santayana diminished
the importance of a once ruling point of American view by naming it. He
forced upon it an identity distinct from all the works and thoughts from
which it had previously been inseparable.

Santayana's imagery evokes and slants. Who would prefer the backwaters of culture to shooting the rapids of imagination? Nathaniel Hawthorne and Margaret Fuller were but two of the American literary figures to see in Niagara Falls some symbol of how the natural in America daunted the artifice of literary culture. Henry Adams brought his fictional heroine, Esther, to Niagara to deny the urgent claims of her intellectual priest-suitor. For Santayana, of course, there was no broad middle way of the Mississippi, but he did not believe what Mark Twain believed about America. The wonderful juxtaposition of colonial mansion and skyscraper loses some of its force in our time, when the superannuation of both the federal and the streamlined have a claim on the aesthetic of nostalgia. This juxtaposition remains a telling scene, even though it signifies cultural change rather than cultural predicament. Santayana's imagery dispatches the genteel tradition powerfully but perhaps unfairly. Like his shrewd assessment of the Declaration of Independence, his picturing of the old house of American tradition reduces something. Hawthorne, at least, gave his mansion seven gables and haunted it.

The genteel tradition itself, the prudish, moralizing, slackened remnant of the old Protestant Hebraized Calvinism, stands for the cultural situation of America. It is because of the shared understanding of this situation that Santayana's method was so successful. From the point of view of his preferred audience, smart and talented young Americans, he points out something they feel to be true. The artist in America famously felt an isolation from audience and centrality. Even the fact of success and centrality seldom soothes the artistic need. But America was a tough place to hoe the imaginative row. The vast democratic public had little time or taste for what the highly specialized imagination might produce in the way of entertainment. The institutionalizing, moralizing custodians of what by the late nineteenth century was as much culture as religion could promise little better.

Santayana granted the reality of the feelings of isolation and neglect that the "superior" individual may feel in a democracy. The cultural tradition claimed that relief would follow upon educating the people to a certain level, and that the artist must commit to that service of moral elevation and social control. Santayana thought otherwise. The genteel tradition counted on a constructed relation between the people and the intellectually advantaged. Advantage meant not only worldly but also moral and intellectual superiority. Feeling none of the democratic—or for that matter, the Christian—moral claim of equality, thinking himself better than almost everybody, Santayana was sensitive to the essential hypocrisy and contradictions of this construction.

The genteel tradition had neither the courage of its feelings of superiority nor the humility of its own precepts. Its compromise was thin and shallow because it did not begin to understand the energies and motives it intended to control. This avoidance was fatal to thinking and art. Santayana's "philosophy" in this context means worldview, ideology, or cultural orthodoxy. The genteel tradition is the middle-class orthodoxy emanating from New England across America. It is the perfumed parlor air one breathes in American letters and art.

The genteel tradition would suborn all "higher things" in its cause. Philosophy and art must mount the same resistance and make common cause against the license and materialism of the people and their arriviste capitalist overlords. They must resist being made "higher," since this elevation will price them out of their natural market; it will enlist them in a competing cause that serves neither truth nor beauty but wishes to use them in its own crusade for moral and social control. It will bind them to something false and barren. The genteel tradition enrages, in part, because it makes the philosophic or artistic or Santayanan claim to rise above horizons; but, as Santayana and Henry James saw, the claim to rise above was made by planting one's feet ever more firmly where one was born to stand. Rising above, for the heiresses of transcendentalism, was singularly earthbound and horizonbound. Indeed, the genteel tradition placed a new screen between the individual and reality. In expression, it mandated a soft focus. It rose above unpleasant facts, unpleasant truths, unpleasant behavior, unpleasant people—the unpleasant—as if life were not, as Santayana wrote to Henry Ward Abbott, a very unpleasant joke at best.

Santayana's lack of interest in a direct relation to the American public or nation improved him as a critic and prophet. It is usually easier to see through things that you do not happen to want and, especially, to see through things that you no longer want. The democracy might be "improved," but this meant that the price of that security in those academic, publishing, and social institutions was for the artist to become a reformer of the public taste. This would mean exhibiting those genteel qualities of taste and morals and learning that the self-constituted cultural elite thought the people required. The reading public was not seen as a public with its own needs and appetites to guide its anointing of its own heroes. The problem for the artist or the intellectual was to write books that "the preachers and the women" would approve, as if that was what the people wanted, too, because the elite knew what was best for them.[22] Writing for a mediating audience that stood between one's work and a public, the artist suffered restraints on what constituted "acceptable" art. Genteel restraints and popular taste constrained the artist from two opposite directions.

The genteel tradition added another and more painful problem to the indifference it was claimed the democracy exhibited toward the beautiful and the true. It was always possible to say that the people did not read and had no taste, that democracy had no high culture, and that the popular taste reflected sensationalist appetites. It has been equally open to the American iconoclast to become an extreme democrat or an equally extreme antidemocrat. Those extremes often keep company within the same imagination. But the genteel tradition masqueraded as civilization in a democracy, claimed to be creating a reading public out of the vast public, went through the motions of sensibility, and dominated the sanctioning institutions. The ministrations of the genteel tradition were enough to make artists long for indifference to their best work.

The genteel tradition was activist about truth and beauty and, in Santayana's shrewd view, was consequently more dangerous than the merely unaware. It was easier for great work to be vulgar than to be genteel. Gentility was as fixed in its resistance to unpleasant truth as to unseemly expression. The population at large might or might not be angry about the extremes of art but could be counted on not to notice most of the time. It was the genteel tradition that was likely to sniff out challenges to its moralistic orthodoxy.

Without in the least advancing an alternative relation to the reader or the people, Santayana outlined the artist's felt dilemma in a society in which an audience (whose likelihood was not great, but the myth of whose existence as a public was) was shielded from the writer by a class of people too frightened of the energy of the society to admit it.[23] The situation fragmented. On one hand, there was the relation between the genteel tradition and the country—one of improvement and reform, which in art opposed moralism to the nation-building passions of expansion. This was part of what Santayana disliked in William James, that a class of traditionalists dared try to suppress the energy of a young nation in the course of its natural rise and fall. Santayana's most attractive argument portrayed the American cultural situation as an artist might see it, as a choice between evils. He detached himself, glad to be rid of both; but, for the American aspirant, the appeal of Santayana's argument was the feeling he understood of facing a dilemma.

Santayana spent the bulk of his lecture talking about the causes of "this interesting situation." He attributed the great influence of the genteel tradition to a kind of debased, denatured, or liberal Calvinism. Calvinism for Santayana was by no means confined to the Genevan dispensation.

Calvinism, taken in this sense, is an expression of the agonized conscience. It is a view of the world which an agonized conscience readily embraces, if it takes itself seriously, as, being agonized, of course it must. Calvinism, essentially, asserts three things: that sin exists, that sin is punished, and that it is beautiful that sin should exist to be punished. The heart of the Calvinist is therefore divided between tragic concern at his own miserable condition, and tragic exultation about the universe at large. He oscillates between a profound abasement and a paradoxical elation of the spirit. To be a Calvinist philosophically is to feel a fierce pleasure in the existence of misery, especially of one's own, in that this misery seems to manifest the fact that the Absolute is irresponsible or infinite or holy. Human nature, it feels, is totally depraved: to have the instincts and motives that we necessarily have is a great scandal, and we must suffer for it; but that scandal is requisite, since otherwise the serious importance of being as we ought to be would not have been vindicated.[24]

Santayana followed this with a wicked account of how a people might come to believe such nonsense, how it might take root in even a deep mind. "It can take permanent possession of a deep mind here and there, and under certain conditions it can become epidemic. Imagine, for instance, a small nation with an intense vitality, but on the verge of ruin, ecstatic and distressful, having a strict and minute code of laws, that paint life in sharp and violent chiaroscuro, all pure righteousness and black abominations, and exaggerating the consequences of both perhaps to infinity." This sounded like, for instance, early New England. He then suggests how this early New England habit evolved into the American, the liberal, the genteel remnant of saving agony:

The nation was small and isolated; it lived under pressure and constant trial; it was acquainted with but a small range of goods and evils.

Vigilance over conduct and an absolute demand for personal integrity were not merely traditional things, but things that practical sages, like Franklin and Washington, recommended to their countrymen, because they were virtues that justified themselves visibly by their fruits. But soon these happy results themselves helped to relax the pressure of external circumstances, and indirectly the pressure of the agonized conscience within. The nation became numerous; it ceased to be either ecstatic or distressful; the high social morality which on the whole it preserved took another color; people remained honest and helpful out of good sense and good will rather than out of scrupulous adherence to any fixed principles. They retained their instinct for order, and often created order with surprising quickness; but the sanctity of law, to be obeyed for its own sake, began to escape them; it seemed too unpractical a notion, and not quite serious. In fact, the second and native-born American mentality began to take shape. The sense of sin totally evaporated. Nature, in the words of Emerson, was all beauty and commodity; and while operating on it laboriously, and drawing quick returns, the American began to drink in inspiration from it aesthetically. At the same time, in so broad a continent, he had elbow-room. His neighbors helped more than they hindered him; he wished their number to increase. Good-will became the great American virtue; and a passion arose for counting heads, and square miles, and cubic feet, and minutes saved—as if there had been anything to save them for. How strange to the American now that saying of Jonathan Edwards, that men are naturally God's enemies! Yet that is an axiom to any intelligent Calvinist, though the words he uses may be different. If you told the modern American that he is totally depraved, he would think you were joking, as he himself usually is. He is convinced that he always has been, and always will be, victorious and blameless.[25]

This was how Calvinism "lost its basis in American life."[26]

Some, in reaction, reverted to inner searchings and revivals, "for any of the radical points of view in philosophy may cease to be prevalent, but none can cease to be possible. Other natures, more sensitive to the moral and literary influences of the world, preferred to abandon parts of their philosophy, hoping thus to reduce the distance which should separate the remainder from real life."[27] Santayana's sketch of the history of what Perry Miller called the "New England mind" was shrewd, and his emphasis on the exchange of pietistic agony for prosperous moralism was especially so. This very bargain had established the genteel tradition.

Santayana characterized Hawthorne, Edgar Allen Poe, and Emerson as types of artistic natures "with a special sensibility or a technical genius in great straits; not being fed sufficiently by the world, [the artist] was driven in on his own resources." Without being part of the genteel tradition, they could not work through it. "They were fastidious, and under the circumstances they were starved." Emerson feasted on books, but "he read transcendentally, not historically, to learn what he himself felt, not what others might have felt before him." And the result for a philosopher or poet of "feeding on books" was "still to starve." And, in all three, the results were unhelpful:

> It was a refined labor, but it was in danger of being morbid, or tinkling, or self indulgent. It was a play of intra-mental rhymes. Their mind was like an old music-box, full of tender echoes and quaint fancies. These fancies expressed their personal genius sincerely, as dreams may; but they were arbitrary fancies in comparison with what a real observer would have said in the premises. Their manner, in a word, was subjective. In their own persons they escaped the mediocrity of the genteel tradition, but they supplied nothing to supplant it in other minds.[28]

Here, Santayana betrayed his own agenda. Not only did he offer an unconvincing reading of Hawthorne, Poe, and Emerson, but also it was a reading back into them of how they came genteelly to be read. The proper subject here was the genteel tradition, which absorbed Emerson's heroic and Hawthorne's delicate and even Poe's fantastic writings, turning them, respectively, into mottoes, fine writing, and ghost stories. To blame the writers for the defanging they suffered at the hands of the genteel tradition reversed the order of blame. But Santayana trained his sights on Emerson and transcendentalism.

Transcendentalism introduced America to the genteel tradition. The churches were tenderizing their dispensation into a liberal sentimentality. "Yet philosophic Calvinism, with a theory of life that would perfectly justify hell-fire and infant damnation if they happened to exist, still dominates the traditional metaphysics. It is an ingredient, and the decisive ingredient, in what calls itself idealism. But in order to see just what part Calvinism plays in current idealism, it will be necessary to distinguish the other chief element in that complex system, namely, transcendentalism."[29] Transcendentalism was part of romanticism, which Santayana execrated. Calling it individualism and pantheism, Tocqueville singled out the same kind of philosophical tendency in democracy that Santayana, two generations later, discerned as transcendentalist. Santayana identified it as the romantic, subjective, egoistic source of the genteel tradition and the cultural situation it signified.

Santayana regarded transcendentalism as the confusion of a method for apprehension with apprehension itself. It was a way of finding out about things but was not a system of things themselves. Like the Germans "who first gained the full transcendental insight," the Americans battened on the romantic egotism of this method, masquerading as a system, for the purpose of reducing reality to the exaggerations of the self. This also became the method of evolution. "Transcendental method, so abused, produced transcendental myth. A conscientious critique of knowledge was turned into a sham system of nature." What with the "individualistic and revolutionary temper of their youth" and their "inherited theology," the Americans grew addicted to this German brew.[30]

The Kantian influence, according to Santayana, was crucial because Kant's own project included preserving a safe speculative place for his own "genteel tradition." The genteel tradition, as Santayana described it, had implied status as a thing in itself, not just an American phenomenon. It constituted a moralistic demand made on the nature of the universe and visited upon artistic and intellectual expression as an orthodoxy. Whether in Boston or in Germany, apparently, a genteel tradition meant to insist that philosophical and aesthetic quests yield the right answers, as if to specific, answerable questions.

These answers generally conveyed the truths of right conduct and decent, conventional, "civilized" behavior. The genteel tradition fashioned the blinders that, in Santayana's view, must be put upon speculation and expression to get these answers from the universe. Nature and history do not teach the leavings of morality in Christianity, let alone the de-agonized order and man-centered moral economy so dear to the self-consequence of the classes whose higher interests the tradition would enforce. The genteel tradition privileged the vain attempt to reduce nature to a situation in which human deserts and luck correspond with, let alone confirm, right human conduct and reward. The universe makes less than common sense and amounts to more than philosophical truth.

Calvinism was a passionate, contradictory attempt to embrace both the sense and senselessness of existence. Santayana condemned it, but he acknowledged its power. The worn-down, genteel version of its already debased liberal version proved still worse. Sentimental and egotistic, it not only tried to make human sense of a world not made by human design, but also it insisted on morals without mystery, moralism without piety. It demanded that philosophy and art return the answers the moralist required. It required that the moral and natural order of the universe endorse the comfortable values of upper-middle-class American life. No wonder Santayana ridiculed the genteel tradition and resented its intellectual sway.

Individualism and egotism in German romanticism or in New England transcendentalism amounted, for Santayana, to philosophically repugnant habits. They crammed the vast truths of things, their irrelevance to the human wish or even to human life, into a small space of convenient human desires. It would only work, this transcendentalist moralism, in a very fortunate place for a very fortunate few, and then only sometimes. The genteel tradition was a heavy filter that among other things filtered out the facts of life—not just sex, but nature. It nurtured the will and the chimeras of informed action in the world, at the expense of understanding. It plundered vitality for false security.

The initial attraction of the transcendental method for the American was understandable. "It embodied, in a radical form, the spirit of Protestantism as distinguished from its inherited doctrines; it was autonomous, undismayed, calmly revolutionary; it felt that Will was deeper than Intellect; it focused everything here and now, and asked all things to show their credentials at the bar of the young self, and to prove their value for this latest born moment. These things are truly American."[31] And Emerson was their prophet.

Santayana was good to Emerson, good and condescending. His version of Emerson makes us wish he had not changed the names and invented the circumstances in *The Last Puritan*, that didactic attack on the didactic.[32] He introduces the character of Emerson indelibly, novelistically, into the history of American thought.

> The romantic spirit may imagine itself to be an absolute force, evoking and molding the plastic world to express its varying moods. But for a pioneer who is actually a world-builder this metaphysical illusion has a partial warrant in historical fact; far more warrant than it could boast of in the fixed and articulated society of Europe, among the moon-

struck rebels and the sulking poets of the romantic era. Emerson was a shrewd Yankee, by instinct on the winning side; he was a cheery, child-like soul, impervious to the evidence of evil, as of everything that it did not suit his transcendental individuality to appreciate or to notice. More, perhaps, than anybody who has ever lived, he practiced the transcendental method in all its purity. He had no system. He opened his eyes on the world every morning with a fresh sincerity, marking how things seemed to him then, or what they suggested to his spontaneous fancy. This fancy, for being spontaneous, was not always novel; it was guided by the habits and training of his mind, which were those of a preacher. Yet he never insisted on his notions so as to turn them into settled dogmas; he felt in his bones that they were myths. Sometimes, indeed, the bad example of other transcendentalists, less true than he to their method, or the pressing questions of unintelligent people, or the instinct we all have to think our ideas final, led him to the very verge of system-making; but he stopped short. Had he made a system out of his notion of compensation, or the over-soul, or spiritual laws, the result would have been as thin and forced as it is in other transcendental systems. But he coveted truth; and he returned to experience, to history, to poetry, to the natural science of his day, for new starting-points and hints toward fresh transcendental musings.[33]

Santayana's Emerson managed to attain detachment, a contemplative distance from the vortex of life. "Our dignity is not in what we do, but in what we understand. . . . On this side of his genius Emerson broke away from all conditions of age or country and represented nothing except intelligence itself."[34]

Unluckily, Emerson had the transcendentalist's reflex of seeing in nature the mirror of his own genius. "Emerson was particularly ingenious and clear-sighted in feeling the spiritual uses of fellowship with the elements."[35] The good part, in Santayana's opinion, of American taste consists in a certain capacity to be enthralled and refreshed by the landscape. This response is, he told his California audience, what they were sure to be feeling when vacationing in their Sierras. A spontaneous taste, the genteel tradition need not necessarily spoil it. Like music, love of landscape showed signs of natural vitality, after all.

Music and landscape make up the spiritual resources of those who cannot or dare not express their unfulfilled ideals in words. Serious poetry, profound religion (Calvinism, for instance) are the joys of an unhappiness that confesses itself; but when a genteel tradition forbids people to confess that they are unhappy, serious poetry and profound religion are closed to them by that; and since human life, in its depths, cannot then express itself openly, imagination is driven for comfort into abstract arts, where human circumstances are lost sight of, and human problems dissolve in a purer medium. The pressure of care is thus relieved, without its quietus being found in intelligence. To understand oneself is the classic form of consolation; to elude oneself is the romantic. In the presence of music or landscape human experience eludes itself; and thus romanticism is the bond between transcendental and naturalistic sentiment.[36]

The idealism of a genteel tradition beclouds that which, in the nature of things, human life disappoints and embitters. The genteel tradition cannot encompass "the joys of an unhappiness that confesses itself," an unhappiness too deep in the nature of human life to seek remedy, too deep for anything but consolation. The genteel tradition believes in happiness, in remedy, and in a worldview that, in Santayana's view, is inescapably mired in the muck of transcendentalist evasion. The unpleasant joke of life is an unhappy-making business. The purpose of a tradition should be to furnish consolation for most people and, for the special few, to encourage that detachment that brings the consolation of true understanding.

Happy American people should live their lives, cherish their luck, and not deprive those who need it of the consolation of higher things. Most people should be provided with a proper system of consolation. The middle classes should be left to enjoy their vitality and vulgarity. Religion should not be tampered with. Better the universal Catholic than the agonizing Protestant, but better still the orthodox than its modern dilutions. Liberalizing only confuses the temporary with the eternal. Let the world go on as it goes on. Implicit in Santayana's argument is a deep and considered resistance to the hope of reform. What reform can change is not worth changing, and it inevitably disturbs what is settled and valuable if only for being settled. This attitude is central and pervasive in Santayana's thought. Although presented as something superior, elegant, diffident, it is persistent and enforced throughout. It reflects a quietism angrier than Tocquevillian doubt.

NO WAY OUT

The fatuousness of the transcendentalist's seeing nature as the mirror of the self was produced by an American prosperity; this delusion offended Santayana and fixed his perception of American culture. The genteel tradition did mediate the tragic and the detached. Hawthorne and Melville would have agreed with Santayana about the conceit of Emersonian optimism. Santayana isolated with brilliant definition the development of an American culture that abandoned the harshness of an earlier Calvinism for a liberal religion that was distinguished by a sheltered worldliness, moralism, gentility, and, especially, by a transcendentally induced belief that the world was best reflected in genteel Americans' own relative good fortune.

Thus was the world to be encouragingly represented in politics, in society, in literature, in philosophy, and in art. Santayana considered that representation as false and corrupting. It elided the true fact of life (thereby subverting the true function of philosophy and art), which is always that the universe does not intend anybody's particular advantage. The very circumstances of American life undermine the somber truths that authenticated philosophic, religious, and artistic pursuits. The genteel tradition launched an unnatural attempt to divert American vitality and to dilute its hardest, best heritage.

What was wrong with the genteel tradition? It refused to accept a serious view of life; so did the Declaration of Independence. The regime is suspended in the animation of the possibility of a view of life that Santayana, like Tocqueville, believed to be false. This view held that the people could be enlightened and be the better for it, and that religion was not merely to be transcended by the few but might be unnecessarily limiting to the many and needed liberalizing. This view held that democracy was a good way of releasing the best in people. It regarded the trade-off between a few superior individuals and a mass of self-focused individuals as well worth making. It also preferred the hopeful notion of happiness as desire, freedom, and materialism. The American understandings were based, as Santayana said, on a notion of the self reflected by the world around one, however modified by the difficult experience of the mortal. He, on the other hand, exalted the detached view of the self in the universe. Santayana never prescribed detachment for everyone—quite the contrary—but he privileged a truth that was tied to elitism, to the assurance that great luck or talent was reason enough for the distinctions societies make. His notions were not a purely private matter. He could have enjoyed his detachment in America, but it would have been just another way of life, a harmless philosopher's eccentricity. This he could not bear: being among, not above. The United States was not congenial to him.

We may wonder if there have been any successful efforts to escape from the genteel tradition and to express behind its back something worth expressing. Santayana posed the question himself. The humorists, "of whom you here in California have had your share . . . point to what contradicts it in the facts; but not in order to abandon the genteel tradition, for they have nothing to put in its place. . . . So when Mark Twain says, 'I was born of poor but dishonest parents,' the humor depends on the parody of the genteel Anglo-Saxon convention that it is disreputable to be poor; but to hint at the hollowness of it would not be amusing if it did not remain at bottom one's habitual conviction." No, the only American writer who "has left the genteel tradition entirely behind is perhaps Walt Whitman." [37]

In his discussion of Whitman, Santayana did two important things. He reasserted his own point of view as that of a "foreigner" trying to discern the representative, and he addressed the democratic. The educated American protests against Whitman's representativeness:

> When the foreigner opens the pages of Walt Whitman, he thinks that he has come at last upon something representative and original. In Walt Whitman democracy is carried into psychology and morals. The various sights, moods, and emotions are given each one vote; they are declared to be all free and equal, and the innumerable common-place moments of life are suffered to speak like the others. Those moments formerly reputed great are not excluded, but they are made to march in the ranks with their companions,—plain foot soldiers and servants of the hour. . . . [Whitman] simply felt jovially that everything real was good enough, and that he was good enough himself. In him Bohemia rebelled against the genteel tradition; but the reconstruction that alone can justify revolution did not ensue. His attitude, in principle, was utterly disintegrating; his poetic genius fell back to the lowest level, perhaps, to which it is possible for poetic genius to fall. He reduced his imagination to a passive sensorium for the registering of impressions. No element of construction remained in it, and therefore no element of penetration. But his scope was wide; and his lazy, desul-

tory apprehension was poetical. His work, for the very reason that it is so rudimentary, contains a beginning, or rather many beginnings, that might possibly grow into a noble moral imagination, a worthy filling for the human mind. An American in the nineteenth century who completely disregarded the genteel tradition could hardly have done more.[38]

Santayana on Whitman made an interesting advance over Tocqueville on a putative democratic poetry. A curious patronizing of a great poet by a failed one, it amounted to an odd appreciation of a gay poet by a gay poet manqué. Santayana also brandished the democratic to gall the genteel. Whitman's inclusion embarrassed the genteel tradition and proved Santayana's own superior worldliness.[39]

Santayana appreciated all kinds of things that were lost on the genteel traditionalists. But, in criticizing their moralism, he did not depart from the genteel in claiming that the application of traditional standards to culture was necessary. He applied a self-described foreigner's standard because the provincial, bourgeois American standard did not understand itself or the world. His indictment made a claim for the possibility of art that rested squarely on a criticism of the conscientious American tradition. Santayana outflanked the genteel in his clear understanding of what the sources of American creative energy must be. He allowed the Americans a great future. But his critical message did not affirm the future he spied. His alternative was cultivation, detached from American narrowness and available only to a few. Is this the reconstruction that justifies revolution? Or does it merely predicate a contempt for democracy as a precondition of intelligent life?

Santayana acknowledged Whitman as the fount of democratic genius. Surely Whitman's affront to the genteel and, perhaps, his homosexual's affront to sexual convention gave Santayana pleasure. Here he was, like Henry James, willing to value and encourage what he could not bring himself to share. The genteel tradition would bowdlerize what was good in America; but it monopolized the only vantage point from which the likes of Santayana might survey so democratic and underdeveloped an expanse. The genteel molehill was a false promontory with a borrowed perspective on a live-wire, urgent reality it was too leery of shocks to touch. To be in America, you had to be in the democratic swim.

Santayana's very awareness of what was exciting in America, and his bitter disappointment in what it might offer him, informed his analysis. His real conclusion was that the genteel tradition mustered a poor substitute for expatriation, and that the detached observer might see things as clearly from Europe as from Boston—better, in fact, because less crowded by democracy. There is a passing, tantalizing suggestion that somehow cosmopolitan detachment can solve the problem one might generalize from Santayana's. But the substitution of distance and a less compromised and freer habit of traditional mind, of an unorthodox indulgence in the history of philosophy, was a lure, not a solution.

To view democracy by the lights of the ideals expressed in the Declaration of Independence, rather than from the detachment of philosophy, was William James's characteristic fault, as Santayana viewed it. James prized the Declaration more than anything Santayana held dear. Better the "impulses of young, ambitious, enterprising America" than that old high-minded American liberalism of a James. Without remembering his grudge and his leave-taking, we mistake Santayana on the genteel tradition, even mistaking his apparent siding with American energy against Philistine moralistic orthodoxies. There was never any love lost between him and the democracy, but there was love lost between him and the proprietor class of the genteel tradition. Santayana did not want to live in either mansion or skyscraper, nor was he about to lie in the grass with Walt Whitman. But was there no way in which the philosophic or artistic mind could connect with the American democratic mind to something other than Whitman's effect? This was where Santayana had to confront William James. In so doing, he revealed what yet inhabits the suave disengagement of his analysis.

Reading "The Genteel Tradition in American Philosophy" prompts a near-melodramatic suspense. Emerson unintentionally encouraged the tradition. Walt Whitman turned out to be an ambiguous savior at best. And Henry James, whose classical method of transcending through understanding shared Santayana's outer and, perhaps, his inner expatriation, offered detachment, not rescue. It is with a sigh, then, that William James is glimpsed as someone who has given "some rude shocks to this tradition" and whose Emerson-like spontaneity and ineffable vitality opened him to a primary relation to the national mind. "Convictions and ideas came to him, so to speak, from the subsoil. He had a prophetic sympathy with the dawning sentiments of the age, with the moods of the dumb majority. His scattered words caught fire in many parts of the world. His way of thinking and feeling represented the true America, and represented in a measure the whole ultra-modern, radical world. Thus he eluded the genteel tradition in the romantic way, by continuing it into its opposite."[40] William James led the genteel tradition "a merry dance." He released its component elements of religion, Americanism, and liberalism from their half-life in its gilded cage.

James took the part of the Americans the genteel tradition could no longer reach. He

> kept his mind and heart wide open to all that might seem, to polite minds, odd, personal, or visionary in religion and philosophy. He gave a sincerely respectful hearing to sentimentalists, mystics, spiritualists, wizards, cranks, quacks, and impostors—for it is hard to draw the line, and James was not willing to draw it prematurely. He thought, with his usual modesty, that any of these might have something to teach him. The lame, the halt, the blind, and those speaking with tongues could come to him with the certainty of finding sympathy; and if they were not healed, at least they were comforted, that a famous professor should take them so seriously; and they began to feel that after all to have only one leg, or one hand, or one eye, or to have three, might be in itself no less beauteous than to have just two, like the stolid majority. Thus William James became the friend and helper of those groping, nervous, half-educated, spiritually disinherited, emotionally hungry individuals of which America is full. He became, at the same time, their spokesman and representative before the learned world; and he made it a chief part of his vocation to recast what the learned world has to offer, so that as far as possible it might serve the needs and interests of these people.[41]

Here, Santayana knew his teacher and knew himself.

The James version of the Jeffersonian natural aristocrat's relation to the people mediates Monticello and Hyde Park. Despite the irony that always provided Santayana his quick exit from feeling, he offered a moving vision of William James's ministry to the troubled souls of modern democracy that overshadowed what Santayana considered its ludicrous aspects. The passage conveys the feelings that made it impossible for Santayana to live on James's terms in America and the truth that no other terms were possible for the clear-eyed. Santayana could not imagine himself ministering to those "spiritually disinherited, emotionally hungry Americans," lest he be counted among them. He least of all would be willing to be mistaken for them, while William James, like Whitman, had no fear of such a confusion.

Santayana saw James's pragmatism as having aided "the normal, practical, masculine American," too:

> Intelligence, he thought, is no miraculous, idle faculty, by which we mirror passively any or everything that happens to be true, reduplicating the real world to no purpose. Intelligence has its roots and its issue in the context of events; it is one kind of practical adjustment, an experimental act, a form of vital tension. . . . Thus all creeds and theories and all formal precepts sink in the estimation of the pragmatists to a local and temporary grammar of action; a grammar that must be changed slowly by time, and may be changed quickly by genius. To know things as a whole, or as they are eternally, if there is anything eternal in them, is not only beyond our powers, but would prove worthless, and perhaps even fatal to our lives. Ideas are not mirrors, they are weapons; their function is to prepare us to meet events, as future experience may unroll them. Those ideas that disappoint us are false ideas; those to which events are true are true themselves.[42]

This not altogether agreeable account of pragmatism verges on caricature. It does indicate where James found an audience in energetic America and, hearing its voice, caught and represented it in philosophy. Again, one sees a philosopher working well with American materials, accepting the American situation because eager to be a part of it, and feeling a part of it—not so much limited by its horizons as bound by commonality. And in the very justice Santayana does to James's accomplishment, one senses Santayana's reserve about the ultimate worth of James's thought.

The third point at which James "played havoc with the genteel tradition, while ostensibly defending it" had to do with the conception of nature and life that replaced "static harmonies, self-unfolding destinies, the logic of spirit, the spirit of logic, or any other formal method and abstract law." Life is conceived as an experienced process, not a progress toward a fixed and preemptively predetermined goal. "Observation must be continual, if our ideas are to remain true. Eternal vigilance is the price of knowledge; perpetual hazard, perpetual experiment keep quick the edge of life."[43] Santayana himself had long since developed his own arguments against James. Here, he patronized him as the best of the Americans. Taking his own place as a philosopher beyond the horizons of the national, Santayana could afford to leave the characteristic American field to James. As he said in *Persons and Places*, this surrender was the easier because he and James did not value the same things.

James was the philosopher of what Santayana could not abide. Santayana diminished the newness of America and the originality of its vision by citing the Book of Ecclesiastes. He reminded the audience that the American was but the natural effusion of the inexperienced, "for to the blinking little child it is not merely something in the world that is new daily, but everything is new all day." The effect of James, Santayana suggested, may have been to lessen somewhat the influence of the genteel tradition.

Santayana was willing to grant that James broke the spell, if not the hold, of the genteel tradition—and yet not really. The very philosophizing that he attributed to James combined a foolish democratic liberalism and a siding with energy against the old mentality. No more than any other American could James attain the maturity of wisdom that was to be found only in detachment. And the failure of detachment was James's true fault. Unlike his younger, smarter brother Henry, William accepted democracy and liberty as American horizons within which to work his wonders. As Santayana wrote in 1931 in "The Genteel Tradition at Bay," "What can a pure poet or humanist have in common with religious faction, or with a sentimental faith in liberty and democracy?" Or, what could he have to do with following the transcendentalist, Kantian path that "reduced religion to false postulates or dramatic metaphors necessary to the heroic practice of morality. But why practice folly heroically and call it duty? Because conscience bids. And why does conscience bid that? *Because society and empire require it.*" [44]

Liberalism and democracy, the available horizons, as James believed, for the intelligent person's participation within America, were out of the question for Santayana. The community James could accept and the ideals by which he could work repelled Santayana personally and philosophically. The clarity of his depiction of the genteel tradition resulted from the distance that a refusal to be engaged by America ensured him. The genteel tradition failed of the detachment required by the wisdom it pretended to. The detached observer might discern this. The genteel tradition could be opposed from within, apparently, only by the childlike, the egoist, or the romantic. The figure who opposed it by acting out his own youth was understandable. Too bad for any American who thought you could be a philosophical grown-up and still be an American.

Any seriously competing allegiance will jam the Socratic transmission. But Santayana was specific about the national allegiance he sought to undermine, making the point about America that it was in several particular ways inhospitable to truth and beauty and that the self-appointed guardians of these were very specifically to blame. His dual attack on democracy and the guardians of institutional culture made Santayana's analysis trenchant and telling for the twentieth-century American intellectual, whose problem was to escape one, and sometimes both, of those things. Twentieth-century American intellectual history shadows liberalism and modernism. Liberalism depended on engagement in an imperfect world, and modernism depended on disengagement. William James was a liberal titan. Santayana gave arguments and a kind of aid to the modernists.

Santayana's proper adversary was not the genteel tradition, which it amused him to denigrate, but the philosopher who presupposed a responsive involvement within the American horizon, representing the distressed individual and the comfortable mass of men, believing that the ideals of the Declaration should restrain wrong national action and foster right—that is, the philosopher who believed all the things that William James did. The genteel tradition, unlike William James, was apart from, without influence on, and misapprehending of the energies and impulses of America. All it could do was keep American middle-high culture to itself.

Part of Santayana's attack was strategic. It aligned with what he prized in America, subverted competing intellectual authority, and maybe paid back the hostile American intellectual and university establishment. In attacking the genteel tradition by giving American high-minded moralism a bad name, Santayana was attacking the intellectual do-gooding of his natural opponents and shrewdly creating terms in which the American would have to think for generations to come. His analysis connected being shrewd about America with despising its native democratic element, with hating both the country and its guardians. It established an understanding that allows only one who is detached not to squirm and twist in its bad company and brutal grip. Santayana had to be as rough on the genteel tradition as he was in order to keep apart from it. It was distance that his distance was meant to establish. Truth was its arguable by-product.

William James did not agree to setting himself apart. But did Santayana think James understood America as clearly as he did? It is interesting to consider in this light the alternative that the final peroration of Santayana's lecture presents. His urgent call that we be content to "live in the mind" stands in striking contrast to Lambert Strether's advice to "live all you can." Although both concede the American adolescence its metabolic due and dispute gentility in its behalf, Santayana, like Henry James, chose not to do what Strether chose to do: to live old in the country of the young. In this, however, Strether resembles William Dean Howells, from a reported remark of whose he was initially fashioned. Strether was also as close as Henry James could come to his brother William. His injunction to Little Bilham is a private adaptation of the Emersonian, not Santayana's substitute for the Emersonian.

Santayana's marvelous ear caught the Emersonian tone. Yet he was hobbled by his address. "You" is anything and everything but "me," in Santayana's language. There is no being Emerson, let alone much of an alternative to William James, without joining the "we." For all its promise, the knowledge Santayana encourages is limited. Santayana told the Californians that they felt in the presence of the natural a consciousness of the irrelevance of human hopes in the scheme of the universe; this imagined response amounted to a manipulative, antiseptic sublime. Santayana understood enough of passion to root it out of himself. He did not understand it well enough to inspire it in others. His elegy to a kind of American epicureanism falters. Unlike Emerson or Whitman or William James, the last thing he was offering was himself. Santayana traded his insight for an exit visa.

CONCLUSION

Tocquevillian interpretation is prophylactic. Democracy must be seen through in order properly to be seen and must be transcended by the intellect in order to be served by the intellectual. The American Tocquevillian sees the problem of American civilization as the consequences of the democratic for the traditional. It further posits Tocqueville-like distance as the model for an American interpretive stance. It is, perhaps, good advice to see oneself as others see one. People who always see themselves as others see them, however, encounter difficulties; and which other's view one chooses can make a fateful difference.

The paradigmatic American Tocquevillian, Henry Adams, appears to have assumed the mantle in a lifelong fit of rejection in which the condition of being unwilling to assume a relation to the democracy—to play by its rules, to do something other than be anointed by it on account of his own superiority—fueled his magnificent, intelligent, but interested writings. Adams defined both the feelings and range of the American Tocquevillian criticism of democracy. His instance also shows that its central claim of being outside and detached is not true. The place of Henry Adams, not only within but also exemplifyingly and even typically within, the American expressive range suggests how much easier it is to claim detachment than to achieve it.

The instance of Henry James suggests, among other things, how the genteel tradition, which he did not name but whose Woollett outlines he discerned, in a significant way replaced the sacred rage. The sacred rage, for all its moralism, was religiously and democratically sincere, albeit stringent and nonegalitarian. It offered the Old Testament as a conscience for the New World but scorned the treasures of the Old World. The Woollett replacement was Tocquevillian in its contempt for democracy as a civilization and conscienceless with respect to freedom of thought or personal liberty.

Its taste in literature ran to the bowdlerized and, as in so much else, folded squeamishness into hypocrisy.

What James had Strether see did not bind James himself to a course of thought or action. He knew where he belonged—and that he did not belong at home in America. James consorted with the genteel tradition, but he did not stop Strether short of challenging the genteel in the name of that old-fashioned sense of American responsibility renewed and reconstituted in Strether—an Emersonian sacred rage. It consoled his return home.

The genteel tradition represented a kind of Tocquevillian compromise that, in turn, prompted Santayana's contempt. Santayana refreshed the Tocquevillian in a way that remains with us. He recognized that American intellectual life had progressed to the point of institutional and professionalized study, and he fashioned a Tocquevillian-like view that rejected institutionalized democratic, philosophic, and artistic life. By identifying American intellectual life as just another aspect of American democratic civilization, he reminded Americans that the issue was what kind of person, artistically and philosophically, you could be in America. Santayana also insisted that the only American worth being was, as Adams came to think, one characterized by energy rather than reflection. Of course, Santayana was not really Tocquevillian; he expressed the view that any culture that you took seriously and that took you seriously interfered with the possibilities of personhood.

Democracy could not afford the room the soul needed to expand. Detachment from the culture was required. The peculiarly tense way in which American realities must have encroached on Santayana's feelings and needs precipitated his critique but does not account for it. The Tocquevillian view is authenticated as much by a particular dislike of American culture as by a theoretical critique of democratic culture.

The Tocquevillian resists the democratic precondition that democracy may not confirm one's sense of specialness or intelligence. Democracy requires that one be prepared to gamble everything all the time and to assume that what one values of truth and wisdom will survive each throw of the dice.

The American in the culture of the United States has the democratic jitters and will not hold still. It continually embarrasses, outflanks, surprises, and disappoints its would-be formalizing adherents. Little of what is perceived as the native American style can give luster and confer distinction as efficiently as the accessioning of the antique. It is also assumed that, in wisdom, as in material things, the American democratic cannot yield what is true, human, and lasting. The desire for line-drawing, for staying the course of democratic metabolism in any individual or group, is plausible and inevitable. The confusing of that desire with the transcending of democratic horizons is perilous.

The great Tocquevillian attraction is that it assumes the traditional as the proper horizon—that best and different horizon from which we can best see ourselves. The danger of seeing from within is solipsistic, self-congratulatory, democratic know-nothingism. The contrary notion that the outside is, perforce, superior may rest on the need to escape the implications of the democratic. The need to transcend democratic horizons characteristically arises in those who have exhausted the democratic's possibility to give them what they want. And one theme of what people want is the privileging of their own desires above those of other people. Democracy requires that one have a certain elemental sympathy with what other people think *they* want. American Tocquevillianism begins by dismissing this community.

Elite culture knows it is supposed to be different from mass culture, but the very nature of mass society means that to function within the culture it must take on democratic aspects. And the problem is how to resist democratic control. This is what Santayana recognized about the genteel tradition. All institutions in the culture function alike once they enter the culture. But how do you make an antidemocratic argument in democratic terms? How do you inscribe antidemocratic ambitions in democratic institutions?

There remains the problem of being "smart" in a democracy. The very fulfillment of individual intelligence and creativity, the very aiming at the Emersonian ideal, makes one's separateness from other people feel more real. The discovery of one's own individuality is, by definition, a process of differentiating oneself from the rest. The democratic dilemma has always been how to rediscover community in a way that does not oppress individuality. The claim that the American Tocquevillian really makes is that the feeling of individuality trumps the feeling of connection. It prefers to make the connection between the individual and the community that traditional civilization understood and soothed. This is possible if you believe that you are one of those individuals privileged by traditional society and that, if you adopt its wisdom, you accede to its status. This also requires that you believe that traditional society in fact accorded status to wisdom and excellence. But the key element remains that the feeling of individuality is encroached upon by the democratic claim to equality.

If "smart" also means feeling one's special personal quality, the irony of the alienated individual in a free democratic society of oppressive equals seems to be the almost definitive cultural tone for the Tocquevillian. The very thing you have to do to make yourself more individual, more philosophic, more creative, and more artistic makes you feel more isolated. The democracy opposes your distinction, and the democratic impoverishes your opportunities for individuality. Self-realization is a democratic delusion founded on a debased derivative of German idealist philosophy that serves a diminished understanding of individuality and false dictates of equality. Such appreciation as democracy offers seldom comes on acceptable terms. The comparisons democracy makes discourage and insult. And the comforts democracy offers to the highly individual are few and far between.

Look around. What an amazing, baffling, crazed culture it is. The alternative to the hierarchy of traditional art and values is terrifying and engulfing. You drive down a street and what do you see, especially if you have no blinders on? How can you focus, given the constant refocusing required by the variety of what is there to be seen? There is no organizing perspective on the world around us unless we have some organized lines of sight. There are too many people, too many apparent differences, too many stories in the naked city of democracy. There may be just too much to pay attention to for the culture, as is, to be understood. There is a loss, as Henry Adams had it, of uniformity. There is a loss of hierarchy. There is a loss of common ground and a terrible loss of perspective.

The height from which tradition enables one to see and judge has vanished. Western civilization teaches its values by creating that height; it is the shoulders of giants over which one is trained to glimpse civilization. Perspective is meant to block some things out so select other things can be seen correctly. The degree to which the mind and art are in fact what human beings have to explain, picture, order, organize, and change their world sometimes becomes irrelevant in a democracy, whose principle of equality makes individual desires abound but which seems to subvert the necessary ordering of values.

Indeed, it seems to be the case that the democracy licenses the wrong values—the material, numerical ones. Popularity is itself a standard. If "the most of the people" right now are pleased and think it makes sense, if they know they like it even though they do not in fact know much about it, then it is good and it works. Democracy presents a baffling and unsettling challenge to traditional, settled values, unless they are susceptible to discovery or adherence by most of the people right now. The moral and artistic damage that democracy does to the individual is real and deserves attention. It has given rise to much of the antidemocratic cultural conservatism in American history. American Tocquevillian solutions that create a kind of gated cultural community for the privileged—whether genteel, modernist, neoconservative, or hip—reflect the same need, after all, to distance thought and perception from the din of democratic life.

And, if detachment is problematic, what is the alternative? Is the answer a neo-Parringtonian attempt to make the good guys Jeffersonian and to make inconvenient complexity or tragedy Hamiltonian? Democracy would seem to offer no hope of escape from the American situation of frustration; that is the whole American Tocquevillian point, which is made with increasing frequency. What else is the demand that Western civilized order be restored to our common core of communication for, if not as preparation for the democracy again to privilege its intellectual betters?

This is the problem of the traditional in the democratic society: a seeing through without the support of the engines that originally licensed and applied the seeing through. The success of American democracy might almost be said to be measured by the availability to ever more of the population of some aspect of the antidemocratic critique of democracy. What a democratic sensibility needs to do is to take account not merely of the self in the culture, but also of the way the self reacts to others. The problem with the American Tocquevillian is that it tends to be as much a judgment of others as the assertion of self in relation to civilization. Its solution to living in democratic America is to create a distance from democratic others. In current literary terms, this amounts to the *othering* of the majority.

This attitude creates enough definition so that the cultural landscape and values are clear again. You learn from great books and can apply to life what you learn. The interaction between learning and living takes place in the detached, quiet place of what some American Tocquevillians like to call the soul. But judging is not experiencing. If your life is what you have, Strether may be right that it is better to understand it by living it, even if you happen to be very smart, indeed.

Morning on the freeway. Morning after morning on freeway after freeway. Everybody is driving to work. Later on, everybody will be driving home. An Americanist caught in traffic, surrounded by Americans. Feeling Tocquevillian, one notices their license plates, their bumper stickers, the false pretension of their cars. One also registers that they have cars and parses the roughshod but generally reliable democratic functioning of the rules of the road. Somehow, the traffic moves and people get to work. They merge as a mass of barely differentiated individuals. What am I doing here? It all feels oppressive. I want to go back home. The FM radio gets the classical station. Good, Mozart.

Maybe one morning the radio breaks or you notice that everyone's car is different as well as the same, or you laugh at a bumper sticker and fantasize your own personalized plate. You break through the American Tocquevillian barrier. You are present on the freeway. You are driving in your own car. You are quivering with awareness that you are one of the thousands, millions, on the road, going to work in a car on a highway in the morning, coming home from work on the highway in the evening. Your awareness of your common lot makes you forget your sense of individuality. Walt Whitman wrote to teach you how to experience your own individual joy in the endless trek and routine. Yes, you are like everyone else, you are and you feel it. You are also yourself, an individual. You need not lose yourself by becoming one of them; remember, rather, that you are one of us.

It is a bad morning. Don't kid me with that Whitman jive. I see the cars, I feel the sameness, I know the regular useless grind of the lives being led, not lived. It is a meaningless, an endless, routine, and it is like capitalism—endless, meaningless reproduction. These women and men are surrendering their precious individualities to false movements, false riches, false ambitions, and false desires. We should stay free and on our own and in the woods. This intense, hostile, beautiful, apprehension of others, and the unhappiness with my lot—making me keenly sensitive to the meaninglessness of your lot—is a Thoreau moment. It is yours to enjoy, the gift of democracy, a moment of complex, sweet self-awareness and differentiation from others. The countryside and the peace and the dream of the self alone appear in russet-colored richness against the horrifying, deadening impulse of the mass of men.

A Thoreau moment is a democratic response to democracy. Its rancor and its dream are available on equal terms to any life. You don't have to be a king to want to be alone, and you don't have to be special to feel tired and angry. But sometimes the sight of all those people in all those cars makes you want to do something. The heat and traffic and relentless demands of ordinary life inspire you with the hope of reform. Like Eleanor Roosevelt abroad in the land of the free, informing herself of the conditions that need attention and change, you realize that life must be shared to be acted on.

The cars, the sheer, proliferating, amazing efficiency of them, their very existence—and the routines of life, the acts of foresight and economy, the chains of cleverness and production, of industry and individual virtue in the homeliest sense they imply—give you Benjamin Franklin spasms. The closed, shadowed windows of a stretch limousine inspire you with a Henry Jamesian curiosity; the bumper stickers inspire a William Jamesian curiosity. The sounds can drive you wild or make you crazy. Their differences make you aware of unjust distributions of property. The beheld sameness of it all can drive you inward or outward. Sometimes you look around you at all the people in all the cars off to do their daily work, off to compass the world with their best intentions and abilities, just as you are. This is an Emersonian moment.

The most challenging and remarkable moment of all is the awareness of them all at once, the encompassing confidence that, by submitting your own intense awareness of the day— of the traffic; of what you have to do; of what you want to do; of the number and variety of people on the road; of the noise and the confusion; of the crowded, encroaching, stultifying, menacing, lurking, dire order; of the intelligence, or the stupidity, or the baffling flexibility—you will find your way. What am I listening to on my radio, what are all these others listening to, how many people are listening to how many radio stations playing how many songs (ads, opinions, news breaks)? How can such questions be asked, let alone answered? At the moment of self- or expansive concentration you have a choice. Driving on the freeway toward your destination, you can choose to see things as if you were there but not a part of it. Or, knowing that you are there, you can see yourself as a part of it. The choice to see yourself in the world around you on the freeway is the beginning of Americanist wisdom, the liberating American choice we owe to the Jeffersonian.

So, have a nice day, have a Jeffersonian day, have a democratic day!

NOTES

INTRODUCTION

1. For an account of their journey, see Pierson, *Tocqueville and Beaumont in America*. Also see Jardin, *Tocqueville*; Schleifer, *Making of Tocqueville's "Democracy in America"*; and Boesche, *Strange Liberalism of Alexis de Tocqueville*.

2. Tocqueville, along with the *philosophes* and the Marquis de Lafayette, was founder of the French interest in American civilization, but he never really showed an affectionate appreciation of the sound and throb of American life. His detachment as an observer was never really compromised by an enthusiasm for American things. It was as grist for the theoretical mill that America inspired him. If his detachment was compromised, it was by his attachment to French and aristocratic things. This ancien régime starch stiffened his detachment into reserve and even contempt for what he saw of American, as well as what he would later generalize as democratic, culture.

3. A series of Star Kist tuna television ads feature Charlie the Tuna devising various plans to demonstrate his "good taste" to the Star Kist folks so that they will catch and can him; his buddy warns him that "Star Kist don't want tuna with good taste, Charlie; Star Kist wants tuna that tastes good." A voice accompanying the inevitable rejection slip at the end of the fish hook says, "Sorry, Charlie."

4. An interesting example—and discussion—of this issue that illustrates both the kind of scheme I am making and, perhaps, just how schematic it can risk being, is in Lionel Trilling's introductory essay to the posthumous collection of Robert Warshow's cultural criticism, *Immediate Experience*: "But the principle by which Warshow worked was never to separate himself from the matter in hand, always to implicate himself in it. His criticism begins with the recognition of the human relevance of even the patently unworthy objects of his attention" (p. 20). Of course, the identifying Tocquevillian mark is the "patently unworthy," bestowed by that most attractive of American Tocquevillian voices, the Trilling first-person plural.

CHAPTER ONE

1. Tocqueville, *Democracy in America*, vol. 2, book 3, chap. 15.

2. One reason people have so much trouble with the idea of the American mind nowadays is its grating lack of specificity. What used to be called the American mind appears to much informed opinion as the white male, elitist, New England mind or at least the white male, middle-class, Protestant, heterosexual mind. Most of the classic accounts of that mind can be read, dissidently, with a sense of the power it exercised as a historical rather than a normative phenomenon. This kind of reading acknowledges its historical domination without granting its claims to continuing exclusive centrality, let alone hegemony.

3. Tocqueville had read James Fenimore Cooper. In "A Fortnight in the Wilds," he mentions his disappointment at his first sight of Native Americans: "I was full of memories of M. de Chateaubriand and of Cooper, and I had expected to find in the natives of America savages in whose features nature had left the trace of some of those proud virtues that are born of liberty" (Tocqueville, *A Journey to America*, p. 329). He did not read, however, with the idea of informing himself, to say nothing of opening himself, to the character and accomplishments of American literature.

4. "In 1840, Tocqueville thus remained uncertain about how exactly *démocratie* would influence intellectual development. In some passages he seemed to foresee the possibility, given free institutions in times of equality, of a unique cultural flowering. Elsewhere he remained pessimistic and predicted a pervasive mental stagnation. But at least he had finally faced the dilemma which he had posed years earlier. Although Tocqueville had not dismissed the possible deleterious effects of *démocratie* on cultural progress, his attitude by 1840 was different from the one expressed in earlier, more emotional drafts. Gone were his more intense fears of barbarian ascendancy and of the immediate, catastrophic collapse of civilization. After an initial delay—possibly once again caused, in part, by an unwillingness to intrude upon areas marked out by Beaumont—further thought had persuaded Tocqueville that Europe under the onslaught of advancing equality, would not go the way of Rome" (Schleifer, *Making of Tocqueville's "Democracy in America"*, p. 232).

5. "Fortnight in the Wilds," in Tocqueville, *Journey to America*, pp. 356–57.

6. Ibid.

7. Ibid., p. 333.

8. James, *Literary Criticism*, pp. 351–52.

9. It is interesting to note James Fenimore Cooper's attempt in *Home as Found* to cultivate a tone of detachment, straying, as is usual with the returning American, into a tone of declension.

10. Pierson, *Tocqueville and Beaumont in America*, p. 579.

11. Tocqueville, *Democracy in America*, vol. 2, book 2, chap. 18.

12. Most academic philosophers, except Stanley Cavell, might agree. See chap. 4, below, on George Santayana's view of Emerson.

13. "The American Scholar," in Emerson, *Essays and Lectures*.

14. Riesman, *Lonely Crowd*; Hofstadter, *Age of Reform* and *Anti-Intellectualism in American Life*; Smith, *Virgin Land*; Marx, *Machine in the Garden*. See also Pells, *Liberal Mind in a Conservative Age*, especially section 4, pp. 183–261.

15. In his remarkable study, *Lost Soul of American Politics*, Diggins has written the most searching contemporary American Tocquevillian view of American political culture. It offers an alternative and a caution to my views of subjects we share.

16. See Eisenstadt, ed., *Reconsidering Tocqueville's "Democracy in America"* and Kramer, "Tocqueville and the Polarities of Intellectual History." Meyers's *Jacksonian Persuasion* is an especially good example of the use of Tocqueville by American historians.

17. See Howe and Finn, "Richard Hofstadter"; Diggins on Hofstadter in *Lost Soul of American Politics*.

18. On Madison, see Adair, "That Politics May Be Reduced to a Science"; Diamond, *Democratic Republic*; Epstein, *Political Theory of the Federalist*; McCoy, *Last of the Fathers*. Also see Diggins, *Lost Soul of American Politics*, pp. 230–36.

19. Peterson, *Jefferson Image in the American Mind*; "The Black Cottage," in Frost, *Complete Poems*.

20. Hofstadter, *Progressive Historians*.

21. Parrington, *Main Currents in American Thought*; Curti, *Growth of American Thought*; Commager, *American Mind*; Schlesinger, Jr., *Vital Center*. Also see Dawidoff, "Commager's *The American Mind*" and "Growth of American Thought."

22. "Reality in America," in Trilling, *Liberal Imagination*, pp. 3–20; Hofstadter, *Progressive Historians*, pt. 4.

23. On the Salzburg Seminar on American Civilization, see Matthiessen, *From the Heart of Europe*; see also Stern, *F. O. Matthiessen* and Levin, *Exemplary Elders*, chap. 3.

24. Edel, *Henry James: A Life*, p. 599.

CHAPTER TWO

1. Friedrich, *City of Nets*, p. 90.

2. Letter to Charles Francis Adams, Jr., 1 May 1863, in Adams, *Letters*, 1:347–50.

3. Ibid.

4. Samuels, *Young Henry Adams*, pp. 138–40.

5. Henry Adams to Charles Francis Adams, Jr., 1 May 1863, in Adams, *Letters*, 1:347–50.

6. "Heritage of Henry Adams," in Adams, *Degradation of the Democratic Dogma*.

7. Samuels, *Young Henry Adams*, pp. 138–40.

8. Persons's *Decline of American Gentility* offers a lucid historical account of the class and cultural context of the phenomenon I call "Tocquevillian."

9. Henry Adams to Charles Francis Adams, Jr., 22 Jan. 1869, Adams, *Letters*, 2:13.

10. Henry Adams to Charles Francis Adams, Jr., 27 Jan. 1869, Adams, *Letters*, 2:14.

11. Henry Adams to John Gorham Palfrey, 19 Feb. 1869, Adams, *Letters*, 2: 18–19.

12. For Adams's teaching career, see Samuels, *Young Henry Adams*, pp 208–98; for remarks to Santayana, see McCormick, *George Santayana*, pp. 376–77; to Ezra Pound, Santayana wrote, "I don't remember my Henry Adams anecdote further than that he said history couldn't be taught" (McCormick, *George Santayana*, p. 405).

CHAPTER THREE

1. On the fin-de-siècle mind, see Lears, *No Place of Grace*; Conn, *Divided Mind*; Nuhn, *Wind Blew in from the East*.

2. On the composition of *The Ambassadors*, see Edel, *Henry James: The Master*, esp. pp. 70–79, and Matthiessen, *Henry James*.

3. It is interesting to compare Strether with Herman Melville's Benito Cereno as the next in the line of American naïfs facing the world.

4. "Realizes" here is the transcendentalist "realizes," as when Elizabeth Peabody, having walked right into a tree, explained that she "saw" it but did not "realize" it.

5. For William and Henry James on one another's writing, see Matthiessen, *James Family*, pp. 315–45.

6. On the subtexts of American generic stories, see Davis, *Homicide in American Fiction*, and Fiedler, *Love and Death in the American Novel*.

7. "Fraternalism" is one term for such male cultural bonding and "homosocial" another I like even better. See Carnes, *Secret Ritual and Manhood* and, especially, Sedgwick, *Between Men*.

8. World War II was the perfect occasion for this kind of transformation, civilizationwide. It could make one's highest ideals look murderously tough and unarguably right, but the human transformation it covered resembled Strether's.

9. Medievalism shimmered with the soft-focus pornographic allure so characteristic of the age and of genteel culture. The willed innocence of its own desires suggests the hypocrisy of American middle-class genteel culture. Its idealism, located,

as Santayana suggested, in its genteel tradition, symbolized its false removal from the real.

10. On the James-Andersen friendship, see Edel, *Henry James: The Master* and Edel, *Henry James: The Treacherous Years*, pp. 306–16.

11. One source for the novel was a remark by William Dean Howells to Jonathan Sturges in Whistler's Parisian garden that, really, one "should live all one can." This remark was repeated to James, in whose imagination it grew. See Edel, *Henry James: The Master*. See also James, *Notebooks*, pp. 225–29, 370–415; Matthiessen, *James Family*, pp. 511–12.

12. James, *Letters*, 2:244–46.

13. It is fun to think of *The Ambassadors* and *The Sun Also Rises* at the same time, American men and some women in Paris . . .

14. See Kazin, *On Native Grounds*, and Aaron, *Writers on the Left*.

15. Howe, "Introduction," in James, *American Scene*.

16. James, *American Scene*, pp. 16–17.

17. "After Apple-Picking," in Frost, *Complete Poems*, pp. 88–89.

18. Justice, *Sunset Maker*.

CHAPTER FOUR

1. Quoted in McCormick, *George Santayana*, p. 97.

2. Ibid., p. 52.

3. Santayana, *Persons and Places*, pp. 362–63. See also Samuels, *Bernard Berenson: The Making of a Connoisseur* and Samuels, *Bernard Berenson: The Making of a Legend*, pp. 226–27, 457–58.

4. Santayana, *Persons and Places*, p. 428.

5. Letter of 16 Jan. 1887, in Santayana, *Letters*, pp. 14–15.

6. "Genteel Tradition in American Philosophy," in Santayana, *Genteel Tradition: Nine Essays*, pp. 62–64.

7. "Some Themes of Countersubversion" and "Ideological Function of Prejudice," in Davis, *From Homicide to Slavery*; Hofstadter, *Paranoid Style in American Politics*; Arendt, *Jew as Pariah*.

8. See Sedgwick, *Epistemology of the Closet*; Dawidoff, "In My Father's House Are Many Closets."

9. The use of "homosexual" and "gay" and "closet" is meant to suggest the importance of lesbian women and gay men in American cultural history. But this discussion does not mean to engross the subject generally, even in discussing ways in which Santayana's closet might bear on general issues of interpretation. I am aware of talking about issues shared and not shared by lesbians and gay men and do

not subsume women when I am talking about one particular man. There are generational overtones. Gertrude Stein, for instance, provides an interesting comparison
with Santayana. Some patterns apply beyond the particular case of Santayana and,
indeed, across gender lines.

10. McCormick tells this story: according to Santayana's confidant, Daniel Cory,
the philosopher remarked to him in 1929 regarding A. E. Housman's poetry, "I sup-
pose Housman was really what people nowadays call 'homosexual.'" He went on to
say, "as if he were primarily speaking of himself: 'I think I must have been that way
in my Harvard days—although I was unconscious of it at the time'" (McCormick,
George Santayana, p. 51).

11. See Wilson, "Roman Diary"; "That Smile of Parmenides Made Me Think,"
in Trilling, *Gathering of Fugitives*.

12. Douglas Wilson in headnote to the poem, in Santayana, *Genteel Tradition:
Nine Essays*, p. 26.

13. See Wilson, "Roman Diary"; Lynn, *Airline to Seattle*, pp. 1–8. Lynn's title
essay is especially acute.

14. Santayana, *Genteel Tradition: Nine Essays*, pp. 26–36.

15. "Genteel Tradition in American Philosophy," in Santayana, *Genteel Tradition:
Nine Essays*, p. 54.

16. On the relationship between James and Santayana, see McCormick, *George
Santayana*, and Kuklick, *Rise of American Philosophy*.

17. Santayana, *Persons and Places*, pp. 404–5.

18. "Genteel Tradition in American Philosophy," in Santayana, *Genteel Tradition:
Nine Essays*, pp. 38–39.

19. Ibid., p. 39.

20. Ibid., pp. 39–40.

21. James, *American Scene*, pp. 83–84.

22. For observations about the climate of American reading, see Brown, *Knowledge Is Power*; Gilmore, *Reading Becomes a Necessity of Life*; Davidson, ed., *Reading
in America*.

23. See Hofstadter, *Anti-Intellectualism in American Life*, and Ziff, *Literary Democracy*.

24. "Genteel Tradition in American Philosophy," in Santayana, *Genteel Tradition:
Nine Essays*, p. 41.

25. Ibid., pp. 42–43.

26. Ibid., p. 43.

27. Ibid.

28. Ibid., p. 44.

29. Ibid.

30. Ibid., p. 46.

31. Ibid., p. 47.

32. For a discussion of Emerson in *Last Puritan*, see Porte, *Representative Man*, pp. 32–46. Santayana's writings on Emerson include "Optimism of Ralph Waldo Emerson" and "Emerson's Poems," both in Santayana, *George Santayana's America*, and "Emerson," in Santayana, *Selected Critical Writings*. See also Santayana, *Character and Opinion in the United States*.

33. "Genteel Tradition in American Philosophy," in Santayana, *Genteel Tradition: Nine Essays*, pp. 47–48.

34. Ibid., p. 50.

35. Ibid.

36. Ibid., p. 51.

37. Ibid., pp. 51–52.

38. Ibid., p. 53.

39. For more of Santayana on Whitman, see "Walt Whitman: A Dialogue," in Santayana, *George Santayana's America*, and "The Poetry of Barbarism," in Santayana, *Interpretations of Poetry and Religion*.

40. "Genteel Tradition in American Philosophy," in Santayana, *Genteel Tradition: Nine Essays*, p. 54.

41. Ibid., p. 55.

42. Ibid., pp. 56–57.

43. Ibid., pp. 57–58.

44. Santayana, *Genteel Tradition at Bay*, pp. 158, 159–60.

BIBLIOGRAPHY

Where possible, I have cited the Library of America editions.

Aaron, Daniel. *Writers on the Left: Episodes in American Literary Communism*. 1961. Reprint. New York: Octagon Books, 1979.

Adair, Douglass. "That Politics May Be Reduced to a Science: David Hume, James Madison and the Tenth Federalist." *Huntington Library Quarterly* 20 (1957): 343–60.

Adams, Henry. *The Degradation of the Democratic Dogma*. Introduction by Brooks Adams. New York: Macmillan, 1920.

———. *Democracy*. New York: Library of America, 1983.

———. *The Education of Henry Adams*. New York: Library of America, 1983.

———. *History of the United States during the Administrations of Thomas Jefferson and James Madison*. 2 vols. New York: Library of America, 1986.

———. *The Letters of Henry Adams*. 3 vols. Edited by J.C. Levenson, Ernest Samuels, Charles Vandersee, and Viola Hopkins Winner. Cambridge: Harvard University Press, 1982.

Arendt, Hannah. *The Jew as Pariah: Jewish Identity and Politics in the Modern Age*. Edited by Ron H. Feldman. New York: Grove Press, 1978.

Boesche, Roger. *The Strange Liberalism of Alexis de Tocqueville*. Ithaca, N.Y.: Cornell University Press, 1987.

Brown, Richard D. *Knowledge Is Power: The Diffusion of Information in Early America, 1700–1865*. New York: Oxford University Press, 1989.

Carnes, Mark C. *Secret Ritual and Manhood in Victorian America*. New Haven: Yale University Press, 1989.

Commager, Henry Steele. *The American Mind*. New Haven: Yale University Press, 1950.

Conn, Peter. *The Divided Mind: Ideology and Imagination in America, 1898–1917*. New York: Cambridge University Press, 1983.

Curti, Merle. *The Growth of American Thought*. New York: Harper and Brothers, 1943.

Davidson, Cathy, ed. *Reading in America: Literature and Social History*. Baltimore: Johns Hopkins University Press, 1988.

Davis, David Brion. *From Homicide to Slavery*. New York: Oxford University Press, 1987.

———. *Homicide in American Fiction*. Ithaca, N.Y.: Cornell University Press, 1956.

Dawidoff, Robert. "Commager's *The American Mind*: A Reconsideration." *Reviews in American History* 12 (1984): 449–63.

———. "The Growth of American Thought: A Reconsideration." *Reviews in American History* 14 (1986): 474–86.

———. "In My Father's House Are Many Closets." *Christopher Street* 12, no. 2 (1989): 28–41.

Diamond, Martin. *The Democratic Republic*. Chicago: Rand McNally, 1970.

Diggins, John P. *The Lost Soul of American Politics: Virtue, Self-Interest and the Foundations of Liberalism*. New York: Basic Books, 1984.

Edel, Leon. *Henry James: A Life*. New York: Harper and Row, 1985.

———. *Henry James: The Master, 1901–1916*. Philadelphia: J. B. Lippincott, 1972.

———. *Henry James: The Treacherous Years, 1895–1901*. Philadelphia: J. B. Lippincott, 1969.

Eisenstadt, Abraham S., ed. *Reconsidering Tocqueville's "Democracy in America"*. New Brunswick, N.J.: Rutgers University Press, 1988.

Emerson, Ralph Waldo. *Essays and Lectures*. New York: Library of America, 1983.

Epstein, David F. *The Political Theory of the Federalist*. Chicago: University of Chicago Press, 1984.

Fiedler, Leslie. *Love and Death in the American Novel*. New York: Criterion, 1960.

Friedrich, Otto. *City of Nets*. New York: Harper and Row, 1986.

Frost, Robert. *Complete Poems of Robert Frost*. New York: Holt, Rinehart and Winston, 1949.

Gilmore, William J. *Reading Becomes a Necessity of Life*. Knoxville: University of Tennessee Press, 1989.

Hofstadter, Richard. *The Age of Reform*. New York: Knopf, 1955.

———. *Anti-Intellectualism in American Life*. New York: Knopf, 1962.

———. *The Paranoid Style in American Politics and Other Essays*. 1964. Reprint. Chicago: University of Chicago Press, 1979.

———. *The Progressive Historians*. New York: Knopf, 1968.

Howe, Daniel Walker, and Peter Elliott Finn. "Richard Hofstadter: The Ironies of an American Historian." *Pacific Historical Review* 43 (1974): 1–23.

James, Henry. *The Ambassadors*. London: Bodley Head, 1970.

———. *The American Scene*. Introduction by Irving Howe. New York: Horizon Press, 1967.

———. *The Bostonians*. New York: Library of America, 1985.

———. *The Europeans*. New York: Library of America, 1983.

———. *The Letters of Henry James*. Edited by Percy Lubbock. New York: Scribner's, 1920.

————. *Literary Criticism: Essays on Literature, American Writers, English Writers.* Edited by Leon Edel. New York: Library of America, 1984.

————. *The Notebooks of Henry James.* Edited by F. O. Matthiessen and Kenneth B. Murdock. Chicago: University of Chicago Press, 1981.

Jardin, André. *Tocqueville: A Biography.* New York: Farrar, Straus and Giroux, 1988.

Justice, Donald. *The Sunset Maker.* New York: Atheneum, 1987.

Kazin, Alfred. *On Native Grounds.* New York: Harcourt Brace Jovanovich, 1982.

Kramer, Lloyd S. "Tocqueville and the Polarities of Intellectual History." *Intellectual History Newsletter* 11 (June 1989).

Kuklick, Bruce. *The Rise of American Philosophy.* New Haven: Yale University Press, 1977.

Lears, T. J. Jackson. *No Place of Grace: Antimodernism and the Transformation of American Culture, 1880–1920.* New York: Pantheon, 1981.

Levin, David. *Exemplary Elders.* Athens: University of Georgia Press, 1990.

Lynn, Kenneth. *The Airline to Seattle: Studies in Literary and Historical Writing about America.* Chicago: University of Chicago Press, 1983.

McCormick, John. *George Santayana: A Biography.* New York: Knopf, 1986.

McCoy, Drew. *The Last of the Fathers: James Madison and the Republican Legacy.* New York: Cambridge University Press, 1989.

Marx, Leo. *The Machine in the Garden.* New York: Oxford University Press, 1964.

Matthiessen, F. O. *From the Heart of Europe.* New York: Oxford University Press, 1948.

————. *Henry James: The Major Phase.* London: Oxford University Press, 1944.

————. *The James Family: A Group Biography.* New York: Knopf, 1961.

Meyers, Marvin. *The Jacksonian Persuasion.* Stanford: Stanford University Press, 1957.

Nuhn, Ferner. *A Wind Blew in from the East: A Study in the Orientation of American Culture.* New York: Harper and Brothers, 1942.

Parrington, Vernon L. *Main Currents in American Thought.* New York: Harcourt, Brace and Co., 1927.

Pells, Richard. *The Liberal Mind in a Conservative Age: American Intellectuals in the 1940s and 1950s.* New York: Harper and Row, 1985.

Persons, Stow. *The Decline of American Gentility.* New York: Columbia University Press, 1973.

Peterson, Merrill D. *The Jefferson Image in the American Mind.* New York: Oxford University Press, 1962.

Pierson, George Wilson. *Tocqueville and Beaumont in America.* New York: Oxford University Press, 1938.

Porte, Joel. *Representative Man: Ralph Waldo Emerson in His Time.* New York: Columbia University Press, 1988.

Riesman, David. *The Lonely Crowd.* New Haven: Yale University Press, 1950.

Samuels, Ernest. *Bernard Berenson: The Making of a Connoisseur*. Cambridge: Harvard University Press, 1979.

———. *Bernard Berenson: The Making of a Legend*. Cambridge: Harvard University Press, 1987.

———. *Henry Adams: The Major Phase*. Cambridge: Harvard University Press, 1965.

———. *Henry Adams: The Middle Years*. Cambridge: Harvard University Press, 1958.

———. *The Young Henry Adams*. Cambridge: Harvard University Press, 1948.

Santayana, George. *Character and Opinion in the United States*. Garden City, N.Y.: Doubleday, 1956.

———. *The Genteel Tradition at Bay*. New York: Scribner's, 1931.

———. *The Genteel Tradition: Nine Essays*. Edited by Douglas Wilson. Cambridge: Harvard University Press, 1967.

———. *George Santayana's America: Essays on Literature and Culture*. Edited by James Ballowe. Urbana: University of Illinois Press, 1967.

———. *Interpretations of Poetry and Religion*. New York: Scribner's, 1960.

———. *The Last Puritan*. New York: Scribner's, 1936.

———. *The Letters of George Santayana*. Edited by Daniel Cory. New York: Scribner's, 1955.

———. *Persons and Places*. Cambridge: MIT Press, 1986.

———. *Selected Critical Writings of George Santayana*. Edited by Norman Henfrey. Cambridge: Cambridge University Press, 1968.

Schleifer, James T. *The Making of Tocqueville's "Democracy in America"*. Chapel Hill: University of North Carolina Press, 1980.

Schlesinger, Arthur, Jr. *The Vital Center*. Boston: Houghton Mifflin, 1949.

Sedgwick, Eve Kosofsky. *Between Men: English Literature and Male Homosocial Desire*. New York: Columbia University Press, 1985.

———. *The Epistemology of the Closet*. Los Angeles: University of California Press, 1991.

Smith, Henry Nash. *Virgin Land*. Cambridge: Harvard University Press, 1950.

Stern, Frederick C. *F. O. Matthiessen: Christian Socialist as Critic*. Chapel Hill: University of North Carolina Press, 1981.

Tocqueville, Alexis de. *Democracy in America*. 2 vols. Translated by Henry Reeve and Francis Bowen, edited by Phillips Bradley. New York: Knopf, 1945.

———. *A Journey to America*. Translated by George Lawrence, edited by J. P. Mayer. New Haven: Yale University Press, 1962.

Trilling, Lionel. *A Gathering of Fugitives*. Boston: Beacon Press, 1956.

———. *The Liberal Imagination: Essays on Literature and Society*. New York: Scribner's, 1950.

Warshow, Robert. *The Immediate Experience: Movies, Comics, Theater and Other Aspects of Popular Culture*. Garden City, N.Y.: Doubleday, 1962.

Whitman, Walt. *Poetry and Prose*. New York: Library of America, 1982.

Wilson, Edmund. "Roman Diary: Arrival—Visit to Santayana." In *Europe without Baedeker: Sketches among the Ruins of Italy, Greece, and England*. Garden City, N.Y.: Doubleday, 1947.

Ziff, Larzer. *Literary Democracy: The Declaration of Cultural Independence in America*. New York: Viking, 1981.

INDEX